STRUGGLE FOR DEMOCRACY

STRUGGLE FOR

To my wife

PREFACE

ALMOST THREE score years have elapsed since the 1911 Chinese revolution took place, and China has in the meantime undergone profound changes. Socially Chinese society is experiencing unprecedented upheaval. Politically China has passed from desiring to embrace Western democracy to an intense commitment to Communism. For this outcome there can be no satisfactory single explanation, and present developments have been and will continue to be measured from major historical landmarks, of which the 1911 Chinese revolution, which overthrew a deeply rooted monarchical system and embarked China on an alien political path, is undoubtedly one. Through an examination of the career of Sung Chiao-jen, a leading revolutionary and political leader of this period, I have examined certain features of China's pre-Republican revolutionary movements and their connections with the political phenomena of the infant Republic of China, in the hope that this will contribute to Western understanding of modern China.

Apart from well-known terms and names of established usage in English, which are retained in their original form, all other Chinese words in this book are rendered in the Wade-Giles system with minor modification (e.g. *Yüeh* for *yo*, *i* for *yi*). The half circle and the circumflex over *u* and *e* are omitted.

The romanisation of Japanese follows the Hebpurn system.

Both Chinese and Japanese names are written in the original order, that is, with the surname first and the personal name second.

To reduce the forbidding look of foreign names in the main text, the umlaut above *u*, and the macron above *e* or *o* in Japanese are left out, but these are retained in the glossary, footnotes, reference notes, and bibliography.

Sources of information are generally given in full in the first instance, followed by shortened forms of their original titles for subsequent references.

Generally the term 'revolutionaries' refers to members of organisations which aimed for the overthrow of the existing government by force; 'reformers' refers to people who advocated peaceful reform; 'constitutionalists' refers to the advocates of constitutional monarchy; and 'bureaucrats' refers to officials of the Manchu régime.

Unless indicated otherwise, all translated terms and passages from Chinese sources are my own.

The research on which the book is based dates back to 1962, when I first entered the Department of Far Eastern History of the Australian National University as a Research Scholar. For encouragement in the early stages I must thank Mr Fang Chao-yin, then Curator of the Oriental Collection of the Australian National University Library, whose knowledge of available materials on modern China greatly assisted my planning. My stay at the Australian National University for the following four years included one year away on field work in the Far East. It was mainly preparation done in this period that made my project possible, enabling me first to complete my thesis on Sung Chiao-jen, and then to write this present volume, after further work and revision. For this modest result I am indebted to many people and institutions. I am grateful to Emeritus Professor C. P. FitzGerald, former head of the Department of Far Eastern History, Australian National University, for his support and encouragement in those initial years; to Professor E. S. Crawcour for his coaching on the Japanese language; to Dr Lo Hui-min and Dr J. A. A. Stockwin for reading and criticising my early drafts. I must also thank the staff of various Australian libraries: the Mitchell Library of Sydney, the Victorian State Library of Melbourne, the National Library of Australia, the Menzies Library of the Australian National University, and the University of Tasmania Library, for their services.

In Japan Professor Chūzō Ichiko of Tōyō Bunko, Professor Sanetō Keishiū of the Chinese Department, Waseda University, and Mr Usui Katsumi of the Japanese Foreign Office have helped me to locate materials in their respective institutions. In Taiwan Mr Lo Chia-lun, Director of the Bureau of National History, kindly gave me access to some materials in the Nationalist Party archives, and the staff of the Academia Sinica let me use their library facilities. Professor Lo Hsiang-lin of the Chinese Department, University of Hong Kong, and the library staff of the Feng Ping-shan Library have also given me generous assistance. To all of them I wish to express my deep appreciation and gratitude. Thanks are also due to Dr Jerome Ch'en of the University of Leeds, Mr Arthur Huck of the University of Melbourne, and Dr J. S. Gregory of La Trobe University for their constructive criticisms.

For help in the final stages I wish to thank the University of Tasmania for its annual research grant since 1966; my colleagues in the History Department, in whose company this work progressed to its present stage; Mrs K. L. Piggott, Mrs D. Caulfield, and Mrs N. Gill for typing; Messrs B. H. Crawford and J. E. Ingleson for proof-reading; and Mrs M. Nicholls for her help in compiling the glossary

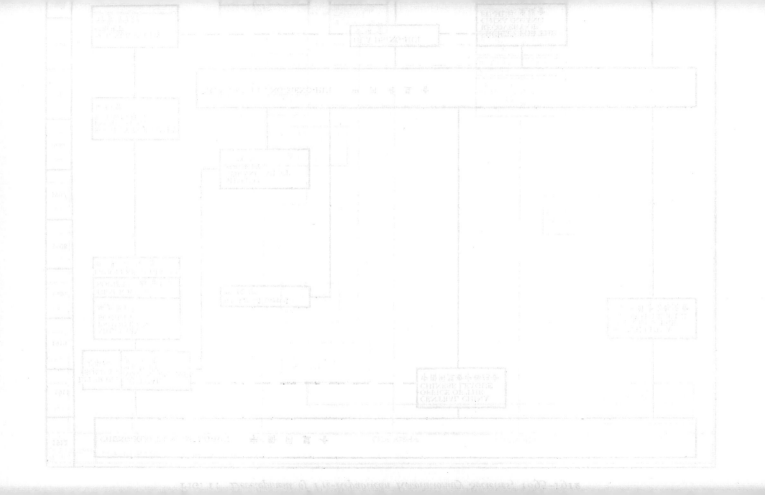

and the index. For final preparation I must thank the staff of the Australian National University Press.

Lastly I must thank my wife, whose sympathy and understanding, as well as her capacity to act as critic, secretary, and proof-reader, have given me invaluable aid in the course of research and writing.

LIEW KIT SIONG

Hobart June 1970

ABBREVIATIONS

CTSTL	*Chin-tai-shih tzu-liao*
HHKM	*Hsin-hai ko-ming*
KMIS	*Ko-ming i-shih*
KMS	*Chung-hua min-kuo k'ai-kuo-ch'ien ko-ming-shih*
KMWH	*Ko-ming wen-hsien*
KSKF	*Ko-sheng kuang-fu*
NCH	*North China Herald*
SLHC	*Hsin-hai ko-ming-ch'ien shih-nien chien shih-lun hsüan-chi*
TMH	T'ung-meng-hui
WHPF	*Wu-hsü pien-fa*

CONTENTS

FIGURES

ONE

Introduction

ON THE night of 20 March 1913, at about a quarter to eleven, an express train was waiting in the Shanghai railway station, ready to move at the chime of the clock. Inside the dim iron-pillared structure, three fashionably dressed men emerged from the doorway of the station's special reception room for parliamentarians. They were soon joined by two others who came out of the ticket office on the right. Together they were moving abreast towards a gate on the far right corner that led to the embarkation platform, when a low sudden pistol shot was heard, then a second, and then another. In the confusion, the gunman, a small man in black military uniform, retreated to the lower left corner in the direction of the refreshment room for first class passengers, and disappeared. Meanwhile, one of the five men staggered. Leaning on an iron seat, he looked in the direction of the ticket-checking point, and called out to his friends that he had been wounded. Thus began the famous, or infamous, political murder case that rocked the foundation of the infant Republic of China.

The victim was Sung Chiao-jen, a prominent leader of the 1911 Chinese revolution and a leading member of the Nationalist Party *(Kuo-min-tang)* which had just won an overwhelming victory in China's first national election. On the last account there was much speculation that he was the premier-elect, who would form the next government. Whether he would have become a premier can now only be a conjecture, but on that fateful night it was beyond doubt that he was on his way to Peking to consult with the President of the Republic of China on matters concerning the formation of the in-coming government.

Why was he shot? What was his role in the building of modern China, and what bearing had his life and death on China's subsequent development? These are questions which form the main lines of inquiry in the following pages.

The Chinese revolution of 1911 was a momentous event in Chinese history. It overthrew a deeply rooted monarchical system that had lasted more than two thousand years, and established in its place a republic which was without precedent in China. It brought to the surface a process which had begun more than a century before, the continuation of which has led to what China is today.

Despite its importance, however, the subject has not until recently been much studied. This is even more true of its personalities. With the exception of Sun Yat-sen (who probably owed his fame more to his persistent efforts over forty years to transform China rather than to his actual role in this revolution), most other personalities of the 1911 revolution were hardly more than names to posterity, even in China.

Recently, developments in China have in many ways caught the world unawares, undoubtedly because of its neglect of much modern Chinese history. As if in an effort to make good this lack, the study of modern Chinese history is now much encouraged in and out of China, and has already begun to bear fruit. The 1911 revolution is one of the topics which have caught the attention of students.

Strictly, the 1911 Chinese revolution refers to an event which began on 10 October 1911, and ended with the establishment of the Republic of China in Nanking on 1 January 1912 and the termination of the Manchu dynasty in the following February. But it is usually extended to include the decade of revolutionary movements preceding it, and also the Republican period from its establishment in 1912 to the second revolution in 1913, when, after the death of Sung Chiao-jen, his colleagues tried and failed to regain leadership of the government by force. It is necessary to take this broader historical perspective in order to understand the single revolutionary event of 1911.

The study of Sung Chiao-jen's career is admirably suited to throw light on this revolution itself. Born in 1882, he was too young to be in the ranks of reformers who were active in the 1890s, while their failure seems to have turned him away forever from the course of peaceful transformation to the road of revolution. This explains why, when he emerged from his quiet country life in 1903, he allowed himself to be engulfed immediately by a movement the propriety of the cause of which he never subsequently doubted. His assassination in 1913, on the other hand, meant that he did not experience the period of warlordism (1916-27) when most leaders fought for no clear purpose or ideal other than wealth and power. This is the reason why Sung has been termed a figure purely of the 1911 revolution.[1] Sung Chiao-jen's life was indeed intimately bound up with the 1911 revolution. His career forms a complete chapter of modern Chinese history.

Besides the significance of Sung's life in the context of China's revolution, there is the controversy among Chinese historians on his role. For years after his death, there has been no agreement about his contribution to the cause of revolution.

During his lifetime he was considered to be a devoted revolutionary. When the republic was formed, he was noted as an 'eminent Republican' by no other than G. E. Morrison, the famed Australian correspondent of *The Times* in Peking.[2] Immediately after his death he was mourned by the whole nation as a great loss to China.[3] But after the collapse of the brief second revolution in 1913, unfavourable criticisms of Sung Chiao-jen began to appear even within the revolutionary camp. As early as 1914, Sun Yat-sen and his followers blamed the 'moderates' for the fate of the 1911 revolution. Sung's name was not mentioned, but it was clear by implication that he was meant, since Sung was regarded as the head of the moderate wing, which favoured compromise with Yuan Shih-k'ai at first and later insisted on controlling him. He was blamed for changing the Chinese League *(Chung-kuo T'ung-meng-hui)* into an ordinary political party, and worst of all for changing it into the Nationalist Party. He was also criticised for opposing Yuan Shih-k'ai in an ineffective manner which endangered the position of the revolutionaries in China.[4]

In the 1920s criticism of Sung Chiao-jen became even severer. He was blamed by some prominent Nationalist leaders for the failure of the 1911 revolution. Feng Tzu-yu, an authoritative historian of this revolution, charged him with forsaking the cause of revolution for material gains and social position.[5] Tai Chi-t'ao went so far as to name him the 'Number one sinner of the revolutionary party'.[6] Despite a resolution of the Nationalist Party in 1925 requesting him to remove this remark, it remains to this day in his writing.[7] Ch'en Tu-hsiu, an influential leftist intellectual of this period, blamed Sung Chiao-jen and his friends for deserting in 1912 the *Independent People's Daily (Min-li-pao)*, an important revolutionary propaganda organ, to become 'high officials and great men', and for submitting to the call of the intransigent bureaucrats to abolish the revolutionary party.[8]

Even today the views of Chinese historians remain divided. In 1961, on the occasion of the fiftieth anniversary of the 1911 revolution, an historical symposium attended by over a hundred historians from all over China was held in Wuchang, to consider the various historical problems of the 1911 revolution. Among the topics discussed was Sung Chiao-jen, who was regarded as one of the representative figures of 1911. The discussion centred around the question whether he was a 'good' revolutionary, or whether his actions after 1911 were in fact retrogressive.[9] Since the primary concern of this study is Sung Chiao-jen's role in the 1911 revolution, the views of this symposium on Sung Chiao-jen are worth quoting in full.

The opinions of the historians split into two, a majority view and that of a minority. The majority held that he had definitely weakened. Four reasons were advanced to justify this view. Firstly, Sung Chiao-jen allegedly lacked resolution in his anti-imperialistic and anti-feudal stand. He opposed Japanese intervention in 1911, but allowed himself to believe in the insincere neutrality of Britain and the United States of America. He opposed the view that enlightened despotism could be a satisfactory alternative to democracy, but on the land question he was very reserved and lagged behind the stand of Sun Yat-sen and Huang Hsing. In fact, according to this view, he never expressed a clear attitude towards the platform of the Chinese League, and Sung's was the least intransigent of the various attitudes towards Yuan Shih-k'ai.

Secondly, after the establishment of the republic, Sung Chiao-jen was said to have devoted himself wholeheartedly to party politics, with the aim of developing capitalism and fulfilling his ideal of a capitalist republic. This was held as concrete evidence of his backsliding from a bourgeois revolutionary to a capitalist reformer.

Thirdly, Sung did not respect the leadership of Sun Yat-sen and did not give his wholehearted support to the unity of the Chinese League. Instead, he precipitated the split of the Chinese League. Three examples were cited in support of this accusation. When Sun Yat-sen was organising armed struggle in south China, Sung went to Manchuria to carry out a separatist action. When the split occurred in the Chinese League between 1907 and 1909, Huang Hsing rose to Sun Yat-sen's defence but Sung's attitude was far from clear. Finally, the establishment of the Central China Office in June 1911 served a positive function, but its formation was the result of dissatisfaction with Sun Yat-sen and a desire to pursue an independent course of action. It was a disintegrating activity, since its formation introduced a further degree of laxity into the organisation of the Chinese League, basically harmful to the revolution.

Fourthly, in reorganising the Chinese League into the Nationalist Party, Sung took a large number of bureaucrats and opportunists into the party. This hastened the disintegration of the revolutionary party. It also reflected Sung Chiao-jen's further compromise with reactionary elements.

In contrast, the minority advanced five points in Sung's favour. Sung was a model revolutionary before 1911. He dared to fight against the Manchus and to hold steadfastly to revolution and democracy, and his philosophy contained a strong element of materialism. After the 1911 revolution, he continued to be anti-feudal. He sought political democracy and actively pursued the political struggle. This could not be said to be backsliding.

Despite the obvious disadvantages of party politics, Sung was using them for progressive ends. To develop capitalist democracy and to establish a capitalist type of democratic republic was the demand of that time. Sung's active struggle for cabinet government was aimed to fulfil both this aspiration and the idea of the Chinese League. Besides, no one else at that time had put forward a more progressive political idea.

The retrogressing in the political planks of the Nationalist Party could not be taken for retrogression in Sung's political ideas. It did not shake his faith in his two principles, nationalism and democracy; neither did it weaken his effort to put them into practice. Nor should one blame Sung alone for the reorganisation of the Chinese League into the Nationalist Party. One should say that the political planks of the Nationalist Party had the assent of all average revolutionaries. They reflect the political attitude for material gains of the capitalists, both great and small. Besides, the Chinese League itself was basically a loose alliance. Its dissolution was a natural outcome. As for the Central China Office, it could not be looked upon as a deviation. It fulfilled the role of the Chinese League in providing leadership to the forces of revolution in the Yangtze valley. When the revolutionary force suffered continuous reverses in its armed struggle in the south, the Central China Office alone noticed the ripening situation for revolution in the Yangtze valley, and proceeded to carry out the work of organising and uniting these forces—a very important positive function.

Sung possessed a noble, unblemished political record. He did not give in to Yuan Shih-k'ai in exchange for high office or money. His assassination by Yuan Shih-k'ai showed that there had been a struggle between them.

At that time the revolutionaries were faced with four alternatives: to resist the transfer of political power to Yuan Shih-k'ai; to seek, under the circumstances which followed Sun Yat-sen's abdication from the presidency, to enforce the provisional constitution of the Republic by political means; to throw aside the revolutionary stand so as to obtain an official post and become Yuan Shih-k'ai's tool; or to retreat to their studies or become monks. The first path appeared to be the most correct, but no one had sufficient courage to follow it. Therefore, under the circumstances, the second course became the best alternative.

Faced with these opposing views, one of the purposes of this study is to clarify them with a re-examination of Sung's role in the revolution.

There were three main components of the 1911 revolution, the young intelligentsia, which formed the leadership sector, the New Army, and the secret societies, which formed the fighting force of the revolutionary camp. The latter two sectors were important, but in this study they are not our main concern. The young intelligentsia, on the other hand, forms the chief arena of this exercise. Sung Chiao-jen was not only a member of this class, but one of its leading figures. Hence a study of Sung Chiao-jen inevitably gives great attention to this sector of the revolutionary movement. Sung's standing in this class, his association with particular groups within it, his relationship with particular individuals, notably Sun Yat-sen, all of which have a significant bearing on Sung Chiao-jen's action in the 1911 revolution, provide much ground for investigation.

Of course, during and after the 1911 revolution, the question of leadership was complicated by the intrusion of non-revolutionary elements such as former bureaucrats and militarists headed by Yuan Shih-k'ai, and former constitutionalists led by enlightened members of the gentry such as Chang Ch'ien. Therefore, the final phase of Sung Chiao-jen's life involved not only the interplay of leadership within the revolutionary party, but also the rivalry between his and other factions for the reins of government.

In terms of the nature of his activities, Sung's career may be divided into two main parts. From 1903 to 1911 he was a revolutionary organiser who sought in a variety of ways the destruction of the existing political order. He formed and helped to form revolutionary organisations, established propaganda organs, and worked hard on his studies to find the salvation for China. From 1912 to 1913 he was a politician. He established a political party in the hope of stabilising the politics of the infant republic through the practice of party government. He sought to consolidate the republic by asserting the authority of China's infant representative institution, and by curbing the executive power of the President through the practice of cabinet government.

In terms of personal development Sung Chiao-jen's life may be divided into five stages. From 1882 to 1902 he was a traditional student learning to master the Confucian studies in the relative calm of his native home in Hunan.

The second stage of his life consisted of two years, from 1903 to 1904. Here we see a major change in Sung's life. He moved from his quiet country life to Wuchang, one of China's bustling political and commercial centres. There was also a major change in the mode of his learning. He had moved away from classical studies to modern scholarship, including Western sciences and technology. Most important of all was his close contact with current affairs, and his exposure to the idea of revolution which, aided by continuous national humiliation at the hands of foreign powers, had begun to influence the minds of a large sector of China's young intellectuals. In less than two years Sung Chiao-jen was transforming thought into action, and thereafter pursued a course from which he never looked back.

The third stage of Sung's life lasted six years, from 1905 to 1910, when he was a fugitive in Japan. Here Sung seems to have been cautious and thoughtful, indicating the maturing of his mind and personality. He did not waver from the course of revolution, but he was no longer the impetuous student in Wuchang who rushed into revolt without a second thought. He had begun to ponder on the methods of revolution which would bring victory, and on problems of post-revolutionary reconstruction which he and his colleagues would have to face. Therefore, this period of his life may be regarded as his period of self-education.

The following period was 1911, the year of the actual revolution. Here we see Sung the revolutionary in action. As the editor of a revolutionary paper in Shanghai, he spared no energy in propagandising the cause of revolution. As an able organiser, he brought into existence an organisation which was to play a major role in the revolution.

With the establishment of the Republic of China in 1912 began the fifth phase, that of Sung Chiao-jen the politician.

Tun-ch'u was Sung Chiao-jen's other name, and Yu-fu was his well-known pen-name.

\

TWO

Formative Years

Sung Chiao-jen was born on 6 April 1882[1] to a Sung family in T'ao-yuan, a district of the Ch'ang-te prefecture in the province of Hunan.

Little is known about Chiao-jen's father, possibly because he died long before Sung Chiao-jen made his name. About his mother, on the other hand, who lived to see the rise of her son to prominence, and then his tragic death, more information is available. Her family name was Wan, and, although orphaned at a very young age, she grew into a woman of virtue and propriety. At twenty-two she was married to Sung Lu-ch'ih, and raised two sons; the elder was Chiao-hsin, and the younger was Chiao-jen himself.[2]

There seems little to distinguish the Sung family except that it owned some land, which put it economically and socially a little above the ordinary landless peasant folk. This small economic advantage had apparently been put to the best use in traditional terms. No effort seems to have been spared to produce a scholar, and Chiao-jen's father studied, and dreamed of literary honours, and of the official career which successful learning might bring. Despite his reputed diligence as a student he does not seem to have obtained any literary degrees. He contracted an illness, allegedly through too much study, and never recovered from it. In 1892, when Sung Chiao-jen was only ten years old, he died, leaving the whole responsibility of bringing up his family to his middle-aged widow.

Mrs Sung was apparently an able and conscientious lady. After her husband became ill, she took complete charge of family affairs. It was said that in taking care of the family's material welfare and the education of her children she never incurred one word of criticism. After the death of her husband she was allegedly strict with her children, particularly with their education. In 1901 her efforts brought reward. Sung Chiao-jen passed his examinations for the first literary degree and was admitted as *Sheng-yuan*, a position qualifying him as a member of the scholar-gentry, China's privileged social élite.[3]

Mrs Sung, while pleased with her son's success, did not appear to regard it as the aim of learning. She was credited with having said to her son on this occasion, 'A Budding Talent* should concern himself with that fate of all under heaven and not with the trivial and unimportant examinations. You may seek for the broad and the distant'. Apparently Sung Chiao-jen himself was also not over-enthusiastic about examinations and degrees.[4] His later life confirms his aversion to them. Why did both mother and son reject the traditional path that Chinese scholars had followed for centuries to fulfil their aspirations for power, influence, and public esteem? With Mrs Sung, the fate of her husband would have weighed heavily on her mind. As for Sung Chiao-jen, for a young *Hsiu-ts'ai* who had successfully crossed the threshold to join the rank of China's élite to turn his back on the normal road to power and fame, there must have been a deeper reason.

Sung Chiao-jen spent his entire boyhood in his village home. There seems nothing extraordinary in his character to indicate his rebellious tendency. One of his childhood friends described his fondness of war games, and how he divided his playmates into opposing teams, with himself standing on a rock to direct their movements.[5] If this is a significant point, it is perhaps because of the quality of leadership which shone through his personality when he was still a boy. Military affairs remained one of his strong interests. Combined with his interest in geography and history, it seems to have given him an acute sense of strategy, which was to serve him well in the planning and instigation of revolution.

When he reached school age he went to a village school, where his interest in geography was first noticed. The district of T'ao-yuan, with its running streams and colourful peach blossoms, was a beautiful one. But it was isolated and far from the centres of learning. Its prefectural capital, Ch'ang-te, to the west of the Tung-t'ing Lake, was more than three days away by river boat from the provincial capital, Changsha. From Ch'ang-te to T'ao-yuan was another day's journey. The town of T'ao-yuan, where the District Magistrate had his office, was only a small market town without walls or big shops. Its streets were narrow, and its houses were small and low, retaining a medieval look. Even this little town was about a day's journey by foot from Sung's home.[6]

In such a place books were hard to obtain. As one of Sung Chiao-jen's childhood friends recalled, Sung once found a folding fan made of bone with a map drawn on it, and played with it all day long. He

---

* *Hsiu-ts'ai* in Chinese, a popular name for *sheng-yüan.*

was so fascinated by the map that he was not willing to part with it even though a cool wind had begun to blow at the end of the day.[7]

While Sung Chiao-jen was undergoing traditional Confucian education in the relative calm of his village, the world around was rapidly changing. Internally China was in an advanced stage of decay. Several centuries of population increase and technological stagnation had created a rent in China's social fabric which was made irreparable by the impact of the West.

Since 1840 China had experienced one major convulsion, the Taiping rebellion of the mid-nineteenth century, which nearly succeeded in destroying the established order. It had also fought and lost two major foreign wars on its own soil, and on each occasion was forced to sign humiliating terms of peace, which are now known as the 'unequal treaties'. They constituted a foreign web which entangled China for nearly a century. From 1840 to 1860 the freshly fallen victim was still struggling. But thereafter it was more or less resigned to its new fate. China was found submissive to foreign demands. Its interior, formerly out of bounds to all foreigners, now became wide open, and its outlying lands were placed under increasing foreign pressures. By 1890 Hong Kong and the Maritime Province had become British and Russian territories respectively. The Ryukyus, part of Sinkiang, Burma, and Indochina where Chinese influence had been supreme, all now lay outside her orbit.

But worse was yet to come. In the 1890s, when Sung was at his most impressionable age, a chain of events took place which electrified China, shattered her ruling class, and jerked the younger generation into action.

The first of these events was the Sino-Japanese war of 1895, in which China suffered a shattering defeat at the hands of its tiny neighbour. The second was the reform of 1898, in which a small enlightened section of the gentry attempted to introduce institutional reform, but failed in the face of overwhelming opposition from the conservatives. The third was the disastrous Boxer uprising, in which peasant discontent was turned into a major anti-foreign upheaval.

China's defeat by Japan revealed to the world the rotten state of the Chinese empire. The collapse of the 1898 reform, on the other hand, furnished the nation with evidence of the inability of the existing leadership either to regenerate China or to revive itself, while the Boxer uprising and its accompanying disasters tended to strengthen these convictions in the younger intellectuals and make them look for a more effective way to save China.

While national disasters and a rapidly deteriorating national position within and without stirred the soul of the Chinese nation, the majority of Chinese as yet had not made up their minds finally on the course of revolution. At the close of the nineteenth century, therefore, no national revolutionary movement was in sight. The seeds of revolution had long been sown, and the general climatic conditions were favourable, yet their germination and growth were uneven.

Thus, Sun Yat-sen began promoting revolution as early as 1894 in South China, but the rest of the country remained quiet for almost another decade. It was only at the opening of the twentieth century that the shoots of revolution began to appear all over China. Even then their strength and density differed from region to region. Those in the Yangtze provinces, particularly Hunan and Hupeh, seemed to gather special momentum, and a uniform rhythm of growth was not attained until 1905 when they converged to form a canopy, the Chinese League, which was to overshadow China for nearly a decade. It seems reasonable to speculate that while the overall climate was conducive to the growth of revolutionary movements, local factors determined the varying rates of growth.

Sung Chiao-jen, a Hunanese, apparently began to express his revolutionary inclinations while he was a student at a Confucian college in his district between 1899 and 1902.[8] This manifestation fitted the general Chinese scene of the time.

Hunan is a rich agricultural province. Subtropical warmth, abundant water supply, and fertile soil make it one of China's most productive provinces, 'a land of rice and fish'. In the nineteenth century, Hunan's riches must have been largely responsible for the size and power of its gentry, the creation of which, under the late Ch'ing dynasty, depended heavily on wealth. The strength of Hunan's gentry can be seen in the comment of a foreign visitor who was impressed by the number of statesmen and high officials Hunan had produced. He wrote in 1912, 'More than a dozen families have a Viceroy on their roll of honour during the past sixty years. Almost as many have had a governor'.[9]

Material sufficiency and the existence of a strong Confucian gentry turned Hunan into a bulwark of Chinese conservatism, and the mainstay of the order in the fight against the unorthodox Taiping rebellion in the mid-nineteenth century.

Geographically, Hunan is a landlocked province. In the north and west it is backed by large stretches of Chinese territory. In the south and east it is cut off from the sea by Kwangsi, Kwangtung, Kiangsi, and Fukien. Until the development of railways in the twentieth century, Hunan's trunk link with the sea was the Yangtze River which, flowing eastward along its northern border, passes through Hupeh, Anhwei, and Kiangsu, to enter the Pacific Ocean at Shanghai. But throughout the nineteenth century the upper course of this waterway was closed to foreign shipping.* As a result Hunan was one of the provinces most impervious to the seaborne influences from the West, a fact that tended to fortify its conservatism and anti-foreignism.

Historically, Hunan belonged to the anti-Manchu south. It was one of China's last provinces to submit to the Manchu rule. It was also one of the provinces which, as China was passing under Manchu rule in the seventeenth century, led China in the expression of feelings and political ideas akin to modern nationalism. Among the premodern nationalist thinkers was Wang Fu-chih (1619-92), a Hunanese who fought against the Manchus until he exhausted all his resources, and then retired into seclusion to teach and write his philosophy. He advocated that race should be the basis of state organisations, and that foreign rulers should be resisted at all costs. He also taught that environments changed with time; consequently, laws and established practices should also be changed from time to time to suit new conditions.[10]

The thoughts of Wang Fu-chih and others† who held similar views had caused much trouble to the early Manchu rulers, and became the object of ruthless suppression. Partly through harsh persecution and partly due to the Manchu's support for Chinese tradition, early nationalistic feelings became dormant, to be rekindled only in recent time under foreign pressures and new challenges.

Thus in 1866 Tseng Kuo-fan, a leading Confucian statesman from Hunan, edited Wang Fu-chih's collected works for circulation, while suppressing the heretical Taiping rebellion on the Manchu's behalf. This apparent inconsistent action aroused wide speculation on his intention. Was it an expression of his inner wish? Was he penitent for saving the Manchus from destruction?[11] Whatever motive Tseng Kuo-fan night have had, at least one fact should be beyond dispute. He shared Wang Fu-chih's views and nationalistic aspirations at a time when China was besieged by foes bigger and more alien than the Manchus, and desired to propagate them to meet China's hour of need.

There must be many others besides Tseng Kuo-fan who appreciated some, if not all, of Wang Fu-chih's teachings. The number of Hunanese advocates for reform and Hunan's lead in the reform

---

* Hunan was not opened for foreign trade until the early twentieth century. The first Hunanese port to receive foreign traders was Yochow, opened in 1899, followed by Changsha itself in 1904.

† E.g. Huang Tsung-hsi (1610-95), Ku Yen-wu (1613-82), Chu Chi-yu (1600-82).

movement towards the end of the nineteenth century must be in some ways attributable to Wang's teachings.

Writing in 1905, Sung Chiao-jen harked back to tradition for his anti-Manchu cause. He wrote:

> Hunanese have all along been known for their insubordination to the Manchus. Since the teaching of Ch'uan-shan [Wang Fu-chih], the great principle of nationalism has been preserved with great respect in Hunan. Tseng Ching-chou, T'ang Liu-yang* and others who attempted risings against the Manchus stand out like shining lights. Last year [following their examples], the students allied with the secret society of Ma Fu-i and others to attempt to detach Hunan from the Manchus and make it independent.[12]

Thus the link between tradition, the reform movement, and the revolutionary movement of modern times seems to be particularly obvious in Hunan.

It has been suggested that the collapse of reform in 1898 convinced many young Chinese of the inability of the established ruling class to regenerate China. This view seems correct, for thereafter doubts about the sincerity and ability of the Manchu court filled the minds of an expanding sector of China's young intelligentsia, and some resolved to overthrow the Manchu régime.

Sung Chiao-jen was one who expressed his disbelief in the possibility of a genuine reform by the Manchus. Thus, in 1905, when, following Japan's victory over Russia, talk of constitutional reform filled the Manchu court in Peking, Sung took great pains to explain its impossibility. He pointed out the incompatibility between constitutional government and the firmly established interests of the Manchus under the existing system. A change to constitutional government from autocratic monarchy would deprive the Manchus not only of their power, but also of the numerous privileges they had enjoyed for the previous two and a half centuries. Like extremists of later days, Sung was of the conviction that the privileged would never part with what they had. He therefore exhorted the Chinese people not to be fooled by the empty talk of Tz'u-hsi, the Empress Dowager. 'Clearly there is absolutely no possibility for the Manchus to practise constitutional government', he declared emphatically, 'Even if they do, it cannot be a genuine constitutional government . . . Also, those of us who still hope day and night for the Manchu government to effect peaceful reform, may they not now cease hoping?'[13]

---

* An unidentifiable figure, unless it meant T'an Liu-yang, a martyr of the 1898 reform.

Following the total collapse of reform in Peking, reform in Hunan met a similar fate. But whereas the central government's effort at reform was confined to imperial edicts and paper work, and had little time to make any concrete impression on the nation, reform in Hunan enjoyed a longer duration. This was partly because it began earlier, but also because it concentrated on education directly fostered and carried out by the provincial administration, thereby exercising an influence on Hunan and on young minds such as that of Sung Chiao-jen, matched in few other places.

Hunan's reform centred around a program of education—the modernising of schools and the propagation of new ideas. It had its headquarters in Changsha and its most important institution was the Current Affairs Academy *(Shih-wu hsueh-t'ang)*, a place criticised by some conservative die-hards as a 'nest of revolution and rebellion'.[14] Apparently, while its program was generally mild, utterances often went beyond the bounds of moderation. Liang Ch'i-ch'ao, a leading reformer and the Principal of the Academy, confessed in his later years that he was then intoxicated with democracy and conscious of his race, and unreservedly expressed his feelings to his students. He discussed the current version of the theory of popular sovereignty with his students, and also talked of historical events of the Ch'ing dynasty, listing episodes of misgovernment, and strongly advocating revolution.[15]

The influence of the reformers was not confined to the perimeter of the provincial capital. To meet the needs of 'country scholars who may be trying to find their way like blind men with a stick and failing to find it',[16] new ideas were carried to them by journals and magazines. Under the influence of its reformist governor, who exhorted all districts in Hunan to acquire these publications for distribution among their schools, undoubtedly some found their way into Sung Chiao-jen's vicinity.[17] Some even spread beyond Hunan. Chang Chih-tung, the Viceroy of Hunan and Hupeh, made a special effort to introduce a Hunan journal to Hupeh, and stopped it only ten months later, when he found its content too radical![18]

Besides the modernisation of schools and the publication of journals, there was a third pursuit, the study societies, which the reformers in Hunan organised with great energy. The most important study society brought into existence was the Southern Study Society *(Nan-shueh-hui)* in Changsha. It was not an ordinary learned society, for its organisers had in view more distant aims than the promotion of learning. Faced with the possibility of China's partition by the powers, the reformers in Hunan envisaged their society as a shadow parliament, capable of governing Hunan as an independent state. For this end the membership of the Southern Study Society included men selected from every prefecture and district in Hunan. It was planned that eventually some of these men would return to their prefectures and districts to establish branches of the society, and bring a network into existence. The reformers in Hunan further hoped that the influence of their society might spread into neighbouring provinces, so that the whole of south China might be drawn into the orbit of their society in the event of partition.[19]

It can be seen that the reform movement in Hunan had a strong regional tendency. It was more concerned with the reservation of the province itself than with the perpetuation of the Manchu empire. The reformers in Hunan had little confidence in the Manchu government, and did not expect the empire to last for long. This is evident in Liang Ch'i-Ch'ao's letter to the governor of Hunan in 1897:

> Today, without reform we cannot maintain our existence at all. If we trust the matter of reform to the ministers in the central government, there is little likelihood it will be brought about. Indeed we may wait until the South Mountain is removed and the eastern seas become dry, and there will still be no reform.[20]

If the reformers in Hunan harboured little hope of reform by the Manchu government in Peking in 1897, and prepared for regional salvation, it is hardly surprising that, after the collapse of reform in 1898, radical men appeared on the scene to advocate the destruction of the Manchu dynasty, and that revolutionary movements should have gathered special momentum in Hunan. Among later dynastic opponents in the twentieth century, quite a few were directly connected with the reform in Hunan in this period.*

During the period of reform in Hunan, Sung Chiao-jen was between fifteen and sixteen years old. There is no evidence of direct contact between him and the reform movement, yet, in view of the all-pervasive nature of the reformers' activities through widely distributed journals and study societies which 'spread like trees in a forest', Sung Chiao-jen could hardly fail to be influenced by them in some ways. In the current zeal for the formation of learned societies, one such group was founded in Sung's vicinity, with the aim of introducing and importing the learning of both East and West to the people, so that, in the words of its constitution,

> they can investigate the phenomena of past and present, Chinese and foreign . . . and develop talents which could serve to reform and deliver us from the perils of this age and save the world.[21]

---

* E.g. T'ang Ts'ai-ch'ang, Yang Yu-lin, T'an Yen-k'ai.

There are, however, almost no records which might throw light on Sung's thought and action in response to the reform current which swept Hunan in 1897 and 1898. His obscurity in these two years and those preceding them must be due to his youth, because of which he had not as yet made enough impression on others to arouse attention. Material on Sung Chiao-jen in the few years after the collapse of the 1898 reform is also scanty, but it is sufficient to reveal his development.

In 1899 he entered a newly opened Confucian college in his district. This college was a partly modernised school. It offered its one hundred students such subjects as mathematics, geography, classics, history, and etymology. Sung Chiao-jen studied here for the following four years, during which his maturing personality began to reveal the influences of his time. He was interested in geography and history, particularly history concerning the development of conservatism and reform. He was credited for his lead in the collection of books for a library in his school, undoubtedly with the promotion of learning in view.[22] His love for books remained with him until his death.

He did not share the interest of the majority of students, who absorbed themselves in the art of writing poetry and formal essays in an effort to meet the requirements of examinations. Instead, he liked to discuss matters in sweeping terms, and was fond of discussing and comparing world affairs, an attitude apparently still much frowned upon by other, more conventional students, who regarded him as an eccentric and refused to associate with him. Years later, one of the students recalled his days with Sung Chiao-jen in this Confucian college:

> When I was young, I studied with Sung Chiao-jen in the Chang-chiang College in our district. At that time the system of examination was not yet abolished. Students concentrated on the study of the Eight-legged essay. In later Ch'ing dynasty the subject matter for examination was changed to 'questions and themes' *(Ts'e-lun)* and we accordingly also studied classics, history, current affairs and other subjects aiming solely to pass examinations and obtain degrees and honours. Only Sung Chiao-jen did not regard them as important and looked for more practical and useful studies in the classics. Generally he liked to read books on military subjects, law and geography in which he often found particular understanding and satisfaction. Sometimes he engaged in discussion with two or three friends and revealed to them his ambition to change and purify the world.[23]

It was during one of these discussions with his intimate friends that Sung Chiao-jen made his first recorded revolutionary utterance. He told his friends:

China suffered long enough under the Manchu administration. If there rises a hero who could take Wuchang as a base, control Kiukiang in the east and Nanking on the lower Yangtze, and then go northward beyond the Wu-sheng Pass* to cut off the railway bridge on the Yellow River, while westward from Hupeh penetrate into Szechuan and further south to secure the food provision of Hunan, then, with the head of the governor of Hupeh hanging at his elbow, his ambition in the world could be fulfilled.[24]

If these were truly Sung's own words uncoloured by the wisdom of hindsight, it would be clear that Sung was not only of revolutionary inclinations, but had already mapped out the strategy which he openly advocated in 1911.

A further mark on Sung Chiao-jen of the time in which he lived was his interest in the modernisation of education. In early 1903, while he was on his way to Wuchang to begin a new page of his life, he was said to have stopped at Changsha to present an address of several thousand words to the governor of Hunan on the modernisation of schools. There is no trace of this address but there seems no cause to doubt the information, given by Sung Chiao-jen's fellow provincial and contemporary. It seems that Sung Chiao-jen's address helped to revive and further the process of modernising schools in Hunan. Chao Erh-hsun was then the new governor of Hunan. He was interested in education and wished to continue modernising Hunan's schools. But he was said to have hesitated because of the opposition of the local gentry, who, since the 1898 reform, had become rather reluctant to see such an undertaking. The address of Sung Chiao-jen, himself an up-and-coming member of the gentry, encouraged the new governor to put his scheme into practice.[25]

---

* Wu-sheng-kuan, an important pass which controls entry into Hupeh from Honan.

THREE

Rebels in the Making

THE OPENING of the twentieth century saw the emergence and identification of two forces, anti-Manchuism and a class of new intellectuals. Before 1900 people hated foreigners, but at that time few dared show contempt for the dynasty. Many people were still very concerned with the fate of the fallen Emperor Kuanghsu, whose zeal for reform in 1898 brought down on himself the wrath of the Empress Tz'u-hsi and her conservative supporters. In 1900 a group of Chinese gentry held a self-styled 'National Assembly' *(Kuo-hui)* in Shanghai to protest against the threat of the Empress to dethrone Kuanghsu. The vacillation between revolution and evolution on the part of its leaders, notably T'ang Ts'ai-ch'ang, who organised both the Independence Society *(Tzu-li-hui)* and the Independent Army *(Tzu-li-chun)* against the Manchu court, marked the transition of Chinese minds from loyalty to the Manchus to opposition to them. The fallen queue which a noted Confucian scholar, Chang Ping-lin, cut off from his own head in protest against the ambiguous aims of the 'National Assembly' signalled the coming breach between the Chinese on the one hand, and, on the other, not only the Manchus, but also tradition itself.[1] Thenceforward there was a mounting pressure of anti-Manchu and anti-dynastic feeling in China.

At this juncture the Manchu government committed a fatal but inevitable act, the introduction of educational reform. It gave birth to a class of men who, drawing their inspiration from the anti-Manchu atmosphere, and imbued with untraditional ideas, undertook to put into effect the nation's hopes.

The Manchu government's educational reform consisted of two important features, which affected China as well as Sung Chiao-jen's personal development. One was the introduction of a modern school system, and the other was the sending of students abroad.

Following an imperial decree of 14 November 1901,[2] which recommended a school system of three levels, various provincial authorities effected it with varying degrees of enthusiasm and success. The Viceroy of Hunan and Hupeh then was Chang Chih-tung, a noted promoter of education who had, a decade earlier, established the College of Hunan and Hupeh *(Liang-hu shu-yuan)* to encourage Confucian studies. In accordance with the new imperial policy, he reorganised the schools in Hupeh.

On the secondary and tertiary levels two types of schools, military and civil, were established. Special emphasis was laid on the importance of secondary education, which Chang Chih-tung regarded as the fundamental stage of intellectual development for either civil or military careers.[3] With this in view he established the the Wuchang Civil High School *(Wu-ch'ang wen-p'u-t'ung chung-hsueh-t'ang)* which, based on his famous enunciation of 'Chinese learning for the fundamental principles and Western studies for practical use', offered a mixed four-year course of twelve subjects: ethics, classics, Chinese language, history, geography, mathematics, natural history, physics, chemistry, legal systems, art, physical education. This school provided accommodation for 240 students between the ages of fifteen and twenty-four. It was primarily intended for students of Hupeh, but thirty places were allocated to successful candidates from Hunan, as the latter was also under Chang's jurisdiction. A small number of students specially sponsored by other provincial governments were also accepted.

The students of the Wuchang Civil High School, selected by competitive entrance examinations, were noted for their above-average qualities and their quickness in learning. Chang Chih-tung was very proud of this fact. A few years later, in requesting the Throne's commendation for graduates and members of the staff of the various schools in his province, he had the following comment to make:

> When the Wuchang Civil High School and the South Road Higher Primary School were first established, the successful candidates were generally of versatile quality. They were fluent in Chinese and were quick in learning and understanding of science and other subjects.[4]

Sung Chiao-jen was one of these students commended so highly by Chang Chih-tung. He was then a mature student of twenty-one years of age who had already obtained his first literary degree in the previous year, which put him four years below the average age for successful candidates for that degree.* He was particularly noted for

---

* According to Chang Chung-li, *The Chinese Gentry: Studies on Their Role in Nineteenth Century Chinese Society*, p. 172, the average age of successful candidates for the first degree was twenty-four.

his talent in essay writing, which was said to have impressed the governor of Hunan, Chao Erh-hsun, who had read his treatise on the modernisation of schools.

Until this time Sung Chiao-jen had moved along the path of the gentry despite the increasing pull of new forces which tended to make him veer off course. In Wuchang, however, he had reached a point in both space and time where the powerful pull of the revolutionary currents steered him ineluctably along the path to revolution. Soon after his arrival he was said to have started holding conspiratorial meetings behind closed doors.[5] In the following year he participated in the founding of two revolutionary societies, the China Resurgence Society *(Hua-hsing-hui)* in Changsha and the Science Study Group *(K'o-hsueh-pu-hsi-so)** in Wuchang, the first to appear in Hunan and Hupeh respectively. Before the end of 1904, unsuccessful plots for armed rebellions against respective provincial authorities were hatched by Sung and his colleagues.

From both the traditional point of view and that of its consequential effects on China, the educational reform was a momentous act. Ever since the establishment in Peking in 1861 of the first foreign language college to train interpreters, the gentry had successfully resisted further acceleration of Western learning, despite the increasing need for it. Thus the Educational Mission, set up in 1872 to send students to the United States of America for special training, was abruptly terminated in 1881 without replacement. Further efforts at the time of the 1898 reform met a similar fate. Therefore, the sanction to the new learning given in 1901 by the Manchu government and the gentry's acquiescence in this amounted to no less than a confession of their own inadequacy.

The speed with which the feared consequences of modernised education manifested themselves perhaps surprised even the most suspicious members of the gentry. Almost immediately after the implementation of the new educational policy, a fast multiplying body of rebellious young intellectuals made its appearance, and seditious literature flooded China's modernised educational institutions.

If foreign ideas were viewed as possibly dangerous to the tranquillity of Chinese minds, travel to the foreign lands where the ideas originated posed an even greater threat. This fear of the Chinese gentry was well justified, for it was in Tokyo, where most Chinese students now went to further their education, that Chinese nation-

---

* Translation follows Hsüeh Chün-tu, *Huang Hsing and the Chinese Revolution*, Stanford, 1961.

alism acquired its first pulse and momentum, and it was mainly from the foreign-controlled part of Shanghai that it was first disseminated within China. It was also in these two centres that China's foreign-educated intellectuals first realised their corporate existence, their identity with China's aspirations, and their mission. A brief account of this process will shed some light on the character of subsequent revolutionary movements, particularly those in the Yangtze provinces, and the final stage of Sung Chiao-jen's personal development before he embarked determinedly on the course of revolution.

Before 1900 there was already a small number of Chinese students in Japan, but it was not until after the introduction of educational reform that their numbers rapidly increased. The temperament of this fast-growing body of men on foreign soil can be seen from the description of a contemporary Western diplomat, who observed that many of these young men, enjoying for the first time government support, a sufficiency of time for discussion, and release from family control, quickly acquired the catchword of this milieu and became themselves vigorous proponents of republicanism for China.[6] This is of course a partial view.* To take a broader approach, it may be argued with equal if not greater validity that they belonged to a select group of men who perceived the perils of their time and took on themselves the task of adjusting China to modern conditions.

Feeling foreshadows action. Among Chinese sojourners in Japan, dissatisfaction with the Manchu régime was first openly expressed in the pages of the *Journal of Pure Discourses (Ch'ing-i-pao)*, a reformist journal established in 1898. Its early issues contain not only attacks on the conservatives of the Manchu court, but also anti-Manchu writings. Thereafter, as the students increased in number, they began to publish their own magazines. Some, like the *Anthology of Translation (I-shu hui-p'ien)*, aimed at introducing Western ideas, and others, like the *Chinese National (Kuo-min-pao)*, founded in Tokyo in August 1901, adopted a more direct anti-Manchu attitude and advocated nationalism and revolution.

From 1902 to 1904 a host of revolutionary publications appeared. A common feature between them was their emphasis on the necessity of removing the Manchu dynasty as a prerequisite for the regeneration of China. The most important revelation in these publications, however, was the display of the students' consciousness of their own role in rebuilding China, and their eagerness to impart this consciousness to others. Thus the author of the *New Hunan (Hsin Hu-nan)* based his hope of saving China on the 'middle class', which to him

---

* For a fuller discussion see Y. C. Wang, *Chinese Intellectuals and the West, 1872-1949*, North Carolina, 1966, pp. 234-7.

consisted chiefly of the young members of the educated class and some small merchants and property-holders, and he preached that 'uplifting the lower strata of the society to rectify the uppermost social class is your responsibility. Destroying the uppermost social class to protect the lowest social class is also your responsibility.'[7] Another writer emphasised the irreplaceable role of the students in China's transition from old to new, and the utter incompetence and unreliability of the existing ruling class in the performance of that function. The latter writer distrusted the masses also, for he regarded them as 'illiterate, barbarous and knowing neither history nor patriotism'. 'Only students', he reaffirmed, 'placed between the upper class and the masses, may be able to save China from total collapse.'[8]

Towards the end of 1903, the general maturity of China's emerging class of young intellectuals for the task of revolution can be detected in an article entitled 'Nationalism and Education'.* Based on Jeremy Bentham's view of the greatest happiness for the largest number as the chief aim of politics, this article advocated revolution as the only means to achieve this aim, and suggested a plan for instigating and organising revolution. It urged that China's revolution should be based on the support of the common people but led by the middle class, and hence that the preparation and indoctrination of these two groups in the principle of nationalism should be the first concern of revolutionary organizers.[9]

According to this article, training the middle class as revolutionary leaders and training the common people as their followers required different methods. It suggested four ways of preparing the middle class: the formation of special societies, the circulation of secret publications, the organisation of headquarters, and the fostering of love for progress. In organising societies diverse forms and methods were permissible provided there was a common aim to unite them and a definite principle to guide their actions. Books and periodicals were means for communicating ideas and for moulding individual as well as group opinions and desires, and the common headquarters were to co-ordinate the actions of the various societies. Within the bounds of a definite principle or principles, and a common goal, various forms might be employed to advance a common cause.

The common people were divided into three main groups. These were members of secret societies, labourers, and soldiers. For their

---

* 'Min-tsu chu-i chih chiao-yü.' Strictly it should be translated as 'Nationalistic Education'. Its author remains unknown. The acknowledgment reveals that it was adapted and rewritten from an article by Kōzai Tadao, a Japanese.

indoctrination and organisation, it was recommended that revolutionary leaders should infiltrate into their midst and seek to influence them through personal contact so as to change their mentality and outlook, to introduce them to modern ideas and knowledge, and to convert them to the cause of revolution. It was pointed out that many soldiers and labourers were also members of secret societies which had their origin in the anti-Manchu movements dating back to the beginning of the Manchu conquest of China. If these elements could be firmly linked together and a unified command established over them, then they would become an unshakable base for revolution.

This essay presents an extraordinarily up-to-date approach to revolution. Much later practice did not go beyond its suggestions. An interesting point to observe is its idea of infiltration of the labouring class and the army. It was apparently drawn from the practices of the Russian Nihilist movement of the nineteenth century, for which the author showed obvious admiration. If this was the case, it marked the first time China looked to Russia for examples, and the idea itself represents a departure from the Parisian citizen-army tradition of the French revolution.

Revolutionary journals formed one channel through which China's rising class of new intelligentsia made its presence felt. Another was their societies, which appeared one after another, and the formation of each marked a new height and intensity of their anti-Manchu fervour.

The earliest Chinese students' organisation in Japan is reputed to be the Mutual Encouragement Society *(Li-chih-hui)*. It is said to have been essentially a social club without racial distinctions between the Manchus and the Chinese. The presence of some radicals, however, seems to have turned it into a trial ground for the dissemination of revolutionary ideas, and the participation in late 1900 by some of its members in the abortive revolt of the Independent Army in Hankow revealed the rebellious strand of the society. Furthermore, Sun Yat-sen, a revolutionary exile, and a member of the Filipino Independent Army *(Fei-lu-pin tu-li-chun)* were recorded to have attended its New Year party in 1901, an evidence of the society's unconventionality. The majority of its members were, however, not definitely committed to radical courses, so that the decision of the Manchu court in mid-1901 to recognise overseas qualifications and to enlist the services of graduates from foreign schools had a disintegrating effect on the Mutual Encouragement Society. To fill its role, the Chinese Nationals' Association *(Kuo-min-hui)* was formed by the founders of the *Chinese National*. It had as its aims the promotion of revolution and the uniting of the overseas Chinese with the revolutionaries in China for concerted action.[10]

Some societies were formed with the promotion of the welfare of the students in view. But there were always radicals ready to subvert its nature at the first opportunity. Thus the Chinese Students' Association on its opening day was likened to the Independence Hall of the United States of America.[11] Some societies were organised in response to specific situations in China. An example of this category was the Co-operation for Kwangtung Independence Society *(Kwangtung tu-li hsieh-hui)*, formed in the spring of 1902 in response to a rumour that the province of Kwangtung was being ceded to France.[12]

Chinese radicals in Tokyo also frequently made use of historical and festival occasions to demonstrate their surging nationalistic feelings. In 1902 an attempt was made to commemorate the two-hundred-and-forty-second year of the passing of the Ming dynasty, and 26 April, the last day of the last Chinese emperor in Peking, was chosen for the event.[13] In 1903, at a New Year party attended by the Chinese Minister to Japan and more than a thousand students, a speaker narrated the history of the conquest of China by the Manchus, and expressed his conviction that nothing, short of the overthrow of Manchu despotism and the restoration of the rights of the Chinese, could save China. He was given a great ovation by the audience, and a Manchu who tried to speak in defence of his race was shouted down.[14]

In China open expression of racial sentiment was impossible except in areas under foreign influence and control. Thus Hong Kong and the foreign-controlled part of Shanghai became the haven of China's young nationalistic aspirants. This was particularly true of Shanghai which, with its position at the mouth of the Yangtze River and its proximity to Tokyo, became a meeting place of out-going and returning students of the central provinces. From 1895 Hong Kong was the operational centre of Sun Yat-sen's Regenerating China Society *(Hsing-chung-hui)*, and since 1899 it was the base of the *China Daily (Chung-kuo jih-pao)*, a propaganda organ of Sun's society. But the Regenerating China Society had never gone much beyond anti-Manchuism in thought and action, and had never gathered a sufficient number of intellectual followers to transform Hong Kong into an outpost of Chinese nationalism comparable to Tokyo or Shanghai. This basic weakness also underlay the failure of its over-seas branches in Hawaii and Yokohama which led Sung Chiao-jen to write of Sun Yat-sen at this period that he was one who was only able to make a lot of noise.[15]

Shanghai, since its opening for international trade in 1842, had been a important centre for the dissemination of Western knowledge promoted by both Chinese and foreign residents through the press and through missionary schools and societies. In the post-Boxer period the increasing traffic of students in and out of China quickly turned it into a second incubator of Chinese nationalism, next to Tokyo. Radical journals began to flourish, and outspoken figures began to gather there.[16]

The best known and probably also the earliest revolutionary organisation in Shanghai was the Chinese Educational Society *(Chung-kuo chiao-yu-hui)*, formed in 1902. In the name of education it established two teaching institutions, the Patriotic Girls' School *(Ai-kuo nu-hsueh)* and the Patriotic Study Society *(Ai-kuo hsueh-she)*. As these names indicate, the welfare of the Chinese nation was the society's chief concern. The Patriotic Study Society was a particularly active group. It consisted of 400 students, half of whom were dissidents who had walked out of a government school in protest against the dismissal of a student for reading reformist publications, while some of the others were dissidents from a military academy in Nanking. Every week they held a public rally during which lectures were given and ideas of revolution enunciated. Their intemperate utterances later in 1903 involved them in a lawsuit brought against them by the Manchu government in Shanghai's foreign court. This came to be known as the *Kiangsu News (Su-pao)* case, the settlement of which led to the death of a young revolutionary, Tsou Yung, while serving his sentence in prison, and the imprisonment of a learned scholar, Chang Ping-lin, who later greatly aided the cause of revolution with his writings. The *Kiangsu News* case itself helped the revolutionary cause. It was unprecedented for an Emperor of China to sue a subject in a foreign court, and Tsou Yung's seditious pamphlet, *The Revolutionary Army (Ko-ming-chun)*, for which he was sued, became a popular piece of literature sought for at high prices.[17]

Thus the rise of Chinese nationalism, the emergence of a class of revolutionary intellectuals in this period, and their connection with Sung Chiao-jen's development may be summed up as follows. Twentieth-century Chinese nationalism is the mixed progeny of a century of internal maladjustments and half a century of foreign aggression and humiliation. Its midwife was the Manchu government's reform edict which sanctioned the new learning, and decreed the establishment of modern schools and the sending of students overseas. Its main hatchery was Tokyo, where most Chinese went after 1900, while its centre of dissemination on the mainland of China was Shanghai, from which the new hatch spread along the Yangtze River to Sung Chiao-jen's school in Wuchang.

Wuchang was on the south bank of the Yangtze River. As it was only a few days away by boat from Shanghai, and steamships shuttled up and down the Yangtze River, it was easily reached by revolutionary publications from both Shanghai and Japan. The recent association of Hupeh students with anti-government activities could be dated back to the abortive revolt of the Independent Army in 1900, in which a number of students sent by the provincial government to study in Japan were involved. This history, together with the humiliation experienced by China after the Boxer uprising, helped to provoke indignation and create discontent among the students of Wuchang towards their incompetent government. The appearance of Liang Ch'i-ch'ao's *New People's Journal (Hsin-min ts'ung-pao)* in 1902, and later the *Hupeh Student Circle (Hupeh hsueh-sheng-chieh)* and others, caused a great stir in the educated circle.[18]

Under the leadership of a returned military student, Wu Lu-chen, who graduated from a Japanese cadet academy and returned to Hupeh in 1903, a group of students still at military academies began the groundwork for revolution. They aimed chiefly to convert to the cause of revolution two groups of people, the students and the soldiers. For the students they imported revolutionary journals. For the second group they pursued a policy of infiltration, inducing many educated comrades to join the army in order to influence the soldiers by persuasion and example. They were apparently very successful. Within a few months more than forty educated men were said to have enlisted in the army, and some were from Sung Chiao-jen's school.[19]

These young rebels were encouraged in their work by their counterparts in Japan, who in 1903 organised a communication centre disguised as a commercial concern based in Shanghai to distribute revolutionary literature and relay external and internal news between overseas students and those in Wuchang.[20] To facilitate further propaganda it raised $2,000 to buy a movie projector to show films in Wuchang and Hankow. Through a careful selection of films and accompanying explanatory notes and lectures at appropriate moments, this novel introduction must have played a very effective role in opening up the minds of the people. At the same time a public reading-room with a significant name, The Armoury *(Wu-k'u)*, was opened; it was one of the important meeting places of the revolutionaries until the establishment of the Science Study Group.

By mid-1903 the movement in Wuchang was reaching the point of action. It was aided by China's difficulty in securing the withdrawal of Russian troops who had entered Manchuria during the

Boxer uprising. In spite of a previous agreement by which Russia was to withdraw its second batch of troops in April, Russia presented China with a series of fresh demands designed to obtain complete control of Manchuria to the exclusion of other powers. The Chinese Youths' Society, formed in Tokyo at the close of 1902 in imitation of Mazzini's Young Italy, seized this opportunity to organise a 'students' volunteers corps for resisting Russia' *(Chu-o i-yung-tui)* and offered to fight the Russians on behalf of the Government.[21] This gallantry was responded to in Shanghai by the Patriotic Study Society, which also organised a corps along similar lines. In Peking the students of Peking University petitioned the Minister for Education, requesting that the Imperial government refuse the Russian demands. They also dispatched letters to all the schools in Wuchang, pointing out to them the urgency of the crisis in Manchuria and the danger inherent in the government's inaction. It was feared that Chinese appeasement would lead to intervention by other powers, notably Japan and Britain, which were willing to undertake to drive the Russians out for the reward of transforming Manchuria into an international territory.[22]

In Wuchang the news of Russian demands led to a huge gathering in a temple to hear speeches and discuss remedies.[23] The students of the Wuchang Upper Civil High School sent a letter to the Viceroy of Hunan and Hupeh, requesting that a telegram be sent to the central government to the effect that the Russian breach of agreement should be exposed to the world, the backing of Britain and Japan should be obtained in the eventuality of war, and that they, the students themselves, were willing to go to the Manchurian front and die for their country.[24]

These demonstrations were quickly suppressed, however, by the Manchu government, which quite rightly distrusted the students' underlying motives. In Japan the students' army was disbanded by the Japanese government at China's request. Realising that it was impossible to win the trust of the Manchu government, and that it was inadvisable to bring their organisation into the open, the revolutionary students thereafter went underground with a clearly stated aim, the pursuit of Chinese nationalism and independence. Accordingly the Association for National Military Education *(Chun-kuo-min chiao-yu-hui)* was organised in May 1903, and secret agents were sent both to China and to southeast Asia to plan revolution and canvass support.[25] This association marked an important stage of development in the history of the Chinese revolutionary movement. It led to the formation of the China Resurgence Society in Hunan, the Science Study Group in Hupeh, and the Society for the Recovery of China *(Kuang-fu-hui)* in Chekiang, and Sung Chiao-jen was actively involved in two of them.

The formation of the China Resurgence Society, and to a lesser degree that of the Science Study Group, were directly connected with the return of one Huang Hsing from Japan.[26] Like Sung Chiao-jen, he was a man from Hunan, but eight years his senior. Also like Sung, after obtaining his first degree he continued his study in Wuchang, but before Sung's arrival in the same city he had left for Japan on a government scholarship for teacher-training. Like many other Chinese students of his time, particularly those in Japan, he soon came to realise the danger facing China, and blamed it on the corruption and inefficiency of the Manchu government. He participated in the organisation of the anti-Russian student corps, and was among those who volunteered to go to the Manchurian front. After the disbanding of the student corps, he was one of the founders of the Association for National Military Education. Shortly afterwards, on 4 June 1903, he completed his course and left for China, no doubt with the aim of his association rather than the duty of a trained teacher foremost in his mind.

On his way to Changsha he passed through a Shanghai excited by the anti-Manchu utterances of the *Kiangsu News*, and then Wuchang, where he paused to pay a visit to his former school, the College of Hunan and Hupeh, now a central teacher-training institution. Here he stayed for eight days, during which time he distributed to students and soldiers more than four thousand copies of seditious pamphlets, and delivered a lecture on the racial differences between the Han Chinese and the Manchus, and the necessity of changing China's entire political structure and institutions.[27]

Sung Chiao-jen and Huang Hsing probably did not know one another before 1903. There is also no direct record to show that they met on this occasion. But judging by their tradition of regional loyalty, the warm feeling between fellow-provincials abroad, and the national aspirations they shared, they probably did meet, and thus laid the way for co-operation in the establishment of the China Resurgence Society later that year.

The school where Huang Hsing was going to teach was the Illustrious Virtue High School *(Ming-te hsueh-t'ang)*, which was Hunan's first private modern school, opened in Changsha in early 1903. Its founder, Hu Yuan-t'an, was a devoted educator who admired Fukuzawa Yukichi's contribution to modern Japanese education and was determined to play a similar role. He was sympathetic to the cause of revolution, though he does not seem to have actually joined any of its organisations. The majority of men on the staff of his school were returned students from Japan with revolutionary inclinations. Hu, as a respected educator supported by an influential local family, was able to provide an effective cover for their activities.[28]

After several months' preparation, a meeting was convened in Changsha on 4 November 1903. It was held in the home of one P'eng Yuan-hsun. To avoid attention it was proclaimed as a birthday party in Huang Hsing's honour. More than thirty people attended, among whom was Sung Chiao-jen.[29]

The outcome of this meeting was the decision to form the China Resurgence Society, with Huang Hsing as its President.* In an effort to escape attention they adopted a semi-clandestine policy. The society was to appear as the Hua-hsing Company, an industrial concern organised ostensibly to promote the mining industry in Hunan, which was then a growing enterprise popular among Hunan's gentry. An ingenious secret code for communication was invented. The 'mining' industry referred to the task of revolution. 'Buying shares' meant joining their organisation, and 'shares' actually referred to their membership cards.[30]

On 15 February 1904 a second meeting was held, and the society was formally established.[31] Its establishment provided an opportunity to test the postulates on the methods of revolution suggested by some Chinese students in Tokyo. The common people under the leadership of the middle-class intellectuals were to form the main revolutionary base. The organisation of intellectuals (chiefly young students) for revolution posed little problem, since the China Resurgence Society consisted largely of members of the intellectual class who were already quite well placed in various schools. But the common populace, defined as consisting of three main groups, soldiers, secret society members, and labourers, might present some difficulties, since most of them were illiterate. To prevent misunderstandings which might result from direct contact between the members of the society (entirely from the educated class) and the uneducated members of the army and secret societies, two special organisations, the Society of Common Hostility *(T'ung-ch'ou-hui)* to the Manchus and the Yellow-China Society *(Huang-han-hui)* were formed. The first, headed by Huang Hsing and Liu K'uei-i, was to act as a liaison body between the China Resurgence Society and the secret societies, and to prepare and organise the members of the latter for taking concerted action in the event of an uprising; the second

---

* Some sources record that Sung Chiao-jen and Liu K'uei-i were elected Vice-Presidents. See *Hunan chin-pai-nien ta-shih chi-shih*, Vol. I, p. 203.

included Ch'en T'ien-hua, Yao Hung-yeh, and several others, whose duties were agitation among the soldiers and their conversion to the cause of revolution.[32]

More important, however, was the China Resurgence Society's recognition of the need for co-ordinating uprisings in Hunan with those in other provinces. In Huang Hsing's own words, if the risings in Hunan were not responded to in other provinces, then Hunan would be fighting against overwhelming odds; it would then be too difficult for Hunan's revolutionary force to direct attacks on Peking and expel the Manchus; members of the society should establish contact with various revolutionary elements both inside and outside Hunan before an uprising could be considered. Accordingly, members of the China Resurgence Society spread out in various directions either to create revolutionary organs or to establish contact with the already existing revolutionary bodies in other regions. Their activities extended to Hunan's neighbouring provinces such as Szechuan, Kiangsi, Kiangsu, Chekiang, Hupeh, Kwangsi, and to big cities such as Wuchang, Shanghai, and Nanking.[33]

After the formation of the society in Changsha, Sung Chiao-jen returned to Wuchang with one other member to establish a branch of the society and to recruit members, paying particular attention to agitation within Wuchang's New Army.[34] It has been mentioned earlier that Wuchang's army and schools had been the objects of agitation for a group of returned students since early 1903, and quite a number of students had given up studies to join the army. Hu Ying was a student of the Ching-cheng School, a second school established by Hu Yuan-t'an in Changsha. He became a member of the China Resurgence Society, and shortly afterwards had to flee from Changsha because the provincial government had discovered his anti-government activities.* He came to Wuchang and joined the army there to convert the soldiers to the cause of revolution.[35] Little effort seems to have been needed to bring a revolutionary organisation into existence. By mid-1904 the Science Study Group was formed. It consisted chiefly of students of the Civil and Military High Schools and some members of the army. A student of a military academy was elected President, and Sung Chiao-jen and Hu Ying were elected Secretary and Business Manager respectively.[36]

By July 1904 the leaders of the China Resurgence Society considered their organisation ready for action. In fact the movement

---

* According to one source he attempted to assassinate Wang I-wu, a notorious conservative. See Ts'ao Ya-po, *Wuchang ko-ming chen-shih*, Vol. I, p. 3.

among the students had only just begun, and the proposed New Army which the provincial government was to bring into existence, and over which the society was confident of gaining control, was not yet formed. But it was pointed out that over 20,000 secret society members in the existing provincial army were ready for action, and that further delay would be unwise.[37]

Huang Hsing, who was returning to Changsha after an ammunition and arms purchasing trip to Shanghai in late July or August 1904, called in at Wuchang and briefed the members of the Science Study Group about the society's intended revolt for 16 November 1904, the occasion of the Empress Dowager's seventieth birthday. Similar messages were passed on to the revolutionary groups in Chekiang and Fukien.[38]

Like the society in Hunan, the Science Study Group concentrated on winning the support of the army, students, and secret societies. In preparation for the coming revolt, a meeting was held that summer to allocate to its members specific responsibilities, such as propaganda and recruiting activities in the army, schools, and secret societies, fund raising, and the supply of arms. Sung Chiao-jen was given the mission of seeing Huang Hsing in Changsha as the date for the uprising was approaching, presumably to finalise their plan for the event.[39]

The China Resurgence Society's plan for revolt was to blow up Changsha's official assembly hall, where the provincial officials would be holding a celebration in honour of the Empress Dowager's birthday. The revolutionary force, composed of converted soldiers of the local army and led by military students, would then capture Changsha with the auxiliary support of the members of the secret societies. The capture of Changsha would be followed by simultaneous risings in five major centres around Changsha. The secret society members in these centres would play a major role in fighting under the command of specially selected students or cadets. Sung Chiao-jen was chosen to command the revolutionary force in his home prefecture, Ch'ang-te, one of the key centres* for the uprising outside Changsha.[40]

Unfortunately, the conspiracy was discovered by government agents about three weeks before the scheduled uprising. A warrant for the arrest of Huang Hsing was issued by the provincial government on 24 October. According to one source Huang Hsing was cooking 'longevity noodles' to entertain his aunts who had come to wish him a happy birthday, when the police arrived at his doorstep.

---

* The other centres were Li-ling, Heng-chow, Yüeh-chou, and Pao-ch'ing.

The police mistook him for a servant, thus giving him a chance to escape.[41] Thus, by a curious coincidence, Huang Hsing's birthday, which marked the beginning of the China Resurgence Society, also marked its end.

Sung Chiao-jen probably left Wuchang for Changsha in early September 1904. Having seen Huang Hsing and received his instructions to take charge of the uprising in Ch'ang-te, he proceeded to his prefecture.[42]

When their plot was detected by the government, Sung Chiao-jen was at home in T'ao-yuan, trying to raise funds for the impending event by selling his family property. Realising that he could not find buyers quickly enough, he left home at the end of October 1904 for Changsha, where he hoped to raise the money he needed. On 31 October he was in Ch'ang-te conferring with his colleagues. Having instructed them to take over his responsibilities in the region during his absence, and having gathered enough money to make the journey by selling his bedding, spectacles, and summer clothes, he left for Changsha with two colleagues on 2 November, with the intention of returning to his post within eight days.[43]

He arrived in Changsha on 5 November, only to find that their plot had been discovered. Two members of the secret society who had fallen into government hands were executed on that day. One of them, Yu Te-sheng, who was Sung's chief lieutenant in the Ch'ang-te region, had confessed to the government that Sung was one of the five regional commanders in charge of the uprisings. However, the name given was Sung Chia-jen and not Sung Chiao-jen.

At this news, Sung Chiao-jen's immediate plan was to send one of his companions back to Ch'ang-te to start the uprising so as to lessen the pressure on Changsha. But he could not solve his financial problem. In the end he gave in to his friends' advice and left Changsha for Hupeh on a coal boat on 7 November.[44]

He arrived in Wuchang on 16 November, the day of the intended uprising. The city, with its lanterns and flags lining the street to mark the Empress Dowager's birthday, appeared to be in a jubilant mood, but the city gates were heavily guarded and the streets were patrolled by soldiers. His friends from the Wuchang Civil High School informed him that the situation in Wuchang was bad, and that he should leave immediately. He also learned that, warned by an early telegram from Huang Hsing, members of the Science Study Group were able to destroy or hide all evidence of conspiracy, and had evacuated their office before the arrival of the police on 28 October. The Science Study Group suffered no loss except the expulsion of Sung Chiao-jen and one other student from the Wu-chang Civil High School.[45]

While in Wuchang Sung Chiao-jen also met Hu Ying, who told him that Huang Hsing and Liu K'uei-i had already gone to Shanghai, where a new organisation called the Ch'i-hua Translation Bureau was set up to conduct further operations.[46] This news helped Sung to make up his mind to leave for Shanghai, where he arrived on 21 November. But to his astonishment, he found that the Ch'i-hua Translation Bureau had been closed down by the governing authorities. It had been involved in an attempted assassination of a former governor of Kwangsi, whose alleged intention to borrow French troops from Indo-china to quell revolts in that province angered some Chinese patriots.[47] Twelve men, including Huang Hsing, were put in prison.[48]

The Shanghai International Settlement authorities' hunt for culprits was intense. Sung Chiao-jen found it expedient to leave China. On 5 December 1904 he sailed for Japan, not to desert the cause of revolution, but, as he expressed it in a poem while sailing down the Yangtze River, 'Desiring to fulfil my sacred principles, the only course is to begin again'.[49]

The period under discussion was an important period for China, as it witnessed the emergence of a new intellectual élite, which began to challenge the existing order and the established leadership of the traditional Chinese gentry. It was also an important period in Sung Chiao-jen's life. He found himself in the midst of a strong revolutionary undercurrent which, stemming from a small Chinese intellectual élite in Japan, led to the appearance of revolutionary societies in his home province as well as in Hupeh where he was schooling, with himself as one of their prime movers.

These revolutionary societies did not in themselves achieve any of their goals, but had three long-term effects on the course of revolution. Firstly, they became forerunners and models for subsequent revolutionary organisations in the Yangtze provinces, particularly Hupeh, leading to the outbreak of the 1911 revolution in Wuchang. Secondly, the failure of the projected Changsha uprising drove a large number of rebellious youngsters, such as Sung Chiao-jen, to Japan. Their concentration in Tokyo was primarily responsible for the formation of the Chinese League in August 1905. The part played by Sung Chiao-jen and his friends in its formation is evidence of this fact. Thirdly, Sung's own connection with these societies in this period was important to the role he was to play at a later stage of his life. It enabled him to renew this connection in

1911, and to claim leadership for his Central China Office over the various largely self-propelled revolutionary forces.

The method of revolution advocated in this period also seems to have determined the character of the revolutionary movements. Guided by the teaching that under one common goal revolutionary leaders might use diversified means and methods, movements tended to develop along separate and independent courses. This contributed to the centrifugal developments within the revolutionary camp after 1911 when the main goal, the destruction of the existing régime, was attained.

Sources on this period of Sung Chiao-jen's life are scarce and mostly indirect. Consequently his personal development is seen in terms of a broad trend of the time, assuming on good ground that nineteenth-century conditions were responsible for the appearance of an identifiable self-conscious class of men whose aspirations Sung shared and in whose midst Sung found himself. Burdened by a sense of national peril and humiliation, and filled with the new ideals of their age, this new class of men strove to attain freedom, equality, and independence for the Chinese nation as well as for themselves. They sought improvement, if not total change, for China, and demanded a substantial share of leadership and power to shape China's destiny.

FOUR

The Theme of Unity

SUNG CHIAO-JEN's arrival in Japan marked a major turning-point in his life, as well as in the Chinese revolutionary movement. There he stayed for the following six years, during which he witnessed the convergence of China's newly risen forces to form the Chinese League, China's first national revolutionary organisation. He also experienced the numerous difficulties which beset this new organisation and threatened it with ruin.

Living in modernised Japan, particularly in its cosmopolitan capital, Tokyo, meant that he came under more direct foreign influences and stimuli, both intellectual and material, both Japanese and European, than ever before. He had for the first time in his life ample opportunities to broaden his own education in various fields, ranging from politics, economics, law, and psychology to world history, geography, and current affairs. Current events, such as Japan's victory and Russia's defeat in the Russo-Japanese war and the Russian revolution of 1905, left indelible marks on his mind and hardened his anti-dynastic attitude.[1] One of the pen-names he used in this period was Kung Ming,[2] which literally means 'just and wise'. But, more significantly, it was the name of a rebel leader in a popular novel, *All Men Are Brothers*,* which depicts the struggle of a group of men against a corrupt and oppressive régime.

This phase of Sung's life began with his arrival in Tokyo on 13 December 1904.[3] He was met by representatives of both the Chinese Students Association and his provincial organisation, as well as his old school acquaintances. With their aid he quickly settled down in his new environment. No one seems to have been worried by the presence in their midst of a rebel wanted by their government. On the contrary, they showed great interest and sympathy towards him and his cause. Ten days after Sung's arrival the Wuchang Civil High School Old Boys' Association held a meeting to hear his

---

* *Shui-hu-chuan* (The Story of the Water Margin), translated and retitled by Pearl Buck as *All Men Are Brothers* (New York, 1933).

account of the happenings in Hunan and Hupeh, and offered to raise money for him to continue his education.[4] This was in marked contrast to the experience of Sun Yat-sen, who, a few years earlier, was thought of as a bandit with red eyebrows and green eyes. Evidently these students were psychologically another step closer to open action.

Sung did not accept the assistance offered to him. His immediate objective was to carry on his campaign against the Manchu government. However, the failure of the Changsha revolt seems to have convinced him that the time was not yet ripe for armed uprisings, and that fuller preparation of the minds of the people through such media as journals, newspapers and books was required before attempting further coups.[5] Apparently this conviction led him to seek to establish a journal, as well as to write for various student publications, such as the *Vernacular Magazine (Pai-hua-pao)* and the *Awakening Lion (Hsing-shih)*.[6]

In early January 1905 Sung Chiao-jen first told his friends of his wish to found a journal. Within a few weeks he had gathered sufficient support to organise the Twentieth-Century China *(Erh-shih shih-chi chih chih-na she)*, to publish a journal of the same name, with himself as its general secretary.[7] Thereafter, however, he encountered many difficulties. Besides financial problems, there were not enough contributors of articles, and there were some who wanted to see the journal changed from a general propaganda organ to a more specialised periodical on law or government. Delay in publication in turn disheartened many supporters, who pressed for the dissolution of the proposed journal and the refund of subscriptions to shareholders. Obstacles in the way of the journal seemed so great that its first editor resigned from his post.[8] But Sung Chiao-jen persisted, and on 24 June, after six months of unrelenting effort, the first issue of the magazine at last appeared.

Twentieth-Century China was a short-lived magazine, but it is worthy of attention for the light it sheds on some aspects of Sung Chiao-jen's life and the revolutionary movements. Firstly, it contains Sung's work, which, written soon after his arrival in Japan, expresses his early thought, and is a good sample of the result of modernised learning in China and the Chinese environment.[9]

The aim of *Twentieth-Century China* was 'to promote national spirit and to import and disseminate modern knowledge'.[10] In the Preface to its first issue[11] this aim was explained more fully. It was to cultivate patriotism, through which to save and regenerate China. Patriotism grew out of a consciousness of the people as a nation, and this consciousness was the result of education. Hence the *Twentieth-*

Century China was founded. With this end in view it was necessarily miscellaneous in character. It contained discourses on philosophy, law and government, history, military and natural sciences, economics and industry, art and literature, news and news commentary, and so on. Its style was scholarly, and its language was generally calm, rational, and persuasive. Since it aimed to educate the people, the ruled rather than the rulers received most of its attention. While criticisms of China's shortcomings often landed in the government's court, the people were held ultimately responsible for what happened to themselves and to their country.

Criticisms, whether of the government, or of the people, or of both together, were often made indirectly and inoffensively. Thus in an article on San Francisco,[12] the Chinese inhabitants of that city were ridiculed for their uncleanliness and senseless gambling habits, on account of which American parents forbade their children to go near the Chinese districts. Yet, while China was exploited by ruthless Western traders, the same Chinese who wasted thousands of dollars in gambling dens and on permits provided China with its only foreign exchange! The journal noted that formerly the Chinese and Japanese were treated equally by Westerners—at one time the Americans even favoured the Chinese—but that now the opposite was true. If some Americans still treated Chinese decently, it was out of pity rather than respect! Japanese business in San Francisco was still small. In contrast the Chinese population approached 10,000, and there was a wide, centrally situated Chinese street. But, the journal pointed out, there were no big Chinese traders. Porcelain was the main Chinese item of its trade. The rest of its goods came mainly from Japan. Even in the China trade, despite the fame of Chinese products, many Chinese preferred to import and sell porcelain from Japan. The American social system, particularly the social status of American women and their magnanimity, were praised in the journal, and were attributed to America's co-educational system and its numerous schools. Furthermore, the adaptability and open-mindedness of the Japanese were used to show the backwardness and rigidity of the Chinese. The Japanese in America dressed like the Americans and were very clean. But the Chinese, excepting the students, all were determined to keep their old habits, and treated the queue on their head as one of their special national excellences; for this they were called 'Mr Pigtails' by the Americans.

Referring to the 4,000-year-old Egyptian mummies in an American museum, the journal pointed out that at one time the proud kings and dukes of Egypt feared their own disappearance after deathlike dead grass and wood, and contrived to preserve their bodies. But now they had lost their country, and their remains became amusing curios. What a reward!

These examples illustrate the style of writing contained in the first issue of the *Twentieth-Century China*. It was simple, direct, mild in tone, and carried its points well.

Some articles were more sophisticated, and adopted a more serious tone. An example of this category was Sung's 'History of Chinese Expansionism',[13] in which he sought to restore Chinese self-respect and confidence by reminding his countrymen of Chinese might and greatness in the past. Expansionism and imperialism were still respectable themes then. Consequently Sung Chiao-jen exalted China's traditional martial spirit, expansion, and conquests, which, Sung proudly claimed, made her a good match for any modern imperialism of the West. He exhorted his countrymen to study their own history, which would show them that the present phase of decline was merely a temporary phenomenon, and would soon pass. With undoubtedly the catastrophic experience of the Boxer Uprising in mind, he asked the Chinese to refrain from taking impulsive action, while remaining anti-foreign at heart. In this he was not original. It was a painful reflection, widely shared among the educated Chinese after 1900, and the resultant maxim was carefully observed by the revolutionaries throughout the pre-Republican era, and was not challenged until long after the 1911 revolution.

Secondly, at the time of its founding, it seems that no similar type of propaganda organ existed among the students in Tokyo. The once prospering student publications appear to have withered away, and, as one of Sung's friends put it, 'the student circle was sterile and lifeless, and no one else was prepared to promote such an under-taking'.[14] It seems that 1904 was the year of attempted uprisings in central China. It could be that the return of the most volatile and energetic student leaders to China had weakened the strength of those in Japan.[15] Furthermore, by early 1905, internal and external events, such as the failure of the attempted uprisings in central China, and the turning of Manchuria into a battlefield by Japan and Russia, depressed many patriots, while talk of constitutional government in the Manchu court tended to strengthen the reformist cause and soften the anti-Manchu feelings of some advocates of violence. A case in point was Ch'en T'ien-hua, a well known radical, who in early 1905 was on the verge of giving up the revolutionary cause in favour of relying on the Manchus to resist China's external foes.[16] In this atmosphere *Twentieth-Century China* served as a booster to the morale of the revolutionary camp. Its unfaltering tone must have sounded like a morning siren awakening the waverers from their moments of slumber.

Twentieth-Century China had reached only its second issue when it was banned by the Japanese government on the grounds that it contained utterances hostile to Japan and detrimental to Sino-Japanese relations.[17] The fact that it was banned so soon after its appearance was, in this case, an indication of its vitality and power. It revealed truths unbearable to the enemies. As in so many other instances, oppression and suppression rarely succeed in controlling the expression of opinions or in daunting the effort of determined men from imparting their message. *Twentieth-Century China* simply adopted another name, the *People's Journal (Min-pao)*,[18] which in a few years was to attain widespread influence in propagating the cause of revolution. In view of the lack of interest of the other revolutionary leaders of this period in establishing propaganda organs, it was no wonder that a year later, on the occasion of the first anniversary of the *People's Journal*, Sung Chiao-jen looked back with sighs of satisfaction.[19] It was mainly due to his initial effort and persistence that this influential journal came into existence. The importance of the journal can further be seen in the fact that the founders of *Twentieth-Century China* were among the founders of the Chinese League, and it would not be an exaggeration to describe the office of *Twentieth-Century China* as a cradle of the Chinese League. It was one of the places where the revolutionaries met to bring the league into existence.[20]

The formation of the Chinese League in 1905 was an important landmark in China's pre-Republican revolutionary movements, and Sun Yat-sen has usually been credited with its establishment. While the importance of his role should be recognised, one must guard against overstating the contribution of any one individual. Many others played at least equally important parts, and there was an unmistakable longing among the modern educated men for unity, a trend increasingly evident since 1903. In that year there appeared in Shanghai a movement to form a Chinese Scholars' League *(Chung-kuo chiao-hsueh t'ung meng-hui)*, with the aim of uniting China's educated class to provide a foundation for the eventual formation of a Chinese Nationals' League *(Chung-kuo kuo-min t'ung-meng-hui)*.[21] At about the same time in Japan, Chinese students began to criticise provincialism and the invisible boundaries that separated them. It was suggested that a United China Association *(Chung-kuo pen-pu t'ung-i-hui)* should be formed to provide a central organisation for the students, and to attend to publication and other activities of common interest. In order to promote and heighten the national consciousness of the students, it was further suggested that the proposed association should observe strictly national boundaries. It would not admit foreigners as members. A regular monthly meeting was to be held, and a national anthem to be sung on each occasion.[22]

The idea of a united students' association quickly found response in Shanghai. On 30 May 1903, a journal in that city published an editorial entitled 'A discussion of the proposal to establish a Chinese Students' League', and urged its formation. It pointed out that China had had modern students for the past twenty years and that they continued to increase in number and improve in quality. 'But', it asked, 'what have these scores of thousands of students achieved?' According to this editorial nothing had been achieved, and the reason was the lack of unity and the absence of a unified organisation. It further lamented that 'if the students whose position, ideals, and interests are not at variance cannot form an united organisation, what chance is there for others to do so?'[23]

The impact of these outcries for unity and for the destruction of regionalism was almost immediately noticeable. Formerly students were fond of naming their publications according to their provincial or regional groupings, such as the *New Kwantung (Hsin Kwangtung)*, the *New Hunan (Hsin Hunan)*, the *Kiangsu*, the *Tide of Chekiang (Che-chiang-ch'ao)*, and the *Hupeh Student Circle (Hupeh hsueh-sheng-chieh)*. After 1903 names with regional connotations were rarely seen. They had given way to titles with broader and more encompassing national implications, such as *Twentieth-Century China*, the *Awakening Lion*, the *New Century (Hsin-shih-chi)*, the *Chinese Flag (Han-chih)*, and, of course, the *People's Journal*. It was probably in response to the demand of the time that in June 1903 the *Hupeh Student Circle* changed its name to the *Voice of China (Han-sheng)*.[24] Even more significantly, an advertisement for an organisation bearing the title of 'Alliance League for regions North and South of the Great Lake' *(Ta-hu nan-pei t'ung-meng-hui)* appeared in the *Hupeh Student Circle* of May 1903, and again in the *Voice of China* in July-August 1903. Except for this suggestive title, nothing else is known, but one may justifiably suspect that it was a partial response of the students to the call of their time, and, if it was, it marked their first move towards unity.

Throughout 1904, however, no major stride towards student unity was discernible. It was a year when some students attempted uprisings in their respective provinces in central China. It was not until after the failure of these separate attempts that the need for unity and concerted action through a unified national organisation was most keenly felt. In 1905 the concentration in Tokyo of leaders, such as Sung Chiao-jen, Huang Hsing, T'ao Ch'eng-chang, and others, made unity physically possible for the first time. Taking these circumstances into consideration, the birth of a national revolutionary organisation in that year seems a logical conclusion. With Sun Yat-sen's aid, the Chinese League was brought into being, with him at its head. Without him a similar organisation would also sooner or later have been created with someone else, possibly Huang Hsing or Sung Chiao-jen, in command.

It should be pointed out that Sun's share, instrumental or otherwise, in the establishment of the Chinese League was no mere coincidence. It represented the culmination of his labour for ten years as an untiring promoter and agitator for the cause of revolution. His association with the Chinese students in Japan began not much earlier than 1900, but the foundation for it was laid in 1895, when he visited Japan for the first time, and founded a branch of his Regenerating China Society in Yokohama.[25] It was not until his second visit in 1897, however, that he managed to establish some contact with them.[26] Between 1897 and 1900 there were fewer than one hundred Chinese students in Japan, and some were said to have visited Sun Yat-sen and been favourably impressed by him. But, with the exception of two, one a school boy of fourteen* who was sworn in by his Cantonese father's order, and the other an ex-reformer and romantic from Hunan,† no other students joined his organisation.[27] This lack of rapport was at least partly due to a continuing mutual distrust between Sun, a foreign-educated man, and the students, who were bona fide products of indigenous Chinese schools.[28] Sun's revolutionary strategy at the time did not include recruitment of members of the educated class. He deemed China ripe for popular revolt and expected a Taiping type of spontaneous peasant rising to occur at the first opportunity. In this anticipation, apart from his doubt on the suitability of Chinese-educated scholars as revolutionary material, the students, who had neither money nor man-power to contribute, must have also seemed to be poor second-rate recruits.

After 1900, following the increase of Chinese students in Japan and after further unsuccessful attempts at uprisings, Sun took greater interest in them. In 1901 in Tokyo he supported the students' Kwangtung independence movement.[29] In 1902 he took part in a plan to commemorate the two-hundred-and-forty-second year of the passing

---

* Feng Tzu-yu. See his *Ko-ming i-shih*, Vol. I, 'Tzu-hsü', p. 3.

† Pi Yung-nien, who was so disappointed by the selfishness and pettiness of some of his colleagues in the abortive Independent Army revolt that he retired to become a Buddhist monk. See Feng Tzu-yu, *Ko-ming i-shih*, Vol. I, pp. 73-6.

of the Ming dynasty.[30] He was also said to have been responsible for an anti-Manchu speech in 1903, delivered by a student from Hupeh to a New Year gathering attended by students and some Manchu officials.[31] If this was true, it was the first instance of Sun's direct influence on the action of Chinese students in Japan. In the same year Sun helped to organise a military school to train students who were barred from Japanese military institutions.[32]

In connection with the establishment of a military school in Tokyo, there are three noteworthy points. Firstly, Sun introduced a new oath which read, 'Expel the Manchus, restore China, establish a republic and equalise land rights'. The last plank was a new addition to the previous oath of the Regenerating China Society. The contents of this oath subsequently became the three principles of the Chinese League, namely Nationalism, Democracy, and the Social Welfare of the People.

Secondly, fourteen students were enrolled in his military school, of whom twelve were from Sun's own province, and the other two from Fukien.[33] This suggests that Sun's influence had not yet gone far beyond the boundaries of his own province.

Thirdly, two of the fourteen students later taught in Hunan, and one actually became a member of Sung Chiao-jen's China Resurgence Society.[34] But there is no evidence of any influence which they might have exercised to bring Sun and Sung, or other Hunanese leaders, together.

Among the more significant events of 1903 were perhaps the appearance in Shanghai of a Chinese translation of the *Thirty-three Years' Dream (Sanju-sannen no yume)*, by Miyazaki Torazo, and an article by Sun Yat-sen in a Chinese students' journal in Tokyo. Miyazaki's book was in fact an account of Sun Yat-sen's revolutionary career. Its translation and publication in Shanghai marked the beginning of interest in him among Chinese intellectuals. Sun Yat-sen's article, entitled 'Discourse on the Preservation or Dismemberment of China', expressed his confidence in the ability of Chinese patriots to save China, and openly attacked foreign imperialism.[35] Sun at last showed positive appreciation of the students' potential, and made an effort to identify his cause with theirs. Sun might even have entertained a bigger rally, for in 1903 it had been suggested to him that a rally of the gentry scholars should begin with rallies among overseas Chinese students.[36] The publication of Sun's article in a student journal in turn suggests that Sun began to find his way into the circle of China's new élite. Thereafter, however, Sun was away from Japan until the eve of the formation of the Chinese League, and, during his absence, the membership of his Regenerating China Society dwindled drastically. Only a dozen men still maintained contact with him.[37] This decline, however, may have been due to Sun's deliberate neglect. He seems to have perceived a new source of strength for his cause, and decided to change his path. In search of this strength, he toured Hawaii and America throughout 1904, and eventually, in early 1905, found the main clue in Europe, which led him back to Tokyo.

Through Liu Ch'eng-yu, significantly a former student in Japan, Chinese students in Europe expressed their desire to meet Sun. They invited him to Europe, listened to him, and then pledged themselves to the cause of revolution under his leadership.[38] This marked the beginning of a major turning-point in both Sun Yat-sen's career and the course of China's revolution. Soon afterwards Sun found acceptance and support among the revolutionary students in Tokyo, and was made head of their movement.

Thus it can be seen that before 1905 Sun Yat-sen had only very slender links with the new student élite, whether in Tokyo or in China. Sung Chiao-jen and other fresh arrivals in Japan in early 1905 had no chance of meeting Sun for another six months, and then they had no time to get well acquainted with him personally before the establishment of the Chinese League. This fact must be borne in mind in the study of later friction within the Chinese League, and the difficulties between him and Sung Chiao-jen.

Immediately on arrival in Japan, both Sung Chiao-jen and Huang Hsing wanted to organise a revolutionary party. They delayed this, however, at the request of one Ch'eng Chia-sheng, a revolutionary from Anhwei, who advised them in the following terms:

> Revolution means conspiracy; we should seek the practice of revolution and not merely the name. Sun Wen (Sun Yat-sen) will visit Japan soon. We should wait for his arrival and let him bear the name of the organisation so that we may return to China to await opportunities for a rising.[39]

Ch'eng's reason for postponing the organisation of a revolutionary party, and its apparent acceptance by Sung Chiao-jen and Huang Hsing, suggests what may have been the motives of some student leaders in supporting Sun Yat-sen as head of their revolutionary movement later. No reference was made to his personality or ideology. Their chief consideration seems to have been that Sun's revolutionary fame might facilitate their activities. With Sun at the head of their party, it would be to him that world attention would be drawn, while they, the real activists, would remain unexposed and would be able to work with greater effectiveness.[40]

It is also significant that this suggestion should come from Ch'eng. He was older than Sung Chiao-jen, and he had known Sun Yat-sen since 1902. Sun's rise to prominence in the students' revolutionary movement depended much on the support of a few acquaintances he had made in Tokyo before 1904. Thus his acquaintance with a few Hupeh students in 1902 had laid the foundation of support for him among the Chinese students in Europe in early 1905, when revolutionary movements among the Chinese students were rapidly reaching the stage of unification.[41] Through this support, and with the aid of a few Chinese and Japanese friends in Tokyo, he was able to obtain the allegiance of student leaders such as Sung Chiao-jen, Huang Hsing, and others who supported his leadership in the newly formed Chinese League.[42]

The news of the students' move in Europe to support Sun as their revolutionary leader, and of Sun's impending arrival in Japan, was passed on to the students by Feng Tzu-yu, one of Sun's first followers in Japan. According to Feng, everyone was frantically overjoyed at the news, though he does not make precisely clear the identity of 'everyone'.[43] Two days before Sun's arrival in Yokohama, Sung Chiao-jen received from Miyazaki Torazo through Ch'eng Chia-sheng an invitation to see him. On 19 July 1905, when Sun arrived in Yokohama, Sung Chiao-jen and Ch'eng Chia-sheng were with Miyazaki. Miyazaki was one of Sun's closest Japanese friends and admirers. He offered to introduce Sun to them, advised them to co-operate with him, and described him as a man of high ideals and honesty unmatched in East or West. He added significantly that Sun Yat-sen's name was too well known; his movements tended to attract the world's immediate attention, which meant that he was very hesitant to take action himself. Miyazaki advised his visitors that they should aim for secrecy and practicability in their future undertakings. This advice was probably intended for Sung's ears, since Ch'eng had expressed the same view. He also warned his visitors of the ambitions of the powers, including Japan, in China. In his opinion, the only Japanese politician with a sincere interest in China's welfare was Inukai Ki, who had aided both him and Sun Yat-sen in their activities.[44]

The meeting was apparently agreeable and absorbing, and Sung was very interested in their discussion, for they arrived in the morning and did not take their leave until dusk. In connection with the meeting it is perhaps worth noting that Sun Yat-sen's initial approach to student leaders like Sung Chiao-jen was through a Japanese rather than a Chinese. This, together with a claim that he was said to have asked his Japanese friends for information on able leaders among the Chinese students in Japan,[45] indicates strongly the absence of more direct contact between Sun and the students in Tokyo, which in turn casts doubt on the accuracy of such statements as 'several hundred Chinese students were waiting to welcome Sun at the dock in Yokohama' or 'numerous students went to visit Sun in Yokohama immediately after his arrival'.[46] It was more likely that this happened after, not before, Sun had established direct contact with student leaders like Sung Chiao-jen and Huang Hsing.

During the week following Sun's arrival, a great deal of negotiation seems to have been carried out to bring Sun and the students together. This perhaps accounts for the frequent travels of some students from Tokyo to Yokohama.

On 25 July 1905 Sung was informed that Sun was in Tokyo, and three days later they met for the first time in the office of *Twentieth-Century China*, in the presence of Ch'eng Chia-sheng, Ch'en T'ien-hua, and Miyazaki Torazo.[47] Sung said little at this meeting, which appears to have been dominated by Sun Yat-sen. Sun spoke on the need for unity among the revolutionaries, and the danger of separate actions. In his opinion, division within the revolutionary forces would lead to chaos which would in turn invite foreign intervention and partition. He also talked about the importance of recruiting people of ability into the revolutionary movement. They were required both for destruction during the revolution and for reconstruction after it.[48]

On the following day members of the China Resurgence Society held a special meeting to discuss the problem of amalgamation with Sun Yat-sen's organisation, for there was no unanimity among its members on this question. Ch'en T'ien-hua favoured amalgamation on a group basis. Huang Hsing suggested a formal union but with the China Resurgence Society retaining its former identity, while Liu K'uei-i opposed the whole idea of union. There were other opinions, but, to Sung Chiao-jen, the only basic difference was that some favoured and some opposed it. Accordingly he suggested that, since there were two groups with opposing views, the future relationship between those who joined the amalgamated organisation and those who did not should be discussed. In the end, however, no satisfactory agreement was reached. The leaders took the easy way out by leaving each member to decide for himself.[49]

As it turned out, this meeting marked the end of the China Resurgence Society, since the Chinese League was formed soon afterwards. The significance of the disagreements which characterised the final meeting of the China Resurgence Society lay not in the number who refused to join the Chinese League but in the number who did. Most of the well known members of the China Resurgence Society, including even Liu K'uei-i, who opposed union with Sun Yat-sen, joined the amalgamated body. Clearly desire for common action far exceeded other considerations.

A series of meetings between Sun and the student leaders followed the meeting of Sung and Sun. The sources are not unanimous with regard to the time and place of these meetings.[50] It appears that the decision to form the Chinese League was reached at a meeting in the house of a Japanese on 30 July 1905. Sung Chiao-jen recorded the following comments in his diary:

> At about 1 p.m. I went to attend Sun Yat-sen's meeting in the office of the Black Dragon Society in . . . Akasaka district. When I arrived the meeting had already begun. There were about seventy people. Sun Yat-sen was the first to speak on the reasons for revolution, and the present trends and methods. He spoke for about an hour. Huang Ch'ing-wu [Huang Hsing] then announced that today's meeting was intended for the formation of a society, and asked the people present to sign their names. Therefore all signed their names. Sun Yat-sen then declared the aims of the society. Each member then wrote his own oath and signed it, and when they had learned the hand-signals [secret signs of communication between members], an election of draftsmen to draw up the society's constitution took place. Eight men, including Huang Hsing, were elected.[51]

During the following fortnight, membership of the not yet officially established Chinese League increased rapidly. Probably encouraged by the enthusiasm of the students, their leaders decided to stage a public welcome for Sun Yat-sen to publicise their cause. This was held on 13 August 1905, with Sung Chiao-jen as its chairman, and was said to have been a great success. More than seven hundred people packed the hall, and many more, who arrived late, could not gain admittance and had to stand outside.[52]

Exactly one week after this public demonstration, a secret meeting was held in the house of another Japanese, Sakamoto Kinya, to bring the Chinese League into official existence. In the presence of more than three hundred people a draft constitution of thirty articles was read, discussed, modified, and adopted. Following the election of office-bearers, the Chinese League was born.[53]

At last the revolutionary students' longing for unity and centralised command was fulfilled. In the hierarchy of the new organisation, Sun Yat-sen became the *Tsung-li*, the equivalent of 'president' or 'chairman', but now a sanctified title reserved for him only. He was also concurrently head of the Executive Department *(Chih-hsing-pu)*. Huang Hsing was the head of the Bureau of General Affairs, one of eight bureaux in the Executive Department. In that capacity he was also the acting *Tsung-li* during Sun's absence from Tokyo. Sung Chiao-jen was made one of two procurators in the Disciplinary Department, with the duty of ensuring party unity and the loyalty of party members.[54]

Sun Yat-sen's chief contribution to the revolutionary movement in China is generally held to be his ideology—the Three Principles of the People. But at the time of the founding of the Chinese League the organisation's political platform was far from clear. Sung Chiao-jen's account of an incident at a meeting in Tokyo illustrates this point:

> On the following day* the inaugural meeting was held in the house of Uchida Ryohei in . . . Akasaka district . . . Someone asked Sun Wen [Sun Yat-sen], 'When one day revolution succeeds, could you please tell us frankly whether you will choose monarchy or democracy?' There were at the meeting nearly three hundred people. The question came in the midst of a flowing speech. On hearing it, like splitting a piece of silk suddenly reaching its end, an abrupt silence overcame the gathering. Sun Wen and Huang Hsing did not know what to say. They were speechless and could not answer it . . . Realising the seriousness of the situation, he [Ch'eng Chia-sheng] came over from where he was sitting and said, 'Revolution is a public affair of the whole nation. How can Sun . . . decide for democracy or monarchy? If we do not in our hearts desire imperial glories, then there is no ground for monarchy to grow on. At today's meeting we will only consider whether the Manchu dynasty should be removed, and not be concerned with questions of monarchy or democracy.' Thus decision was reached. Membership papers were signed with enthusiasm, and the society was named the Chinese League. . . .[55]

Clearly, in 1905 nationalism was the main driving force of China's revolutionary movements. The other goals, democracy and social welfare, were hardly emphasised or defined, and became later a source of disagreement within the organisation.

Apart from its ill-defined aims and the absence of a more positive ideology as the basis of revolution, there were apparently basic differences in attitude between Sun Yat-sen and the students over organisation. Sung thus described another of his meetings with Sun, held in the house of his friend, Ch'eng Chia-sheng:

---

* According to Sung Chiao-jen's diary, this meeting was held on 16 August 1905.

When Sun Wen arrived in Japan, he [Ch'eng Chia-sheng] gather-ed together Ch'en T'ien-hua, Huang, Sung, Pai Yu-huan, Chang Chi, Tan T'ao, Wu Yang-kung to confer with Sun . . . Sun still insisted on his twenty-man organisation. From noon to dusk no decision could be reached . . . Ch'eng said, 'Open up the mountain in order to reach the spring and tap its water. Why should we restrict ourselves to twenty men? The canal has since reached the size of a big river, so why still use the former method of measuring shallow depths with animal hoofs?[56]

It is not clear what this 'twenty-man organisation' was, but Ch'eng Chia-sheng's words indicate that Sun wanted a smaller and tighter organisation or inner ring, rather than a loose and broadly based organisation as desired by the students. There is no way of ascertain-ing the degree of difference between them, nor whether the structure of the Chinese League was in fact a victory for Sun, or for the students, or whether it was a compromise. But the significance of this dissension became meaningful almost ten years later, when Sung Chiao-jen reorganised the Chinese League into an overt political party with a broadened base, a move Sun later disagreed with. Sung was severely criticised, and, after his death, Sun organised the Chinese Revolutionary Party, requiring his followers to swear personal obedience to his leadership.

The hard core of the Chinese League consisted of men from three pre-1905 societies: Sun's Regenerating China Society, a Cantonese group; Huang and Sung's China Resurgence Society, a Hunan-Hupeh body; and the Society for the Recovery of China, from Chekiang. Each of these had its own regional basis and was subject to specific gravitational pull. Formal unity was achieved among the revolutionary forces within a month of Sun's arrival in Japan. But its maintenance depended greatly upon extensive homogeneity in thought, which would take longer to attain. It was precisely the absence of the latter which created difficulties for the Chinese League shortly after its formation. It gave rise to separatist move-ments, and eventually separated Sun Yat-sen from the Tokyo group led by Sung Chiao-jen and his friends.

FIVE

Education and Revolution

FROM ITS establishment in 1905 until 1910, the Chinese League carried out a series of unsuccessful revolts in China's southern provinces. Sung Chiao-jen, however, did not take part in them. After the abortive Changsha revolt, he appears to have been convinced that more solid groundwork should be carried out before making further armed attempts. He was against rash undertakings.

In September 1906, when Huang Hsing returned to Tokyo after visiting Hong Kong and Saigon, Sung Chiao-jen attempted to persuade him to moderate his activities, but without success.[1] Sung feared that impatience and recklessness might lead to a situation where the strength of the Chinese League could be gambled away in one stroke. It was probably partly due to this conviction that Sung remained in Tokyo throughout this period. Another reason for his decision to stay in Tokyo was probably his desire for higher learning. He frequently said, 'Brave men and men who can be in the vanguard of revolution are easy to find, but those who can think clearly and carefully are few. Unless the foundations are first laid the fall of the Manchus will create more problems for us than we had before.'[2]

Because he realised the need for men of ability to engage in post-revolutionary reconstruction Sung felt he had to devise plans to produce them. Thus in the summer of 1906 he organised a society to study politics and government. On many a Sunday Sung and his friends apparently gathered at Enoshima, an island resort on Tokyo Bay, or in the Temple of the Twelve Gods in Shinjuku-ku, to discuss political problems.

In pursuit of knowledge Sung at this time not only stayed away from the battlefront, but also tried on several occasions to hand over to others the offices he held in the Tokyo headquarters of the Chinese League. In this, however, he rarely succeeded. His leadership and his organising ability often seemed indispensable to his colleagues in the movement's activities.

The first act of the Chinese League after its formation was to set up a propaganda organ. Sung Chiao-jen's *Twentieth-Century China* made its first appearance in June 1905. The magazine at once caught the attention of the student circle, so that when it was offered to the Chinese League as its party organ, it was received enthusiastically. The method of handing it over was first discussed on 27 August, when it was decided that Sung Chiao-jen would officially present it to the Chinese League and Huang Hsing would receive it on behalf of the organisation. On the same day the second issue of the magazine was ready for distribution, but unfortunately an article entitled 'A discussion of the Japanese politicians' designs on China' offended the Japanese authorities, and the magazine was confiscated, so that, on the day set for its official handover, Sung only had the ledger, cash, books, office equipment, and official seals to deliver.[3]

Having failed to persuade the Japanese authorities to return the confiscated magazine, Sung suggested reprinting it for circulation. It was not, however, the policy of the Chinese League to antagonise foreign powers. On 19 September it was decided to continue publication under a different name. The new magazine would thus appear as something separate from and indeed totally unrelated to *Twentieth-Century China*. On the following day Sung wrote to advise his colleagues on the procedure for terminating the journal, and the next day he learned that it was renamed the *People's Journal (Min-pao)*. New personnel were added to the staff of the journal, among whom was Chang Chi, who was made publisher and manager because he was fluent in Japanese. It seems, however, that the actual management of the journal continued to be Sung's responsibility, until he relinquished it in early 1906 to pursue his own studies.[4]

The objectives of the *People's Journal* were twofold: to propagate the cause of revolution, and to counteract reformist influences. Among the six planks of the journal, one aiming to 'promote closer relations between the peoples of China and Japan' and one to 'campaign for international approval and support for China's revolutionary cause' were departures from the platform of Sung's *Twentieth-Century China*, which aimed to promote 'moral patriotism, independence, and self-reliance'.[5] These departures were important because they represented some of the concrete imprints of Sun Yat-sen's influence on the character of the Chinese League, and also some of the basic differences in attitudes between Sun's Cantonese group and Sung's Tokyo or Central China faction concerning nationalism and foreign relations. The nationalism of the young Chinese intellectuals had its root in anti-foreignism, which led to demands for the removal of the incompetent alien Manchu government and the restoration of the seat of power to the Chinese. To Sung and his friends it was essentially a Chinese affair. To them foreigners were basically untrustworthy, especially when there were conflicting interests between them and China. It followed that their aid should not be accepted lightly. Sun Yat-sen, in contrast, saw China's revolution in the light of world progress and as a part of modern international developments. He saw no conflict of interests between foreign powers and an enlightened, modernised China. To him their interests were mutual. He did not fear foreign imperialism. Instead he had actively sought their aid and co-operation, sometimes even at the expense of some national interests. This difference between Sun and the Tokyo group was a basic cause of later friction in their revolutionary movement.

Since 1902 Liang Ch'i-ch'ao's reformist journal, the *New People's Journal*, had dominated the Chinese press in Tokyo, and met only sporadic challenges from some revolutionary publications. The *People's Journal* of the Chinese League represented the first organised effort of the revolutionaries to counteract its influence. The wider goal of this challenge was to woo public opinion, both national and international, but the immediate prize was the minds of the Chinese students in Tokyo. There were about eight thousand students in Japan in 1905, but only a few hundred had joined the League. Only by demolishing the views of their reformist opponents could the revolutionaries hope to extend its influence.

The duel between the two journals lasted nearly three years, but for the revolutionary camp the reward was rich. The revolutionaries' more concrete political and economic plans, based on current belief in progress and evaluations of China's relative position and capabilities for change, seem more attuned to the mood of the students and the nation at large. The focus of resentment on corruption, chaos, weakness, and backwardness was far more tangible to an average mind than the reformers' theory of gradual evolution or their uncertain fears of the future. Thus the influence of the *People's Journal* was well established within the first year of its existence. When a celebration was held for its first anniverary on 2 December 1906, it boasted an attendance of ten thousand enthusiasts, and in addition its voice was echoed far and wide by a number of other publications.[6] By 1907 the harassed reformers were ready to seek peace, and approached Sung Chiao-jen for this purpose, but their bid was rejected by the leadership of the League.[7]

In the first two years the *People's Journal* contained a series of well presented, cool-headed articles. From the twentieth issue onward, however, emphasis was laid on nationalism and heroics. This seems to have been a reaction to repeated failures suffered by the revolutionaries in their risings in south China. Their numerous defeats had, as feared by Sung Chiao-jen, begun to affect the morale of his colleagues, and drove some to advocate heroics and assassination in place of careful groundwork and systematic group action. The call for assassinations, terrorism, and individual action had untold adverse effects on the fate of the revolution. Thus the assassination in Canton of Fu Ch'i, a Manchu military commandant, by an overseas Chinese, Wen Sheng-ts'ai, immediately before the Canton uprising of 27 April 1911, alerted the Manchu government and hampered the revolutionaries' plan.[8] The immediate effect, however, was the suffocation of the *People's Journal* itself. As a result of an article in its twenty-fourth issue, entitled 'The Psychology of Revolution', which called on the revolutionaries to further their cause by assassination, the journal was banned by the Japanese government for 'endangering public peace and security'.[9] Sung Chiao-jen attempted to save it by legal means, but failed. Plans to continue its publication in the United States were conceived but did not materialise. In early 1910 two more issues of the journal were secretly published in Tokyo, but thereafter it ceased to exist. Nevertheless, after the voluntary suspension in 1907 of the opposition organ, the *New People's Journal*, the *People's Journal* had already fulfilled its main mission.

Only three months after its establishment, the Chinese League was faced with a crisis which threatened to split its ranks and might well have led to its complete collapse. This was the Chinese students' boycott of Japanese schools at the end of 1905, an incident sparked off by the Japanese government's attempt to exercise stricter control of its guest students.

In 1905 the Chinese student population in Tokyo was approaching ten thousand. Amongst such a large number there were undoubtedly some whose conduct left something to be desired. On the other hand, the presence of such a large group of foreign visitors meant wealth to many Japanese. Some realised this opportunity for gain, and did not hesitate to introduce commercial exploitation by the establishment of irregular institutions of learning and hostels, and by the sale of diplomas. To meet the needs of this large and fast-increasing number of foreign students, private schools and hostels sprang up, many of which were primarily profit-seeking institutions, which not only plagued the conscience of many well-meaning men, but were also feared lest they should irreparably damage the reputation of Japan. Rumours of stricter control of Chinese students had been circulating for some months before the publication by the Japanese Ministry of

Education, on 2 November 1905, of regulations concerning state and private schools open for admission of Chinese students.[10]

The new regulations were ostensibly aimed at correcting the evils noted above. To the students, however, this was an act fraught with malicious intent and aimed at curtailing their freedom. Had not the Chinese in Tokyo been the most vocal group from China to voice their opinions on controversial issues, particularly their objections to Japan's new position in Manchuria after the Russo-Japanese war? The new regulations seen in this light were no less than a wilful act of vengeance, a deliberate reprisal against the students. Their timing, soon after the formation of the Chinese League and at about the same time as the publication of the *People's Journal*, gave additional grounds for suspicion. Might they not have been introduced at the request of the Manchu government, which, fearing the radical tendency of the Chinese students in Japan, hoped to curb their dangerous inclinations in this way? It was well known that the Chinese government had wanted Japan to control the Chinese students in Japan. Only two years previously a high-ranking Chinese Viceroy, Chang Chih-tung, had approached the Japanese Minister for China in this connection.[11]

Two months earlier, when news of the new regulations for the control of Chinese and Korean students was circulating, the Chinese Students' Association held a meeting to examine the issue.[12] A query was lodged with the Japanese Foreign Ministry, which promptly denied that any such move had been contemplated. For ten days after the publication of the regulations in the press the students took no action. The Student Council of the Chinese Students' Association then decided to raise objections only to Article 9, which appeared to restrict the students' freedom of residence, and to Article 10, which forbade schools designated for Chinese students to admit students who had been expelled from other schools for 'bad conduct'. In a communication to the Japanese Ministry of Education, the students objected to being forced to live in hostels, on the grounds of their different health requirements and habits, and to the vagueness of the phrase 'bad conduct'. But many students felt that their Council's action was tardy and useless.[13]

On 26 November notices appeared in various schools, requiring students to register and supply detailed personal information about themselves within three days. It suddenly dawned on the revolutionary students that the sinister hand of the Manchu government might be behind the Japanese action. This suspicion led them to reconsider the implications of the whole affair. Discussions began within each school group, and each came basically to the same conclusion, that the new law should be resisted. The students at the Kobun Institute seem to have been the first to decide on a strike if the regulations were not withdrawn. It was then 30 November 1905.

On 3 December student representatives from eight schools met at the Students' Association's office and decided on total rejection of the regulations. A strike plan was adopted as their first line of action, to be followed by a mass exodus from Japan if necessary. On the same day Sung Chiao-jen's own regional association met and decided independently on the same measures.[14]

Following the refusal of the Chinese Minister to press for the withdrawal of the regulations, the students were left to their own resources. The students at the Kobun Institute began their strike on 11 December, and were immediately followed by others. To ensure unity and order, and to avoid disturbances which might be used against them later, all students were required by the Students' Association to observe certain rules, which included staying away from public places, such as parks, restaurants, theatres, and shops, and minimising noise in hostels. For the maintenance of discipline, a student squad was formed by the militant members of the Chinese League to patrol school grounds, hostels, and other public places. It was reported in the Japanese press that some members of the squad were actually armed with pistols and knives.[15]

The behaviour of the Chinese students irritated many Japanese. On 7 December a Japanese newspaper attacked the Chinese students in strong terms. It described indulgence and meanness as Chinese characteristics, and contemptuously remarked, among other things, that the Chinese were incapable of unity. This added insult to injury, and caused Ch'en T'ien-hua, a sensitive patriot, to commit suicide, in the hope that his death might serve as a constant reminder to Chinese students of their precarious position as subjects of a weak nation, and that it might kindle in them the fire of patriotism, the desire for unity, and the resolution to strive for progress and national regeneration.[16]

Ch'en T'ien-hua was Sung Chiao-jen's close friend, and also a founder of the Chinese League. His death strengthened his colleagues' resolve. They felt that there was now no turning back. On 10 December, one day after the discovery of Ch'en's death, Sung's Hunanese association resolved to leave Japan *en masse*. That afternoon, in the presence of Japanese police officials, the several thousand students flocked to the Chinese Students' Association for a special meeting. The same conclusion was reached, and the students began preparations to leave Japan. The first batch of 300 students sailed on 13

December 1905, and a further 2,000 students had booked their passages.[17]

The situation was serious. The loss of life, the determination of the Chinese students, and the imminent loss of income for some Japanese after the departure of the students combined to affect public opinion in favour of the Chinese students. The Japanese government decided to clarify its regulations, and as a result cleared up most of the points obnoxious to the Chinese students.[18] By then, however, the students had shifted their point of argument from substance to psychology. Their complaint was not so much how they would be affected by the regulations but why they should be the targets of these control measures. Thus Sung Chiao-jen's close friend, Ch'eng Chia-sheng, in a public statement on behalf of his colleagues, pointed out that the grievance of the students was not against the contents of the regulations but merely that the Japanese government should single out Chinese students for special control.[19]

The fate of Korea, which had virtually become a Japanese state after the Portsmouth Conference,* aggrieved the Chinese students. Flushed with their recent victory over Russia, and believing that Japan had not been adequately rewarded for her sacrifice in the war, the Japanese public of 1906 was in an angry and arrogant mood, much to the discomfort of the Chinese students. Chinese sensitivity and patriotism were further stirred by negotiations in Peking over Japan's newly found position in Manchuria. Besides, the regulations reminded them of a previous episode when the Japanese press reported the intention of the government to introduce regulations for the control of Chinese and Korean students. The association of China with Korea, now officially recognised as a Japanese protectorate, could hardly be viewed as a compliment. It gave rise to speculation on the intentions of the Japanese government. When the report was queried, the Japanese authorities denied any intention of introducing regulations for the control of students. Now the regulations had become law, it did not matter to the students if the title did not indicate actual control. The primary motive behind the regulations left room for doubt, and their future application could not be ascertained.

It was against this background that sharp reactions occurred. With students' feelings running high, the Chinese Students' Association, then still under conservative, or at best neutral, influences, failed to respond adequately to the needs of the students. In fact Yang Tu, the Chief Secretary of the association, failed to attend a

---

* The Portsmouth Peace Conference was held at Portsmouth, New Hampshire, between 9 August and 5 September 1905 to settle the Russo-Japanese War.

conference with school representatives, with the result that a special
inter-school body, composed of representatives from eight schools,
was formed on 3 December to take charge of the situation. Hu Ying
was elected its Chairman, while Sung Chiao-jen and K'ang Pao-
chung were elected Secretaries. Soon afterwards the staff of the
Chinese Students' Association was reshuffled, and the conservatives
were replaced by radicals.[20]

Unfortunately, most students rushed into drastic decisions in the
heat of the moment. When a showdown was imminent, differences
of opinion slowly emerged. Senior students who were near the end
of their courses were reluctant to leave without their diplomas. Worst
of all, there was no unity within the League on the measures to be
taken. Sung Chiao-jen and Hu Ying led the radicals; they do not
seem to have regretted their decision to return to China if necessary.
They could then carry out direct revolutionary activities. But Hu
Han-min and Wang Ching-wei, significantly both Cantonese,
opposed it, on the grounds that the infant Chinese League would
collapse if they all returned to China. They insisted that, for the sake
of the revolution, the radical wing should abandon its suicidal course
and seek other solutions to the dispute. Hu Han-min had cause to be
more conciliatory. He was involved in a similar action in 1902, which
interrupted his education without positive gains for the students'
cause.[21] This division of opinion, however, between Hu Han-min and
Wang Ching-wei on the one side, and Sung Chiao-jen and Hu Ying
on the other, also reflected basic differences between two main
regional groups, central and south China, or, more narrowly,
Hunanese and Cantonese. This suggests that ideological differences
were at play, the fervent nationalism of the central Chinese provinces
clashing with the internationalism of Sun Yat-sen and the Cantonese.

For advocating a peaceful settlement of the dispute, not a few,
including Hu Han-min and Wang Ching-wei, were said to have been
'sentenced to death' by the radicals. At least one case has been
recorded of the radicals pursuing an official of the Chinese Students'
Association to his hideout in a hospital and beating him up.[22]

The militant students' stand was further weakened by the influential pen of Liang Ch'i-ch'ao, a leading reformer. In mid-December
Liang published 'A description of the common grievances among the
student circle in Tokyo and my opinion', in which he argued that,
while the Japanese government's action was taken under dubious
circumstances, he could find no serious objections in the contents of
the regulations. He continued that they aimed more to control the
schools for the benefit of the students than to control the students.
If there were some points that lacked clarity or were unpalatable

to the students, they perhaps could be amended. In his opinion there was nothing to justify the students' demand for complete abrogation, especially after their queries had been answered, and ambiguities clarified. He criticised the destructive nature of the students' plan to return to China *en masse*. It would only cause harm to all concerned—to themselves as well as to the nation.[23]

Liang's argument tended to strengthen the hand of the moderate students, who seized the opportunity to form a second student body, with the aim of seeking a separate settlement of the dispute. The body consisted of Hu Han-min, Wang Ching-wei of the Chinese League, who insisted on a peaceful settlement in order to preserve the revolutionary base in Tokyo, and some senior students who wished to stay to complete their studies. As Hu Han-min put it, 'They shared the same bed but not their dreams'. They were using the senior students, who had closer contact with school authorities, to conduct secret negotiations with them. Thereafter the radicals and the moderates fought for their respective causes with meetings, circulars, speeches, and sometimes threats.[24]

In the end the moderates won, for three reasons. Firstly, the radicals gave in to the argument that the cause of revolution should be foremost in their considerations. A substantial number of students favoured staying to continue their education. The revolutionaries felt that they could not and should not abandon them to the reformers. Secondly, unity could no longer be maintained. It was senseless to continue to bicker. Thirdly, some influential Japanese politicians had stepped in to mediate, and had taken the edge off the dispute.[25]

Agreement to return to school was reached on 11 January 1906. On 13 January a formal meeting was held by the militant students to dissolve their militant inter-school body. On this occasion, Sung pointed out that 'at the beginning of the dispute, we could certainly fight for our convictions. But now we can no longer continue the fight. Neither reason nor sentiment nor present developments justify its continuation.'[26] If he and his colleagues had not given the dispute enough thought at the beginning, as the opposition claimed, at least he was now prepared to redeem himself. As he spoke in favour of reconciliation, there was still a great deal of opposition to it.

There seems little doubt that Sung Chiao-jen was one of the radical leaders in the dispute. Yet, as late as 2 December 1905 a diarist who went to see him about the dispute recorded that Sung had not yet formed any opinion on the matter.[27] There are few direct records on his attitudes and actions in this period. Apart from the above reference in his diary to the dissolution meeting of the militant inter-school body on 13 January 1906, the only other diary entry concerning the dispute was on 4 January 1906, in which he recorded that Ch'eng Chia-sheng asked him to raise a sum of money to meet the expenses of entertaining journalists for the purpose of communicating their opinions to the Japanese public.[28] For the crucial months of October, November, and December 1905, there are no entries in his published diary. Was he too preoccupied with other activities to attend to his diary? Or perhaps they were omitted from the published version because of what they had to reveal?

When the students' strike against the introduction of fresh regulations by the Japanese government was coming to an end, a Sino-Japanese Student Association was formed to 'promote friendship, knowledge, and virtue'. At a meeting on 28 January 1906, attended by a number of distinguished Japanese and Chinese personalities and fifteen hundred students of both nations, a Chinese speaker coined the famous phrase: 'while being patriotic let no one forget his studies; and when studying, let no one forget patriotism'.[29] These words not only won the applause of the audience, but remained for many years the most popular phrases in China's student movement. At the time of their utterance they must also have won loud acclaim among the Chinese students in Tokyo who had just demonstrated a great patriotic gesture, and have smoothed the return of many students to their school institutions. Sung Chiao-jen, who had always recognised the importance of learning, was among the first to turn his thought to education after the dispute.

After the Sino-Japanese War of 1895 the Chinese government was attempting to create a modern army, and a large number of students were encouraged to study military science. By 1900 the plotters of revolution had realised the importance of the army and had begun infiltration. Therefore military studies were foremost in the minds of students seeking advanced education in Japan. When Sung first arrived in Tokyo, he also considered military training, and actually planned with his friends to set up a school to provide short courses in military science. The proposed school did not materialise, but his interest remained. He joined a Japanese physical fitness society and participated in its exercises and military drills.[30]

In June 1906 he enrolled at the Hosei University for courses on law and economics, which he apparently studied until the time of the strike. As Sung later revealed, this did not represent a switch of interest from military art to law, but was because his desire for military training could not be fulfilled. Following the formation of the Chinese League, the need for men of ability for post-revolutionary reconstruction engaged his attention. He thus carefully recorded in his diary Sun Yat-sen's conversation with him and his colleagues at their first meeting:

At present, the spirit of the people of Kwangtung and Kwangsi is high and secret societies are powerful and numerous. They have been a problem for the Manchu government for more than ten years, and the Manchu army has failed to quell them. It shows that their destructive power is more than sufficient. Their weakness is that there are too few men of ability among them . . . In last year's Liu-chou* uprising, they sent representatives to Hong Kong to seek men of talent. But I was then in the U.S.A. and therefore could not assist them. If we have now several thousands of men to join them to take charge of various activities before and after the task of destruction, and everything is attended to by specialists, then as soon as the revolution occurs, a civil government will be established, and the affairs of the nation will be immediately stabilised and consolidated.[31]

The emphasis on ability naturally led people to appreciate and cultivate gifted men. Sung's intellectual quality was well recognised and admired by his friends. No sooner had he set foot in Tokyo than friends offered to aid him with his education. Now that their attention was drawn once more to ability, they again considered Sung's education. When his fellow-provincials found that there were two scholarships available, one was given to him.[32]

After the strike, Sung still clung to the idea of military studies, but his friends advised him to study law and government, which, in their opinion, were more suited to his inclinations. In the end he gave in to his friends' persuasion and entered the Waseda University under a pseudonym Sung Ch'ien.[33]

In China there was nothing unusual in giving oneself a new name. It was particularly common practice among the educated who had a special appreciation for elegant or meaningful words. However, in Sung's case, one suspects it was as much due to necessity as to caprice. For various purposes, including the scholarship and the official sponsorship he needed for furthering his studies in Japanese institutions, he could ill afford to reveal his true identity. A little later, in May 1906, he was found to have been using another name, 'Lien', which means 'in-training'. He was called to the Chinese legation to explain whether it was also his name, for it was suspected that it might be Sung Chiao-jen's alias! Sung admitted that both Sung Ch'ien and Sung Lien were his names but denied that he was Sung Chiao-jen. To disarm the legation's suspicion, he had to invoke the assistance of

---

* A major town in Kwangsi.

an official from his provincial association. Needless to say, this official who came to Sung's aid was also his personal friend.[34]

At Waseda University, the class he joined was a preparatory class for Chinese students. Its curriculum consisted chiefly of Japanese language but also some general subjects. As an advanced student, he must have found the course onerous. Hence we find him paying particular attention to the acquirement of Japanese and English, which he regarded as necessary for higher learning. In addition he planned for himself a program of self-education, and untiringly engaged in widening his knowledge as well as increasing his depth of understanding of Chinese history and philosophy. Throughout 1906 he dabbled in a wide range of subjects from law and government to psychology and economics. He was particularly interested in the study of the lives of great men such as Gladstone, Washington, Napoleon, Bismarck, and the three much admired unifiers of modern Italy, Mazzini, Garibaldi, and Cavour, as well as such Chinese thinkers as Wang Yang-ming, who taught intuitive knowledge as the principal guide for human action, and Tseng Kuo-fan, a renowned Confucian whom he admired not so much for his deeds as for his capacity as a scholar for assuming political and military responsibilities. Sung's serious attitude towards his studies can be seen in his constant effort to reduce his social activities and party duties. He relinquished his post as general manager of the *People's Journal*, and refused an appointment to teach in Java.[35]

In July 1906 he completed the first part of his preparatory course. As it turned out, however, this also marked the end of his formal university education. As an exile in a foreign country, he seems to have been subject to emotional strain of various kinds which gave him periodic mental depressions. In one such attack he gave up his study of English, a prerequisite for normal courses at the Waseda University. He planned a little later to resume his study and to prepare himself for entering the Tokyo Imperial University, but his health broke down and he had to stay in hospital for treatment. When he recovered in November 1906, after nearly three months there, he still wished to continue his education, but seems to have given up the idea of attending university courses. The problem of finance had taken a great deal of his time throughout 1906. To meet his own and sometimes his friends' financial needs, he engaged in the translation of various constitutional systems for the Manchu government's commission which was sent abroad in 1906 to study governmental systems of foreign countries. From March 1906 to January 1907 he translated the constitutions of Britain, Russia, Austria, Hungary, Germany, and the United States, which undoubtedly contributed much to his own understanding of constitutional government.[36]

When Sung Chiao-jen arrived in Tokyo, war was raging in Manchuria between Russia and Japan. A great deal of writing and reporting on this region appeared in the Japanese press and journals. They naturally attracted the attention of Chinese patriots, particularly Sung, who was interested in geographical and historical studies, and aggrieved to see Chinese territory turned into a battleground by foreign powers. He followed closely the progress of the war, and took careful notes of all reports on the land and the people of Manchuria.

One report on the Mounted Bandits* in Manchuria caught his special attention. Towards the end of the nineteenth century, internal weakness and foreign intrigues combined to cause great instability and disorder in China's outlying regions. In Manchuria, devoid of government protection, the inhabitants banded together to safeguard their own lives and property. Later, some groups were, perhaps of their own free will, but more probably compelled by poverty, also engaged in lawless pursuits. Roaming the wide plains of Manchuria on horseback, they won for themselves the title of 'Mounted Bandits'.[37]

Just as the Japanese and the Russians saw the usefulness of the Mounted Bandits in their own battles and exploits in Manchuria, Sung perceived in them potential material for revolution. Besides, in accordance with the strategy of the Chinese League at the time, Manchuria in the north had as many possibilities as the southern provinces bordering Hong Kong and Indo-china. Sung Chiao-jen saw further advantages in Manchuria. The bandits, who were hostile to the Manchu government, were a ready army for revolution when converted, and Manchuria's proximity to Peking meant that, in revolutionary hands, it would pose a far greater threat to the Manchu régime than could revolutions in the south. Furthermore, the Mounted Bandits were mostly Chinese settlers who had nothing to lose in a revolution. Sung saw the possibility of winning and transforming them quickly into a force for his cause. In this conviction he studied the geography and history of Manchuria and its people, particularly the organisations and locations of the bandits.[38]

Sung had great sympathy for the Mounted Bandits, whom he regarded as oppressed men like the heroes in a popular Chinese novel, *All Men are Brothers*, who were driven to the jungle by a bad government. The corrupting influences of Russia and Japan in their

---

* *Ma-tsei* in Chinese. They were also called 'Red-beard men', because of the red material attached to the muzzle of their guns.

respective attempts to enlist the bandits' support for their wars
angered Sung. In an article about the bandits, he compared Russia
and Japan to house robbers, and the Manchu government to a
traitor who collaborated with the robbers to loot China. He appealed
to all Chinese, including the bandits of Manchuria, to unite to put
their house in order by punishing the traitors and resisting the
robbers.[39]

Sung Chiao-jen's sympathy for the outlaws, his confidence in their
fundamental goodness and their capacity to follow and support the
righteous cause, is noteworthy. It seems to have been the result of
his study of Wang Yang-ming's philosophy of the universal mind and
intuitive knowledge which taught universal goodness in men. It was
an attitude of importance in the revolutionary movement, as it
tended to separate Sung Chiao-jen from his colleagues. According to
one source, after the establishment of the Manchurian branch of the
Chinese League by Sung Chiao-jen and his colleagues, Wu Lu-chen,
Lan T'ien-wei, and Chang Shao-tseng (all returned students from
Japan and serving as army officers in Manchuria), disagreement
arose between them on the question of recruitment. Most leaders
favoured concentrating their propaganda and recruiting activities
within three social groups—the educated, the inter-village and
inter- or intra-district pacts, and the army. No one except Sung
wished to bring the Manchurian outlaws into their movement.[40]

This divergence of opinion was apparently due to the fact that the
other leaders looked upon these outlaws as born criminals, basically
mean, selfish, lawless, and cruel, whereas Sung believed in their
innocence and their capacity to do good once they were made aware
of the social causes of their misery and the proper remedies for them.
Sung alone believed that through indoctrination and re-education
these men of the jungle could be put on the right path and fight for
the cause of revolution.

Sung actually had no chance of testing his theory at the time.
In fact he had not even worked out an effective method by which he
could realise his goals. But the same assumption seems to have
underlain his actions in 1912, when he reorganised the Chinese
League into an overt political party and attempted to rest it on a
popular basis.

After the Russo-Japanese war, Korea became a Japanese pro-
tectorate, and Manchuria fell further into its orbit of influence.
Consequently there was an increasing number of Japanese travellers
to Manchuria who brought back tales about the land they saw.
On 5 May 1906 an article entitled 'An Independent Nation at the
Source of the Yalu River' caught Sung Chiao-jen's attention. It was

said to be a region bordering Korea and about the size of Japan's Kyushu Island, known as Chien-tao, or, in Japanese, Kanto. Its ruler was said to be one Han Teng-chu, a man from the province of Shantung. Moreover, it was reported as a rich region, full of minerals, timber, and ginseng.[41]

Sung's interest was aroused. A further report supplied him with more information. He learned that it was a territory of about 22,000 square miles. It was said to have been given to Han Teng-chu's ancestor by a Manchu emperor for some service he rendered in a conflict with the Russians. Sung also learned that in 1900 Han Teng-chu had tried to resist Russia's entry into Manchuria. He failed, but managed to negotiate a truce. Han was said to be about thirty-six years old, and Chien-tao under his rule was orderly and peaceful, no bandits daring to encroach on it. Sung, however, soon found discrepancies in the information he collected, and decided that the only way to verify the true situation was to visit Manchuria himself.

After the failure of the Chinese League to establish bases in south China in 1906, Sung offered to Huang Hsing his Manchurian scheme, in which he suggested the possibility of obtaining the independent region of Chien-tao as a revolutionary base. In his opinion the revolutionary party could seek either complete control over the region or merely domination over its economy, but either would be difficult to achieve; a simpler but less reliable method was to send a delegate to persuade the ruler of the region to give financial support to the revolutionaries.

Sung's suggestions were vague possibilities only, but the Chinese League was then looking for support. Sun Yat-sen sought it among the Chinese in southeast Asia, which was a long way from China. Huang Hsing sought it among military officers in the Manchu army, but with little result. Manchuria, with its roaming bandits, foreign oppression, and weak central control, offered good prospects for revolutionary movements. If Chien-tao was as rich and defiant of the Manchu government as reported, then its allegiance was worth seeking.

Huang Hsing approved Sung's idea. But for the following few months the party's attention was drawn to revolts on the border to Hunan and Kiangsi, and many of its members left Tokyo to join them. The idea was not taken up again until February 1907, when the failure of the uprisings was followed by internal disputes within the Chinese League, and the organisation's activities seemed to have come to an end. On 6 March 1907 a decision was reached between Sung Chiao-jen and Huang Hsing on their Manchurian scheme. Sung was to go to Manchuria to enlist the support of the bandits, and join anti-Manchu forces to found a revolutionary base for the Chinese League. Fukugawa, a former Japanese sergeant who had lived in Manchuria for many years and knew some bandits, was to be his guide on this mission. As Sung was preparing for his journey, Huang Hsing brought the news that some Russian revolutionaries were also planning something in Manchuria and hoped to obtain the League's assistance. Sung's trip was assuming a wider goal.

The way Sung raised money to finance his trip is worth noting. He was entirely left to his own resources. He attempted to borrow money from banks and money-lenders, but without success. He even tried to persuade the Chinese legation to give him in advance his school fees included in his scholarship. Had he not had a particular stroke of luck it was questionable whether he could ever have begun his trip. But luck was on his side. On one of his fund-raising runs he ran into one Pai Yu-huan, a student from Hupeh and a member of the Chinese League, who had been entrusted with a public fund of $2,000 to help students from his home town, but desired to divert it to some better use. He approved Sung's project and offered the money. This enabled Sung to begin his trip, and it was further planned that when he and his companions, Fukugawa and Pai Yu-huan, reached Antung in Manchuria, they would co-operate with the bandits to rob the government treasury of the T'ung-hua district, and use the loot to finance their great forward policy. Obviously, Sung's Manchurian trip was almost a personal undertaking, even though it had the approval and support of Huang Hsing. Only a few participated in Sung's plan, and Sun Yat-sen does not seem to have been informed or consulted.

Sung and his companions left Japan on 25 March 1907. On their arrival in Antung on 1 April, Sung immediately communicated with a bandit leader there. When a reply came, inviting him to proceed to the bandit's headquarters, Sung decided to go, and sent a letter ahead to prepare the bandits' minds for negotiation.

Details of Sung Chiao-jen's subsequent exploits are not known. For security reasons Sung gave up his habit of keeping diaries. It seems that Sung had succeeded in obtaining the co-operation of some bandits, and managed to establish a branch of the Chinese League. In the summer of 1907 a series of revolts took place in south China. Sung is said to have planned to respond with uprisings in Manchuria. He envisaged the possibility of occupying Mukden and Shan-hai-kuan, the pass controlling the entrance from Manchuria to China Proper, to pose a direct threat to Peking. His plot, however, was uncovered by the government. His colleague, Pai Yu-huan, was caught, though Sung himself managed to escape and return to Japan.[42]

This period of Sung Chiao-jen's life was filled with varied activities. He founded a journal which became the most influential organ of the Chinese League. He played a leading role in the activities of the Chinese students in Tokyo, and was one of the founding members of the Chinese League. The major theme in this period of his life, however, was education, through which he hoped to prepare himself for the task of rebuilding China after the revolution. Thus he worked hard on his study of social sciences, and at the same time sought the friendship of all students of ability, irrespective of their political colouring. As one of his friends recalled in 1913, after Sung's death:

In the spring and summer of 1907, the sounds of action filled south China. When all failed and I again fled to Japan, many colleagues groaned and moaned indignantly at the failures. Tun-ch'u [Sung] alone held that the Manchu dynasty with all its weaknesses would in the end be destroyed with ease. To him the important question was government and reconstruction which as yet had not received any attention but was a responsibility our party must shoulder. He further held that learned scholars might not be of use in the work of destruction, but their uses after it were unlimited. Therefore, with these views in mind, he paid special attention to men of ability. If he noticed one he would seek his acquaintance and friendship with all humility even though he belonged to a different political party. Consequently, Tun-ch'u alone knew the qualities of all the students who studied in Japan in these years, a fact well known to and admitted by even members of the Republican and the Democratic parties.[43]

Therefore this period was an important period for Sung Chiao-jen's personal development. It was in these years in Japan that he acquired most of his modern political knowledge and formed his political convictions which later enabled him to play a more important role in the Chinese revolution.

Sung's emphasis on the importance of scholarship and scholars in national affairs received almost immediate justification in his own performance—the contribution of his knowledge of Manchuria to the solution of the Chien-tao question, a territorial dispute between China and Japan in 1908.

Chien-tao was a stretch of territory at the source of the Yalu and north of the Tumen, the two rivers which separate China and Korea. It was the original home of the Manchus, who, after their conquest of China, reserved their original homeland as their own exclusive hunting ground. The Korean king forbade his subjects to cross the Tumen, and similarly the Manchus prohibited intrusion into their reserve. In 1869 the order of prohibition was broken when a famine in Korea drove many Koreans to seek food across the river. The

Manchu government did not interfere except by requiring them to register with local officials, to pay taxes, and to comply with its laws. In 1885, in an effort to increase government revenue, more land was thrown open to both Koreans and local inhabitants. At one time the Korean government attempted to withdraw its migrants, but without success. The Koreans were reluctant to leave their newly acquired properties. Instead of leaving them, they tried to turn the land they occupied into Korean territory, thus giving rise to a dispute at first between Korea and China, and later between China and Japan, when Korea became a Japanese protectorate.

Japan began the frontier dispute with China in August 1907 under the pretext of settling the Chien-tao question between Korea and China. Formerly the dispute was confined to the selection of a tributary of the Tumen River as boundary, and the determination of the ownership of about three hundred acres of sandbank in the lower Tumen River. But, under the new Japanese claim, all the land north of the Tumen River which had come under Korean cultivation was Korean territory.[44]

It seems that Sung Chiao-jen learned of Japan's claim on Chien-tao from Han Teng-chu, the reputed ruler of Chien-tao, whom he tried to persuade, whether successfully or not is unknown, to support the cause of revolution. But from him Sung heard of Japan's intrigue, and he decided to investigate the matter. According to one source, Sung disguised himself as a Japanese called Sadamura, and, through the introduction of a Japanese acquaintance in Tokyo, he managed to get inside a Japanese organisation, the Long-White Mountain Development Society, to find out its secret activities, which included the falsification of boundary evidence in preparation for Japan's claim on Chien-tao. He subsequently visited Seoul to collect documentary evidence to refute Japan's claim, and, with the information he thus collected, he wrote his *Chien-tao Question*.[45]

In this book he used historical and geographical facts to prove beyond doubt Chinese ownership of Chien-tao, and the legitimacy of the existing boundary along the Tumen River. In addition he warned the Chinese that grave consequences would follow if Chien-tao were lost to a foreign power. It was the back gate of Manchuria, and its loss would open Manchuria to greater Japanese pressure, and would destroy the balance of power in the region. He even suggested methods of dealing with Japan. He thought that China should first prove its ownership with historical and geographical evidence. If these were not acceptable to Japan, China should take the case to the international court at The Hague.[46]

Apparently Sung's book was sought by both the Chinese and the Japanese governments, and the latter tried to convince Sung that, in the interests of the revolutionary movement, he should aggravate, and not help to solve the Manchu government's difficulties. Sung, however, was not persuaded, since for him, as a nationalist, patriotism and territorial integrity should come before internal squabbles. Through one Hsu Hsiao-shou, Sung's work managed to reach the Manchu government. It apparently both impressed and aided the Manchu government, for Sung was subsequently rewarded with 2,000 yen, and the Manchu government even sought to recruit him for its foreign office. Allegedly, on the order of Empress Tz'u-hsi, who had read his book on Chien-tao and was greatly impressed by his scholarship, he was offered the rank of a fourth grade official in the department of External Affairs.[47]

Following the settlement of the Chien-tao dispute in China's favour on 14 September 1909,[48] Sung's aim in writing the *Chien-tao Question* was fulfilled. But this apparent aid to the Manchu government and the honours and reward bestowed on him by the latter gave rise to rumours and misapprehension within and without the revolutionary camp. To clear himself, he found it necessary in his letter to the Manchu government to declare his uncompromising stand on domestic affairs, and invited that government to strip him of his student title and withdraw his scholarship.[49] These drastic steps reflected his extreme plight at this time. The revolutionary movement seemed to advance no closer to its goal; instead, the Chinese League was beset with distrust and division. It was no surprise that he suffered frequent depressions in this period, and is said to have frequently sought relief in alcohol and opium.[50]

SIX

Intra-party Disputes

THE CHINESE LEAGUE was a product of exigency. It was a conglomeration of diverse and incongruous elements brought together by the needs of the time. Their main objective, the overthrow of the Manchu dynasty and the restoration of the Han Chinese to power, was the strongest bond which kept them together. To establish a democracy and to solve the problem of the people's livelihood were also their professed aims, but they were vague and ill-defined, and ultimately became the main source of disagreement and friction which weakened the party.

When the League was first formed its initial membership was claimed to be about three hundred, consisting of students from seventeen of China's eighteen provinces. Kansu alone had no man in the party, as it had no students in Japan.[1]

Within two years its membership increased to about a thousand, and branch organisations were established in various places in southeast Asia as well as in China. Irrespective of the accuracy of the figures recorded, it was certainly clear that the members of the League came from diverse provincial backgrounds, each carrying a certain amount of regional prejudice with him. If all members had joined the League as individuals, perhaps it would have been easier for it to combat deviation and to ensure unity in its ideas and actions. Unfortunately, the provincial organisations existed before the League, making it more a federal union of the provinces rather than a unitary organisation composed of individuals. The recruitment of members on a basis of provincial divisions, entrusted to the respective provincial leaders, sharpened further the provincial lines within the League. It elevated the influence of provincial leaders, and enhanced the centrifugal tendencies of the provincial groups to the detriment of central authority.

The first loyalty of party members was to their respective provincial leaders rather than to the central authority. The central leadership of the League was also primarily concerned with retaining the loyalty of the provincial leaders rather than soliciting direct support from the rank and file. Sun Yat-sen lost the support of some of the provincial leaders in 1908 when his leadership was challenged by them. Undoubtedly this was one of the reasons for his request in 1914 for personal loyalty from all his followers.

Sun Yat-sen was a man from Kwangtung, the province with the longest period of contact with the outside world, and among the most cosmopolitan of Chinese provinces. He had been to foreign lands, and was educated in foreign schools. In their dealings with foreigners the Cantonese were generally willing to adopt a co-operative attitude, and Sun seems no exception. He was always ready to give and take. He admired Western democracy and institutions, and wished to borrow them for China. His knowledge of the history of other nations convinced him that it was both proper and necessary to enlist foreign aid in the task of reshaping the destiny of China. Did not America receive French assistance in its war for independence? For the Chinese revolution an American 'Lafayette' would be most welcome. He saw nationalism and revolution as universal phenomena, inevitable developments in the transition from tyranny and backwardness to democracy and modernism.

Sun greatly admired Western materialism and industrialisation, and hoped to achieve the same for China. He would have liked to see the Western capitalistic system transplanted in China, with perhaps a few adjustments to suit Chinese conditions and to eliminate evils bred by the system. He believed that there could be no peace or harmony in the world as long as disparity between the nations existed. It followed that the advanced nations had an obligation towards the weaker ones. They should help to close the disparity gap by assisting peoples who were striving for modernisation and progress. A strong and independent China would at once eliminate all conflicts in the Far East and restore stability and peace in the interests of all nations. These beliefs were the basis for Sun's appeal to Japan, Britain, and America for aid during this period.[2]

The Hunanese group, headed by Sung Chiao-jen and Huang Hsing, came from an inland province not in direct contact with foreign influence until the turn of this century. They were educated in China prior to coming to Japan, and were mostly steeped in Chinese classical learning. Their revolutionary enthusiasm was fired by nationalism and patriotism, the intensity of which was heightened by contact with fervent Japanese nationalism.[3]

The Society for the Recovery of China of the Chekiang-Anhwei group, led by such thoroughly Chinese-educated men as Chang Ping-lin and T'ao Ch'eng-chang, and mainly supported by secret societies which were firstly anti-foreign and only secondly anti-Manchu, was an even more uncompromisingly nationalistic body. Chang Ping-lin was a distinguished master of Chinese learning. Although theoretically he did not object to the absorption of selected elements of Western civilisation, he was bound to emphasise the excellence of things Chinese, and tended to look inwards to seek guidance in China's past. He doubted the value of parliamentary democracy, and regarded it as a form of oligarchy worse than despotism.[4] He had no high regard for material advancements, and so opposed industrialisation, preferring to see China remain a static agricultural society.[5]

These were but some of the ideological differences between the leading personalities who ultimately determined the fate of the Chinese League. Conflicting opinions respecting democracy and policies for reconstruction were not immediate problems, however, as they loomed large only after the overthrow of the Manchu dynasty. In 1907-8 the internal disputes of the Chinese League arose primarily out of the problems of leadership, finance, and the differing attitudes of its members to the question of foreign financial assistance. Undoubtedly financial hardships, regional prejudices, jealousies, disappointments resulting from repeated failures, and Sun's long absence from his Tokyo headquarters, all played their part.

Ideologically Sung was primarily a nationalist and a patriot. He paid a great deal of attention to the problems of political reconstruction after the revolution, for which purpose he studied law, government, and economics. But he said little and wrote nothing during this period concerning the issues of democracy and land rights. Judging by his later attitude, he fully accepted constitutional democracy and parliamentary institutions but had reservations on the principle of the equalisation of land rights.

Hunan, Hupeh, Chekiang, and Anhwei formed a geographical unit in the Yangtze valley, and the people of these four provinces had more in common with one another than they did with the people of Kwangtung over the mountain range. Historically, the members of the China Resurgence Society and the Society for the Recovery of China were closely associated, and together conspired in the abortive uprisings in 1904. The leaders, too, such as Sung Chiao-jen and Chang Ping-lin, became friends as soon as they met.[6]

The first signs of weakness in the League showed themselves in February 1907, just a little over a year after its establishment. It took the form of a personal clash between two top leaders of the League, Sun Yat-sen and Huang Hsing, over the design of the national flag. There was no lack of suggestions for the flag. Some thought it should show drawings of ancient Chinese weapons to symbolise the expanding spirit of the Han Chinese, others suggested the use of eighteen stars to represent the eighteen provinces, or a flag bearing China's five traditional colours. Huang Hsing favoured a design with the character 'Ching', to symbolise the principle of the equalisation of land rights. 'Ching' refers to a much idealised method of land distribution in ancient China, the so called well-field system. It not only indicated an important goal of the League, but would serve maximum propaganda value, since it was familiar to all Chinese. Sun, on the other hand, insisted on a blue sky and white sun flag designed by his deceased friend and comrade, Lu Hao-tung, who died for the cause of revolution. Sun criticised Huang's flag as reactionary and unaesthetic, and Huang replied that Sun's proposal resembled too closely Japan's 'rising sun'. Sun claimed that his flag had the support of tens of thousands in southeast Asia, and if it were to be removed he would have to be removed first.[7]

This sparked off the first crisis of the League. Huang walked out of the meeting and seriously considered leaving the party. He accepted a compromise offered by Chang Ping-lin and Liu K'uei-i, however. They were to shelve the issue for the present and he was to remain in the party.[8] In practice Sun won the day.

Sung Chiao-jen, a close friend of Huang Hsing but working closely with Sun in his capacity as Treasurer, made the following observations with regard to the flag question:

> I have thought carefully over the causes of Ch'ing-wu's unhappiness and come to the conclusion that it has a deeper origin. An indescribable resentment has accumulated in his heart for a long time before exploding under the present dispute which is after all a trifling matter; for Sun Yat-sen has never been sincere, open, modest or frank with others and his way of handling things is almost dictatorial and intransigent to an unbearable degree.[9]

Sung was not only dissatisfied with Sun's leadership but he was also extremely disappointed with the general behaviour of party members. He observed that an atmosphere of suspicion and distrust prevailed among the rank and file of the League, a most disturbing feature. He almost gave up hope for the success which he had envisaged for the party, and half thought of extricating himself from involvement to spare himself the onus of failure and ridicule. He made no effort to mediate in this dispute, but instead insisted on resigning his office of Treasurer, to the dismay of Sun Yat-sen. He rested his hopes on a successful outcome of his Manchurian scheme.

At about the same time as the flag dispute, the Manchu government approached the Japanese authorities, requesting the expulsion of Sun Yat-sen from Japan, on the grounds that his activities were endangering the security of China. The Japanese complied with the Manchu government's request, but handled the case tactfully. A party was thrown in Sun's honour and the Japanese Foreign Minister explained to Sun personally Japan's diplomatic difficulties with China and Japan's regret for having to ask Sun to leave the country.[10]

As a gesture of goodwill the Japanese government offered Sun a sum of money to meet his travelling expenses, and a Japanese stockbroker sympathetic to the cause gave a further 10,000 yen. From the money he received Sun gave 2,000 yen to Chang T'ai-yen to meet the expenses of the *People's Journal*, and left Japan with the rest of the money on 4 March 1907.[11] His concealment of the money and the cause of his departure was certainly not calculated to please his colleagues in Tokyo. When truth came to light, they were understandably greatly irritated. It looked as if the head of the Chinese League had taken a bribe and absconded. At any rate he should not have accepted any form of foreign aid without consulting them. Sun was denounced, and charged with misappropriating for his personal use funds subscribed by a revolutionary sympathiser. The leading dissenters were Chang Ping-lin and T'ao Ch'eng-chang, both of Chekiang, and Sung Chiao-jen, T'an Jen-feng, Chang Chi, T'ien T'ung, Pai Yu-huan, and Hirayama Shu.[12] Chang Ping-lin, then Chief Editor of the *People's Journal*, was particularly angry. He took down Sun's picture from the wall of the office of the *People's Journal*, and, believing that Sun was still in Hong Kong, sent it to the Hong Kong branch of the League with the following words: 'Sun Yat-sen, traitor to the *People's Journal*, should immediately be removed'.[13]

The dissenters threatened to oust Sun, and put pressure on Liu K'uei-i, the acting head and acting Treasurer of the League in Tokyo, to convene a congress to elect a new *Tsung-li*. They wanted to replace Sun by electing Huang Hsing as head. A heated argument ensued, during which Liu Kuei-i single-handedly resisted the demand and fought a first battle with Chang Chi before the dissidents quietened down.[14]

Liu K'uei-i was one of the foundation members of the China Resurgence Society who did not favour merger with Sun Yat-sen before the establishment of the League. He was a follower of Huang Hsing, but was working closely with Sun at this time, and had at his disposal more information respecting Sun's activities. Thus he dared to stand alone for the sake of unity. He explained his position many years later:

I understand that when Sun Yat-sen received this money he left two thousand yen for the maintenance of the *People's Journal*, and used the rest to meet the urgent needs of the party members who were organising revolts in Ch'ao-chou and Hui-chou in eastern Kwangtung. He had indeed no alternative. Besides I know quite well that Huang Hsing was devoted to the cause of revolution and would never assume the empty title of Tsung-li. He and Sun were at the time organising a revolt in eastern Kwangtung; if by any chance a change of *Tsung-li* gave rise to misunderstanding and hampered the future of the revolutionary forces, it would mean suicide for the party. Therefore I alone opposed the opinion of the majority.[15]

Although Liu K'uei-i refused to give way, he did not think the actions of Sun blameless. This was clear from his attempt to secure an apology from Sun Yat-sen for the dissenting colleagues in Tokyo. Liu K'uei-i hoped that Hu Han-min and Feng Tzu-yu, followers of Sun and fellow Cantonese, would use their influence to persuade Sun to send a letter of apology. Hu and Feng also deemed it proper that Sun should apologise. Sun, however, refused to submit, insisting that facts alone could settle the dispute.[16] In the end it was Huang Hsing who prevented a showdown. For the sake of unity he had acquiesced on the flag issue. Now, for the same reason, he wrote to his fuming colleagues in Tokyo, entreating them to resolve their misunderstanding and bury their differences. He wrote:

The life and death of every party member affects the revolution. It is not merely a problem involving the name and position of one man. Sun Yat-sen's virtue is worthy of respect. If you want the revolution to succeed I beg for your understanding and whole-hearted support to spare me the dishonour of disgrace.[17]

As a result of Huang's intervention the dispute subsided, but was not settled, and remained to flare up anew when the occasion arose.

The next quarrel occurred during the summer of 1907 over an arms deal. Sun Yat-sen sent Kayano Chochi to Japan to buy weapons and ammunition to support a projected revolt in Kwangtung. Kayano purchased 2,000 karuta 1905 model rifles with 600 rounds of ammunition each, plus 30 pistols with 100 rounds each, and a number of bayonets and swords. For some reason the Japanese members of the League regarded these weapons as obsolete and unsuitable. Sung, always a cautious man, apparently believed that the obsolete weapons would endanger lives at the front, and he joined with Chang Ping-lin in sending an uncoded message to the *China Daily*, a revolutionary newspaper in Hong Kong, saying that these weapons were not suitable for use in revolts. As a result the secret leaked out, and Kayano Chochi had to delay shipment.[18]

According to Hu Han-min himself, he threatened to invoke party discipline against the offenders, and regretted later that he had not done so. Sun, justifiably displeased with his colleagues in Tokyo, was heard to have said frequently that he was not afraid to face the ignorant masses; what worried him were the half-baked revolutionaries.

After this incident, Sun decided to conceal all his activities from those in Tokyo. He gave Miyazaki Torazo his Power of Attorney, with full authority to raise funds, purchase equipment, and obtain supplies in Japan for the revolutionary army. He made Miyazaki directly responsible to himself, and instructed him to consult no one else in Tokyo, Japanese or Chinese, member or non-member.[19]

This measure had grave consequences. It reveals the personal character of China's revolutionary movement. Sun preferred to operate through friends rather than through his official organisation, a practice unlikely to encourage the growth of institutions. It was not surprising that members of the Chinese League in Tokyo felt neglected and demanded a fuller share in the organisation's activities. It became one of the major causes for dispute in the League. With Sun and Huang away in southeast Asia, the centre of power seemed to have shifted with them, and the Tokyo headquarters enjoyed only nominal authority. A group of members, mainly from the central provinces of Hunan, Hupeh, and Szechuan, formed a separate organisation significantly named the Mutual Advancement Society. T'an Jen-feng points out that the formation of this society was clearly a reaction of the members to Sun's disregard of the League's headquarters.[20]

There were, however, more fundamental aspects underlying this separatist movement within the League.[21] Sun Yat-sen's whole plan of campaign began with the seizure and control of two southern provinces, Kwangtung and Kwangsi. This area was chosen partly because it was farthest from Peking. It was thought that distance, together with the traditional anti-Manchu sentiment of the southern Chinese and their long contact with the outside world, made it the most vulnerable spot of the Manchu empire. In addition, their long shore-line, their accessibility by sea, and their contiguity with Hong Kong, Macao, and Indo-china, all controlled by powers either neutral or friendly to the revolutionaries, contributed to make it an ideal region for anti-government operations. But the most decisive factor influencing Sun's choice was the consideration that these two provinces were closest to the sources of his power, namely the overseas Chinese in southeast Asia who provided him with most of the funds for his campaigns.

Sun's argument in favour of concentrating operations in this region was strong. By contrast, central China seemed devoid of all these advantages, and the setback to the revolutionary cause following the disastrous uprisings of late 1906 and early 1907, plus Sun's own expulsion from Japan, decided the swing in Sun's favour. A group of revolutionaries from central China, notably Huang Hsing, followed Sun to the south. But there were some who disagreed with Sun's plans, and they, including Sung Chiao-jen, remained sceptical of his methods. By autumn 1907, when operations in the south had made no apparent progress, the Mutual Advancement Society was formed in Tokyo. In the following few years, further fruitless attempts in the south tended to strengthen the case of the separatists, and eventually led Sung Chiao-jen to undertake semi-independent measures.

If the overseas Chinese provided the financial basis for Sun's movement, who were the mainstay of the dissidents in central China? Evidence suggests strongly that the leadership of the Mutual Advancement Society was closely connected with wealthy landowning families. For this reason Sun may be said to be the political representative of businessmen and city and plantation workers, while the central China group was that of land-owners and emerging industrialists. That this difference between them was important is evident in their respective attitudes towards the lower strata of Chinese society. Both camps expressed an interest in enlisting the allegiance of the secret societies, and recognised that they had a role to play in the revolution. But it was here that differences reflecting their own backgrounds arose. These differences concerned two issues, namely the secret societies' duties in the revolution, and the responsibility of the revolutionary leadership towards the welfare of these under-privileged followers. On the first only shades of difference existed, and it seems natural that an internal-based organisation had a closer tie with people in the lower social strata than an external-based and differently powered movement. Hence the Mutual Advancement Society was actively engaged in incorporating the secret societies into its structure, while Sun Yat-sen would give them no more than a minor supporting role in his operations. On the second issue, however, the two camps assumed almost reversed stands. The platform of the Chinese League embraced nationalism, democracy, and the equalisation of land rights. The Mutual Advancement Society retained the first two but discarded the third plank and put in its place the equalisation of human rights. This change was said to have been deemed necessary because it was more tangible to the down-trodden who made up the secret societies.[22]

But the fact that the bulk of secret society members were peasants in origin makes it an unconvincing explanation. It is more likely that the crux of the matter lies in the nature of the leadership itself. One does not have to be a Marxist to see that it is easier for Sun and his overseas supporters, more detached from land than the leadership of the Mutual Advancement Society, to accept the doctrine of the equalisation of land rights. At a later date, and for the same reason, Sung Chiao-jen, in canvassing support for his designs in central China, also had to leave out the question of land rights from his political platform.

Neither Huang Hsing nor T'an Jen-feng approved of the breakaway organisation. Huang feared the rise of factionalism within the revolutionary camp, while T'an simply regarded it as retrogressive, probably because the new society expressed its intention of modelling itself on the secret societies. Sung Chiao-jen took note of the formation of the Mutual Advancement Society, and was probably even involved in it in a limited way, but expressed no opinion, for or against.[23] Judging by his sympathy for Huang Hsing after the 'flag dispute' and his momentary wish to extricate himself from the Chinese League, he was probably not averse to it.

Huang Hsing, worried by the formation of a separate society, put the following question to Chiao Ta-feng: 'Since you have formed this separate society there are now two streams in the revolutionary movement; which is the main stream?' Chiao was said to have answered, smiling, 'War hasn't begun yet; why are you in such haste? When that day comes and you prove to be the stronger and more successful, we will follow you. Otherwise you can follow us.'[24] Unless this was meant as a joke, Chiao had made it clear from the start that his society was not to be subordinate to the Chinese League. True, Chiao's view might not be representative. The Hupeh branch of the Mutual Advancement Society, for example, was said to have actually recognised the head of the Chinese League as its own.[25] But actions were inevitably more telling than words. The Mutual Advancement Society had not only rejected one of the League's three main principles, but proceeded to introduce a separate system of control throughout China under the direction of their own appointees. For all intents and purposes it was a rival to the Chinese League. A thread of co-operation was maintained while the common enemy lasted. No sooner had this enemy disappeared from the scene than independence and separatism were vigorously asserted by these early dissidents.

An internal dispute of a more serious nature, which shook the foundation of the Chinese League, was that between Sun Yat-sen and T'ao Ch'eng-chang.

T'ao (1877-1912) was one of the founders of the Society for the Recovery of China, an ultra-nationalistic party composed chiefly of people from Chekiang and Anhwei. When the Chinese League was established, T'ao and many of his followers joined the League. Because of certain differences, however, they were never really amalgamated. According to the recollection of an old participant in T'ao's society, the main difference was a question of action. The leaders of the League, mostly exiles at this stage, could do no more than carry out verbal propaganda and instigate inconsequential uprisings from foreign bases, such as Hong Kong and Indo-china. T'ao's society favoured attack from within. Since it had good connections with the secret societies, it preferred to maintain its former status and name, and continue to exploit these connections. According to Sun Yat-sen, however, only a slight difference in the principle of social welfare existed. Whatever they were, the fact remains that full amalgamation was never attained.[26]

T'ao joined the League in late 1906 or early 1907. In the autumn of 1907 he and Chang Ping-lin, together with exiles from India, Annam, and Burma, organised a United League of the Conquered Nations of East Asia, with Chang Ping-lin as Chairman. That winter T'ao and Chang Chi joined a group of socialists to promote studies of socialism. From April to July 1908 T'ao was the Chief Editor of the *People's Journal*, and through it advocated terrorism and assassination as means of revolution. The League's headquarters and the *People's Journal* were then in need of money. Since Sun had stopped assisting, T'ao went to southeast Asia in August 1908 to raise funds.

Reports of the encounter between Sun and T'ao are confused, and the truth is not easy to ascertain.[27] According to Sun, T'ao approached him and asked for $50,000 to finance his projected revolt in Chekiang, and a further few thousand yen to subsidise the *People's Journal*. According to T'ao's biographer, Chang Huang-ch'i, T'ao approached Sun Yat-sen for a letter of introduction to enable him to go on a fund-raising tour, but Sun refused. Whatever the truth was, it is a fact that after this meeting T'ao turned against Sun. To make himself and the activities of his society known to the Chinese in southeast Asia, he wrote and published an account of his society's exploits in Chekiang and toured southeast Asia to stage an anti-Sun campaign. Because of the support of a group of Hunanese teachers in Indonesia, then the Dutch East Indies, he obtained considerable support from a wide section of overseas Chinese and a number of discontented men evacuated from Yunnan, Kwangsi, and Kwangtung. When Wang Ching-wei and Teng Tzu-yu tried to raise money on Sun's behalf, they were unsuccessful, owing to the opposition of T'ao and his friends.

In 1909 T'ao succeeded in getting some members of the League in southeast Asia, representing seven central Chinese provinces in the Yangtze valley, to petition for the dismissal of Sun as head of the League. It listed nineteen charges against Sun Yat-sen, including the misuse of party funds and discrimination against non-Cantonese members of the League. The letter ended with a request that Sun be replaced by Huang Hsing. T'ao personally delivered the petition, with a number of Sun's letters as evidence, to the League's head-quarters in Tokyo, and asked for a meeting to discuss the petition. However, either his accusations were grossly excessive and lacked substantial evidence, or the leaders in Tokyo were anxious to maintain unity, and T'ao's move received little support. The presence of Huang Hsing in Tokyo at this time and his staunch support for Sun Yat-sen was undoubtedly a stabilising factor. The quarrel did not become a burning issue.

Having failed to oust Sun in this manner, T'ao and his supporters carried their campaign a step further by publishing their charges against Sun and distributing leaflets among all overseas Chinese communities. This measure, while causing the League to sag in influence, was not sufficient to remove Sun. Thereupon T'ao decided to revive his former society. He established a head office in Tokyo, with Chang Ping-lin and himself as Chairman and Vice-Chairman.

Li Hsieh-ho, who became the executive officer for southeast Asia, completed the break with the League by transferring the allegiance of all branches of the League under his control to the Society for the Recovery of China.

From 1908 to 1910 the League was at its lowest ebb. Sun was not allowed to land in Japan or Hong Kong. The overseas Chinese in Indo-china and southeast Asia seemed to have been exhausted financially, and were torn by internal dissensions in the party. The Tokyo headquarters of the League suffered from a shortage of staff and money, and by the autumn of 1908 had practically ceased to exist. When the *People's Journal*, the symbol of the League, was closed down by the Japanese in October 1908 on a charge of sedition, the League had in fact ceased to operate as an organised body. The extremely demoralised state of the revolutionaries could be appreciated from the defection of some of its members to the Manchu side.

Sung Chiao-jen, having tried to save the *People's Journal* by legal means and by planning its transfer to the United States, also became very down-hearted. He was said to have resorted to drinking and smoking, and borrowing money from a maid-servant. This state of affairs affected even the close friendship between Sung Chiao-jen and Huang Hsing. When Huang returned to Japan in mid 1908, he avoided meeting Sung until a third party intervened.[28] In an effort to save the situation, Huang Hsing secured the agreement of the League's provincial heads to contribute to the upkeep of a new headquarters, named The House of Diligent Study. But the new headquarters had nothing to do, and its supporters soon stopped contributing to its maintenance. Huang then tried to maintain it with loans borrowed at usurious rates, and as a result was forced to hide from his creditors for two months in Miyazaki's house, until T'an Jen-feng raised enough money to settle his debts.[29]

It was in this atmosphere of hopelessness and desperation that Wang Ching-wei resolved to carry out his scheme for assassinating high-ranking Manchus in Peking. He came to Japan at the end of 1908, and secretly published two more issues of the *People's Journal*. His action unexpectedly incurred the hostility of Chang Ping-lin, and caused further ructions in the League. At the beginning of 1910, Wang and a few of his colleagues left Japan for Peking to make an attempt on the life of the Regent. His plot was discovered, and he and one other were to remain in prison until the overthrow of the Manchus in 1911.

During this period of despondency and dissension within the League in Asia, Sun Yat-sen was touring Europe and then North America in an effort to win fresh support. Sun's task was by no means easy, because of T'ao Ch'eng-chang's anti-Sun campaign. He wrote to Wu Chih-hui in 1909:

From my observation of the Overseas Chinese in the U.S.A. I find that since the collapse of the Society for the Protection of the Emperor, their attitude has turned towards revolution. The only obstacle is that the leaders in the various cities have heard T'ao's rumours and are inevitably rather sceptical at present. Therefore we cannot hope to obtain their co-operation quickly. Once this bad period is over, people will surely co-operate again. There are about seventy thousand overseas Chinese in this country and over half might be persuaded to join the revolution . . . Once the foundations are laid we may expect support from overseas Chinese in other parts of America. Therefore my plan at present is to build up the influence of the revolutionary party. There is in fact no alternative.[30]

This letter also reveals Sun's attitude towards the League, and in particular its Tokyo head office. His emphasis was now on the Chinese in America, and he showed signs of discarding his quarrelsome Tokyo headquarters. When he succeeded in establishing a

revolutionary organisation in San Francisco in early 1910, its members were sworn in as members of the Chinese Revolutionary Party
(Chung-hua ko-ming-tang) and not of the Chinese League, and the
oath was not the official oath of the League, but a new eighteen
character oath which read: 'To extinguish the Ch'ing dynasty of the
Manchus, establish a republic of China, and promote the principle
of social welfare'.

Sun made these changes without reference to Tokyo before or
after—an extraordinary act which can only be explained as a result
of his reaction to the confusion in the League and the spread of
general dissatisfaction with his leadership. Perhaps he had already
given up the League as a lost cause.

In the middle of 1910, when he managed to 'sneak' into Japan
under an assumed name, 'Dr Alaha', he was still full of resentment
against his colleagues. When Sung Chiao-jen approached him with
a proposal to revitalise the organisation, Sun bluntly replied that
the League had been dissolved, and that those who were able, might
start their own society. The following is T'an Jen-feng's account of
the episode:

> In July* Sun, hearing that Katsura Taro was forming a govern-
> ment, secretly came to Japan. Huang Hsing and Chao Po-sheng
> also arrived. I saw Sun and asked him to reform and revitalise the
> party. He consented. Unexpectedly, when Sung Chiao-jen went
> to hold discussions with him, he said, 'The League has long since
> been dissolved. Those who felt strong enough to do so could
> organise independent establishments of their own'. When Sung
> asked him to explain these remarks, he said, 'Party members
> attacked the *Tsung-li*, how could there be a League without me?
> As all funds are raised by me, party members have no right to
> question me about them, still less to make them the object of
> attack.' Sung did not argue with him but returned and told me.
> I was rather angry and went with Tun-ch'u [Sung] to see him the
> next day. His tone was unchanged. I therefore replied, 'The
> League was formed by determined men of the nation. How can
> it be abolished by your words alone? There are no rules by which
> the Tsung-li can directly punish party members, and neither can
> you blame the party members, since no one in Tokyo supported
> the charges of T'ao Ch'eng-chang. As for money, it is the direct
> result of our organisation. Since it is raised in the name of our
> organisation, its expenditure should be made known to all mem-
> bers. How can you say that it should not be questioned?' There-
> upon Sun agreed to call a meeting of all the provincial heads of
> the League for further discussions.[31]

---

* It should be June 1910 (see *Kuo-fu-nien-p'u*, Vol. I, pp. 266, 222).

Sun's promised meeting with the provincial heads never eventuated. The Japanese government's five-year ban on Sun was still in force, and the Manchu government had found out about his return to Japan and put pressure on the Japanese to secure his departure. Once again Sun had to leave Japan without a proper settlement of the differences with his colleagues, and the League's head office in Tokyo never regained its former prominence.

Sun's secret return to Japan was prompted partly by reports of the mounting tension in China at this time, and partly by a wish to discuss certain matters with his friends in Tokyo. He also wanted to find out the attitude of the Japanese government towards his party. Tokyo was also the best place from which to establish connections with provinces of north and central China. Therefore, to re-establish his organisation and to reunify the various provincial groups were in fact the chief aims of his return to Japan. Unfortunately he stayed for only two weeks, and then was ordered to leave on 25 June.[32]

From Tokyo Sun travelled to Singapore and Malaya, where he began to introduce the new constitution and the new oath he had adopted in San Francisco. He renamed all his organisations 'The Chinese Revolutionary Party'. When questioned about this change, he gave the following explanation:

As for the change in the oath, it is not a case of giving up the essential for the less important, but making it more comprehensive. The former oath of four sentences is reduced to three so that each contains one principle to coincide with our doctrine of The Three Principles. The former title, 'Members of the Chinese League', is now changed to 'Members of the Chinese Revolutionary Party' so that the name agrees with the fact. Besides, this avoids interference from the various colonial governments. In the colonies there are laws prohibiting the formation of illegal societies. Two years ago, some members of our party deported from French Indo-china were taken into the British colonies as political refugees. It was, in effect, a *de facto* recognition of the political nature of our activities, and provided us with an excellent precedent for future claim for assistance or protection in foreign territories. But we cannot do so under the Chinese League, which has not been registered with the British colonial authorities, and can thus be taken as an illegal organisation. To make our claim legitimate, we should use the name 'The Revolutionary Party' in our official oath, as is used already in U.S.A. and Hawaii. As for intra-party communications, members are free to use either name.[33]

Despite the reasons advanced above, one could reasonably doubt Sun's real motive in changing the name of the party. It happened at the height of internal disputes within the League, and the new name was first used, not in the colonies, but in the United States of America. Besides, the Chinese League had been established in southeast Asia for nearly five years without having been declared illegal by any colonial government. Not only was the act of changing the name and oath of the party, without reference to the party hierarchy, highly unconstitutional, he even failed to inform them afterwards. It also appears that Sun had never liked the name 'Chinese League'. His original suggestion had included the word 'revolutionary', but had been over-ruled for reasons of secrecy and diplomacy.[34] Since the League was no longer an integrated whole, he must have deemed it time to revert to his favourite name.

While Sun was reconstituting his organisation in southeast Asia, Sung Chiao-jen was in Tokyo, conferring with eleven provincial leaders and other members of the League, mostly from central and lower Yangtze regions, on plans to revive the League.[35] On this occasion it is recorded that Sung Chiao-jen put forward his famous theory of zonal strategy for the revolution. He suggested that China be divided into three alternative zones for the purpose of instigating uprisings. In his opinion the central or capital zone was the first and best place for revolution; a successful uprising there would immediately overthrow the government and take control of the nerve centres of the nation; Turkey and Portugal provided the most recent examples of this type of revolution. But it was also the most difficult zone in which to initiate revolt. Therefore a second alternative might be considered.

The second zone, consisting of the central provinces of the Yangtze basin, was Sung's next choice. In his plan these provinces close to the capital were to begin uprisings simultaneously, organise a government, and then march north. This theory was not new to Sung—he had developed it while still at school in Hunan several years before— and the China Resurgence Society had in fact attempted to carry out his plan.

The third alternative meant instigating uprisings in the border provinces, including Manchuria in the north and Yunnan, Kwangtung, and Kwangsi in the south. He suggested that revolutionaries were to establish secret cells in these provinces, occupy the border regions as bases, and then gradually extend control and influence.

The third method had, however, been tried and had failed. The idea of a central revolution to be carried out under the nose of the government seemed too difficult to accomplish in China. It was not surprising that the meeting chose the second measure, the instigation of revolution in the Yangtze basin.

It was decided to invoke article sixteen of the 1906 constitution, and to reorganise the Tokyo office into a regional office for central China, with Shanghai as its operational centre.[36] This was no doubt partly intended as a reply to Sun's provocative challenge to the able members to organise independent movements, and partly to dethrone Sun from his office of *Tsung-li*. But more significant was the recognition of the strategic importance of the central provinces. They at last openly disapproved of Sun's concentration on the southern provinces. Just as previous failures in central China swung the movement southward, repeated failures in the latter region in turn forced back the lever of action in the original direction.

To meet the financial needs of the new organisation, a proposal to sell to Japan the sole agency rights for antimony produced by the mines in Hunan was endorsed. Sung Chiao-jen was appointed to conduct negotiations with the Japanese, while two other Hunanese, Tsou Yung-ch'eng and Chang Tou-shu, were sent to discuss the proposal with mine-owners in Hunan. On their way to Hunan, Tsou and Chang, acting on the instruction of Sung Chiao-jen, organised the Kuang-hui Mining Company[37] in Hankow, with Chang in charge. It later became an important command centre of the revolutionary movement in Hunan and Hupeh. Tsou continued his journey to Hunan. In Changsha he visited Liu Wen-chin, a lieutenant in the mounted troops of the twenty-fifth Mixed Regiment. He briefed him on the plans of the revolutionaries in Tokyo, and asked him to assume the responsibility of recruiting and organising soldiers in his army. According to Tsou, Liu responded and laid the foundations for revolution in his regiment. The proposed regional office for central China was not actually formed until almost a year after this Tokyo meeting. But preparatory activities had already been extended to Hupeh and Hunan before the end of 1910. Sung Chiao-jen himself returned to Shanghai at the beginning of 1911, and thereafter the office of the *Independent People's Daily*, for which he worked as an editor, was used as a liaison centre.[38]

It seems that Sung's departure from Japan was primarily for financial reasons, and he intended to return shortly. Yu Yu-jen recalled that when he met Sung and invited him to be editor of the *Independent People's Daily*, Sung at first declined, because he was an anti-Manchu revolutionary, and might not be able to stay for long in Shanghai.[39] Finally, however, he decided to stay on in Shanghai as editor of the *Independent People's Daily*, and from this vantage point he lashed out at the Manchu government's internal and external policies. He was also seen carrying out a number of financial activities, including a deal in antimony with a Japanese agent. The Japanese intelligence service, which had been keeping a close check on everything concerning the Chinese, reported between February and April 1911 that Sung was interested in the price of hide in Canton.[40] Obviously few things ever escaped the notice of the watchful Japanese, for then was the eve of a brewing storm in Canton. The revolutionaries in the south were pooling all their resources to launch their biggest assault on that city, and Sung was called in to give them a hand.

SEVEN

Prelude to a Storm

THE EVIDENCE indicates that both reform and revolutionary movements in China were spurred on by foreign aggression. Sun Yat-sen's Regenerating China Society and K'ang Yu-wei's reform movements began during or after the Sino-Japanese War of 1895. The Boxer Uprising of 1900 followed on the heels of the Powers' 'battle for concessions' in China, while Russia's demands in Manchuria in 1903 provoked the establishment of the Volunteer Corps for Resisting Russia by Chinese students in Japan, and set in motion revolutionary movements among China's young intelligentsia in and outside China, culminating in the formation of the Chinese League in 1905. As a result of Japan's victory over Russia in 1905, China's constitutional reform movement gathered momentum. The Manchu government was forced by public opinion to make gestures of preparation for constitutional government, an act to which the reformers in exile enthusiastically responded by establishing a Political Participation Society *(Cheng-wen-she)*.

The apparent willingness of the Manchu government to consider constitutional reform naturally removed some of the assumptions for revolution and impeded its progress. This sharpened the already intense conflicts between the reformists and the revolutionaries. In their efforts to check this unfavourable tide, the Chinese student revolutionaries in Tokyo extended their war of words to physical combat. Sung Chiao-jen was involved in at least two known cases. One occurred on 17 October 1907, during the inaugural meeting of the reformers' Political Participation Society. According to one eye-witness, this meeting was attended by about a thousand people, and among them were some prominent Japanese political leaders. There were about a hundred members and officials of the Political Participation Society, each wearing on his chest a triangular red insignia. About four hundred revolutionaries armed with walking sticks turned up for the meeting. In the middle of an opening address by the reformist leader, Liang Ch'i-ch'ao, the revolutionaries broke loose and drove out the constitutionalists. The gathering was turned into a meeting of the revolutionary camp, with Sung Chiao-jen on the rostrum, expounding the aims of revolution.[1]

A similar event took place in the autumn of 1910 when about a thousand Chinese students met in Tokyo under the chairmanship of Sung Chiao-jen to voice an attack on the Manchu government for its inability to protect Chinese territory against British encroachment on the Yunnan-Burma border (the P'ienma Dispute). A reformer who spoke in defence of the Manchu government provoked the anger of the revolutionaries and was knocked down. Confusion ensued when the Japanese police tried to intervene by arresting the attackers. It developed into a fight between the students and the Japanese police.[2]

Both verbally and with fisticuffs, Sung Chiao-jen and his colleagues had the upper hand. The *New People's Journal*, a reformist organ in Tokyo which had, for some years prior to the appearance of the revolutionaries' *People's Journal*, dominated the minds of young Chinese, stopped publication voluntarily in the autumn of 1907. Thereafter, neither journals nor societies of the reformist camp regained popularity among the students in Tokyo.

Unfortunately the revolutionaries' triumph over the reformists in Tokyo was not matched by victories in the battlefield against the Manchu government in this period. Instead they suffered many disheartening reverses. The failure of the uprisings on the Hunan-Kiangsi border in December 1906, and the abortive revolt of the Society for the Recovery of China in the following summer, seriously jeopardised the foundation of revolution in the central provinces of China, and caused the centre of the revolution to swing to the southern provinces bordering Hong Kong and Indo-china.

During 1907 and the first part of 1908 the Chinese League launched no less than six unsuccessful uprisings in south China.[3] Repeated failures then led China's revolutionary movement to its darkest phase of inaction and internal dissension. Fortunately China's other factions fared no better. Following the deaths of the Empress Dowager Tz'u-hsi and Emperor Kuang-hsu in 1908, the reins of government fell into the hands of younger, inexperienced Manchu princes, whose intolerance and animosity towards non-Manchu statesmen, particularly Yuan Shih-k'ai, and whose overhasty and indiscreet execution of a centralisation policy, cost them the service and affection of some loyal and able Chinese officials. At the same time the reformers discredited themselves by internal squabbles over money.[4]

In 1910 foreign pressure on China was once again mounting. China's diplomatic difficulties with Japan, Russia, and Britain over border and dependency disputes placed the Manchu government in the spotlight of criticism and opposition. The constitutionalists succeeded in forcing the government to concede to them the right to serve in an advisory capacity in both provincial and national affairs, and to advance the date for full constitutional government from 1917 to 1913.[5]

The revolutionaries, after a lull of two years, wished to strike at the Manchus again. In early 1910 a *coup* was planned for Canton where the revolutionaries had secured the sympathy and support of a few new army units. But their plot did not work out as planned, and the revolt collapsed after a short struggle. The revolutionaries were deeply disappointed, not only because it was their first action after a long lull, but also because it was their first revolt for which they had the support of government troops of considerable strength. While they were lamenting their latest defeat, China's foreign relations were worsening. British troops had entered Tibet and P'ienma on the Burmese border, while Russia pressed for treaty revisions respecting its trade and diplomatic relations with Mongolia and Sinkiang. Just as the constitutionalist felt that the court should call a special session of the National Advisory Assembly (*Tzu-cheng-yuan*), and request its aid in the solution of these difficulties,[6] the revolutionaries felt the urgency of overthrowing the Manchu dynasty as a prerequisite for settling China's difficulties with foreign nations. They felt that their time for saving China was running out, and they must exert their last effort to drive out the incompetent Manchus. Huang Hsing, in a letter to his colleagues in Thailand on 11 January 1911, emphasised this point. He wrote:

Japan has annexed Korea and has reached an agreement with Russia respecting Manchuria and Mongolia. Britain, seeing China's weakness, has sent troops to Tibet and the Yunnan-Burma border. It is only a matter of days until western China is lost. The Germans are in Shantung and the French in Yunnan. Wherever their railways run the territory ceases to be ours. The U.S.A. have not occupied any of our land and have not done us any harm but they are monopolising foreign loans. . . . The Manchu government, however, remains in a drunken state. Unaware of the dangers (sugar-coated in sweet gestures), it welcomes the American policy while tacitly consenting to the demands of other powers. Towards the people, however, it pursues a policy of deceit by announcing its adherence to constitutionalism while in fact depriving its subjects of all kinds of rights in order to put its policy of centralisation into effect. China's present situation is that if it is not conquered by partition it will be lost through invisible financial control by foreign powers. Indeed, how can we tolerate this state of affairs? This autumn, Mr Chung-shan [Sun Yat-sen] called a special meeting of representatives from various branches of our organisation to decide on a plan of attack and its immediate execution. We are making an all-out effort to strike.[7]

Sung Chiao-jen, who had been the editor of the *Independent People's Daily* since his return to Shanghai at the end of 1910, also wrote profusely in his daily editorial on China's external relations and the general international situation in Asia, to show how they were all dangerous to China. The result was another major offensive of the Chinese League against the Manchu government in the Canton Uprising of 27 April 1911, in which Sung Chiao-jen took part in person.

Sun Yat-sen had left Japan for southeast Asia in July 1910. After four months of reorganisation in southeast Asia, Sun gathered his chief lieutenants, Huang Hsing, Chao Sheng, Hu Han-min, and others, for a conference in Penang on 13 November 1910, which decided on an all-out strike against the Manchus. The target was again Canton, as they felt that their connections with the New Army units in Canton, though somewhat impaired by the previous abortive attempt to capture the city, could be revived. The New Army units in Canton were to be the revolutionaries' main fighting force. But, as past experience had proved the difficulties in the initial stages of their revolts, the revolutionaries decided to select 500 men from their own ranks to form a vanguard unit charged with the specific duty of starting the uprising and providing leadership to the army and the militia. It was also planned that, following the capture of Canton, an army led by Huang Hsing would advance through Hunan to Hupeh, while Chao Sheng with a second army would proceed through Kiangsu to Nanking. It was hoped that their past association with these regions would invoke the sympathy and support of the local people, particularly members of the New Army units stationed in these areas.[8]

In January 1911 a Central Command *(T'ung-ch'ou-pu)*, headed by Huang Hsing, was set up to carry out the overall planning of the projected uprising. It consisted of eight departments, in charge of finance, secretarial work, transportation of arms, propaganda, communication, espionage, the drafting of laws and regulations, and general affairs.

In view of the importance of Hunan and Hupeh to the second stage of the projected campaign, T'an Jen-feng, who arrived in

Hong Kong on 4 January at the invitation of Huang Hsing and Chao Sheng, insisted that the revolutionary organisations in these two provinces should be informed of the plan beforehand. Consequently he was sent with $2,000 to make the necessary preparations. Before his departure, T'an further suggested that Sung Chiao-jen's aid should be enlisted. Here the extent of ill-feeling and disagreement between Sung Chiao-jen and the Cantonese faction of the Chinese League was revealed. Chao Sheng seems to be the only person in favour of T'an's idea. Huang Hsing was said to have consented with reluctance because of the ill-feeling between Sung and Hu Hanmin.[9]

Sung was sufficiently keen on the projected revolt to consent to participate. But when T'an Jen-feng passed through Shanghai for Hupeh and Hunan and urged him to go to Hong Kong, he expressed reservations, apparently also doubting his welcome in Hong Kong. He told T'an that he would rather wait until he heard directly from Hong Kong. The expected invitation never came, so that, when T'an reappeared in Shanghai after his mission, he found Sung still waiting. At T'an's urging, however, Sung agreed to depart with him at once.[10]

On arrival in Hong Kong, Sung was put in charge of the department for drafting regulations. In this position he drew up a set of laws pertaining to the organisation and system of the revolutionary government and administration, which later provided a basis for the formation of revolutionary governments in Hupeh and Kiangsu.[11] It was, in fact, the only tangible achievement of this Canton uprising, which ended in complete failure and inflicted serious losses to the revolutionaries in men, money, and morale.

The revolt was originally intended for 13 April 1911. Unfortunately things did not go as planned. The assassination of a Manchu General in Canton on 8 April by a revolutionary from Malaya alerted the government.[12] This, together with delay in the shipment of arms from Japan, and in the remittance of funds from America and Indonesia, forced the postponement of the uprising to 27 April. This date was chosen after considering the following factors: firstly, the arms from Japan and Indo-china were expected to reach Canton on that day; secondly, the 'vanguards' would all be in Canton by that date, their presence would make further delay impracticable and unwise, since such a large body of men would make their secrets difficult to conceal, and their maintenance would also be a serious problem; thirdly, it had been reported that the Second Battalion of the New Army, sympathetic to revolution, might be repatriated at any moment.[13]

Huang Hsing came to Canton on 23 April to take charge on the spot. Finding that the situation was far too hot, he wired Hong Kong to stop his colleagues, who were scheduled to leave Hong Kong for Canton in the following couple of days. On 25 April the Canton government was seen dispatching troops to strategic points. It was also reported that the Second Battalion of the New Army had been disarmed. Suspecting that there was a leakage, Huang Hsing had in fact decided to suspend the revolt. More than three hundred party fighting men had been sent away when it was reported that the government had ordered a house-to-house search for rebels.

It was apparent that the only way for the revolutionaries still in the city to save themselves was to start an uprising immediately. In desperation Huang Hsing, encouraged by the arrival of three Patrol Battalions *(Hsun-fang-ying)*, which were reported to consist of many revolutionary supporters, reversed the decision to suspend the revolt. He decided that the uprising was to take place on the afternoon of 27 April 1911, and the Hong Kong office was accordingly notified on the eve of the uprising to send all the men available.

The Hong Kong office was faced with a difficult problem. There were only two sailings a day from Hong Kong to Canton, one in the early morning and the other in the evening. To send more than 300 men, most of them without pigtails and many of them non-Cantonese, was clearly impossible. It was decided that a small number of men would sail in the morning, while the majority would catch the late sailing. Huang Hsing was accordingly informed, and asked to withhold the revolt until the following day.[14]

Sung Chiao-jen went with the majority of the 300 men by the evening boat. When they arrived in Canton on the following morning they found that the revolt had collapsed and they had to turn back to Hong Kong on the same day.[15] Apparently Huang Hsing had failed to comply with Hong Kong's request to postpone the uprising, for three reasons: firstly, repeated postponements were bad for the morale of the participants; secondly, government arrests were imminent; and thirdly, with the aid of the newly arrived Patrol Battalions as assured by a party liaison officer, the revolutionaries felt sure they could capture Canton without the men from Hong Kong.[16]

Unfortunately, the expected aid from the Patrol Battalions was not forthcoming. Instead, most of them were hostile. The revolutionaries found themselves not only greatly outnumbered, but also confused in the execution of their plan, owing to the three changes in dates. The uprising had failed and the revolutionaries sustained the heaviest loss of life they had yet suffered. Seventy-two 'young and talented' men had died in this revolt, causing Sun to write some years later that this Canton uprising had virtually plucked the 'flowers' of the Chinese League.[17]

The Canton uprising of 27 April 1911, despite its failure, is generally held to have had far-reaching influences. Hu Han-min went so far as to remark that 'as a result of it the Manchu court was shaken and the will of the people steeled to follow the footsteps of the dead. It precipitated the Wuchang uprising, to the first shot of which the whole nation echoed.'[18] In view of the heroic deaths of those selfless and idealistic youths, this was a fitting tribute. In the context of historical evidence, however, the contrary holds true. The final effort of the League under Sun Yat-sen's direct leadership had failed, and its resources had been exhausted. There was a general demoralisation among its rank and file. Chao Sheng, a gifted soldier of the League, died disappointed. Huang Hsing, a determined revolutionary leader, was on the point of parting with the whole revolutionary movement, wishing only to revenge the deaths of his friends on his most hated enemy, Li Chun, a naval commandant in Canton. Even Hu Han-min, a resolute and sophisticated man, had changed his attitude towards assassination, and actively co-operated with Huang Hsing in the latter's scheme to assassinate Li Chun. T'an Jen-feng, a man of great determination, was also depressed, and decided never again to participate in the affairs of the League.[19]

Luckily for the cause of revolution Sung Chiao-jen and a number of revolutionaries in the Yangtze provinces were unaffected by the failure. Sung was disappointed but not disheartened. He completed the draft of his provisional constitution as requested by Chao Sheng, and continued his search for answers to the problems of revolution. When he returned to Shanghai, he said to his colleagues, 'although this rising has not been successful, it has provided us with much experience to assist our preparations for next time'.[20]

In a sense the Wuchang uprising owed its success to the martyrs of the Canton revolt, that is, the disaster of the latter restored the centre of conspiracy to the Yangtze region. Sung and his colleagues finally made up their minds to push ahead their revolutionary activities in central China by bringing into existence their Central China Office of the League, as planned in Tokyo.

According to the revised 1906 constitution of the Chinese League,[21] nine main regional offices, five in China and four outside, were to be set up, each with the responsibility of directing, supervising, and co-ordinating activities of local branches of the League within its jurisdiction. The five intended offices in China were: the West China Office, which, based on Chungking, was to take charge of

Kueichow, Tibet, Kansu, Sinkiang, and Szech'uan; the East China Office, with its headquarters in Shanghai, which was to direct operations in Chekiang, Kiangsu, and Anhwei; the Central China Office, based on Hankow, which was to lead the movement in Honan, Hunan, Hupeh, and Kiangsi; the South China Office, with its head office in Hong Kong, which was to assume responsibility for Yunnan, Kwangtung, Kwangsi, and Fukien; and the North China Office, based on Yent'ai, which was to lead operations in Mongolia, Shensi, Shansi, Shantung, Chihli, and Manchuria.*

Because of the shortage of staff and money, this plan was not carried out until the autumn of 1909, when Sun Yat-sen, after a lull of a year and a half in military activities, was ready to strike at the Manchu government again, and instructed Hu Han-min to set up the South China Office.[22] After its establishment, the South China Office immediately carried out preparations for a revolt in Canton, the so-called New Army uprising, which took place prematurely in February 1910, and failed, causing great damage to its foundation in that city. It was followed by another year of military inaction while Sun Yat-sen tramped around the globe to canvass support. He had some success in America, and even succeeded in reviving his organisations in Malaya, which had fallen to a low ebb following the internal disputes and inaction of the preceding two years. But his failure to overcome his differences with his colleagues in Tokyo led to a resolution by the League's members in Tokyo to organise the Central China Office as stipulated in the 1906 constitution of the League. Chu Cheng was immediately sent to prepare the groundwork in Hupeh, while T'an Jen-feng went to Hong Kong with a view to securing some financial assistance from the South China Office for this project.[23] It was said that Huang Hsing, on hearing of this plan, did not oppose the project, but thought it workable only if money could be found. But Hu Han-min, a henchman of Sun Yat-sen, opposed the whole plan. He thought that it would create further dissension within the League with regard to the office of *Tsung-li*. He was said to have remarked:

> The members in Tokyo could not even maintain a small establishment such as the House of Diligent Study, how could they talk of doing anything else? The post of *Tsung-li* is only a temporary device. If, as a result of changes in the organisation, worthless disputes in this regard occur, will it not become a laughing stock?[24]

---

* The four main offices outside China were based on Singapore, Brussels, San Francisco, and Honolulu.

Provoked by this contemptuous remark, T'an retorted angrily: The headquarters [of the League] are in Tokyo, but the *Tsung-li* has been wandering about in the South and East [southeast Asia, Europe, and America] continuously without a fixed address, and has never given it any attention. What sort of *Tsung-li* is he? The maintenance of the Tokyo Office entirely depended on the contribution of the residing colleagues, who had never resorted to bragging and deceit in order to raise funds. But you, in the name of the League, had obtained from the overseas Chinese huge funds. How dare you belittle everyone else merely because you have set up this office filled with a few idle men, and a paper to print a few brazen words.[25]

Ill-considered remarks and heated exchanges of this kind revealed the extent of ill-feeling between the Tokyo group and the Cantonese faction under Sun Yat-sen. They at once marred the chances of closer co-operation between them. T'an recalled that, if Chao Sheng had not been there to restrain him, he would most certainly have used his punitive fists on Hu. Instead, he left Hong Kong at the first opportunity, swearing that he would never again return. His unpleasant experience in Hong Kong had no doubt been transmitted to his colleagues in Tokyo, and partly accounted for the discord between Sung Chiao-jen and Hu Han-min.

During the months following T'an's trip to Hong Kong, acute financial difficulties prevented the Tokyo group from carrying out their scheme of reorganisation at their headquarters. The following account illustrates the plight of Sung Chiao-jen and his colleagues in Tokyo:

When I [T'an Jen-feng] returned from Hong Kong, K'e-ch'iang [Huang Hsing], who also had financial difficulties, only managed to raise for me 300 dollars, which was not even sufficient to meet the interest on his debts. Therefore we continued to borrow money by using scholarship students' allowance passbooks as guarantee. Because we had to run day and night seeking loans, the task of reorganisation had to be shelved. However, fearing that inaction might drain away the enthusiasm of our members and cause them to change their minds about implementing our plan, we began holding weekly meetings. When winter came, we were no longer able to dodge the daily mounting debts. We were forced to sell the copyright of *The Comparative Finance*, a book edited by Sung Tun-ch'u, translated and published under my management, to our creditor, Lin Chao-tung. Tun-ch'u already owed Lin a thousand dollars. After clearing this debt and the interest I still owed him with the proceeds from the book, we had only a few hundred dollars left, an amount which would not last for very long. I therefore instructed the students to report to the Chinese Legation the loss of their allowance passbooks, which had been given over to the creditor in payment for interest. In this way we avoided paying him the arrears. This was done because the amount of interest we had paid had already exceeded the actual loans, and we were rather annoyed by the creditor's ruthless exploitation. It was an action my conscience could face without guilt or shame. The hardship we endured in those days was indeed beyond the power of words.[26]

As a matter of fact, the scheme of reorganisation was never carried out in Tokyo. Shortly after the events described by T'an Jan-feng, Sung Chiao-jen left for Shanghai. Here he worked as a journalist, and used to the best advantage his knowledge of international politics and economics gained during six years of exile in Japan, in order to protect Chinese national interests against foreign encroachment as well as to promote revolution. He had not forgotten the Tokyo plan to form the Central China Office. In fact, he was in the process of reintroducing it when he was called away to participate in the Canton uprising of 27 April 1911.[27]

Sung and T'an's participation in the Canton uprising should not be taken to mean reconciliation between the contending factions. They responded to the call of Huang Hsing and Chao Sheng, both of whom were from the Yangtze provinces, rather than to that of Sun and Hu. Above all, they answered the call of their nation, for which they and their colleagues in Tokyo were willing to bury any differences for the time being. Even a breakaway like Li Hsieh-ho, who two years earlier joined T'ao Ch'eng-chang in opposition to Sun Yat-sen and went to the extent of transferring the allegiance of all branches of the League under his control to T'ao's society, took part in this revolt.[28]

After the disastrous Canton uprising, all hope of success in initiating revolutions in the south seemed to have vanished. The South China Office of the League informed the revolutionaries in Hunan and Hupeh that it had been so weakened by the Canton attempt that it could not start a revolt within the next five years, and that, if any members or groups wished to take immediate action, they would have to do so on their own.[29]

The turn of the central provinces had come. The Mutual Advancement Society, an off-shoot of the League, had been active in the central provinces, particularly Hunan and Hupeh, since its establishment in Tokyo in 1907. Owing to the unceasing efforts of its members, as well as those of other societies, the revolutionary forces in this region had gradually built up their strength and influence. They had originally planned to rise in response to a successful *coup* in Canton, but did not do so, as a result of the latter's unexpected collapse. Therefore they remained intact and provided a good foundation for any future plans the revolutionary leaders might adopt.

For some weeks after the Canton uprising, however, the government was vigilant, and the revolutionaries either found it expedient to lie low, or were recovering from the shattering blow they had suffered. Sung Chiao-jen, after his return to Shanghai, was busily planning and working. Apparently he was deeply grieved by the losses in Canton. A close friend of his said of him that 'he was filled with sadness and indignation after his return; happy smiles rarely crossed his face'.[30]

The final impetus for bringing the Central China Office into existence seems to have come from the revolutionaries in Hunan and Hupeh. Immediately after the Canton uprising, the leaders of the Mutual Advancement Society in this region held a meeting in Hankow and passed three important resolutions: firstly, that henceforward Hunan and Hupeh were to assume a central role in China's revolution—initial uprisings might begin either in Hunan or in Hupeh, provided one supported the other in the event, but the ideal was to start uprisings simultaneously; secondly, the backbone of the revolutionaries' fighting force was the New Army in Wuchang, supported by subsidiary forces composed of secret society members; thirdly, the Literary Society *(Wen-hsueh-she)*, a rival revolutionary organisation in Wuchang, should be informed of the Mutual Advancement Society's plan, and a *rapprochement* should bring the two organisations together to fulfil a common objective.[31]

In accordance with the last resolution, a meeting was held between the societies on 11 May 1911, at which the basis of co-operation between them was discussed. By the time T'an Jen-feng, a deeply disappointed man after the Canton uprising, reached Hankow from Hong Kong, the foundation for the formation of a Central China Office was already laid.

Sung Chiao-jen, T'an Jen-feng, and Ch'en Ch'i-mei, who were to play key roles in establishing the Central China Office and in the revolutionary movements in the Yangtze basin, left Hong Kong for Shanghai together.

On reaching Shanghai, Sung resumed his editorship of the *Independent People's Daily*, while T'an made his way home. He arrived in Hankow in May or June and was met by a group of Hunan and Hupeh revolutionaries who, disagreeing with the instruction of the Hong Kong Office to suspend large-scale uprisings, and also with T'an's pessimism, persuaded him to remain in the movement. He and another Hunanese, Tseng Po-hsing, were charged with the duty of recruiting and organising support in the lower Yangtze basin (Anhwei and Kiangsu), while other members of the Mutual Advancement Society attended to affairs in Hunan and Hupeh. By July 1911 preliminary understandings between the various revolutionary organisations in the Yangtze basin from Changsha to Nanking were achieved. The time was deemed ripe for the organisation of a head office. On the last day of July 1911 the Central China Office of the Chinese League was formally established.[32] A declaration was issued, in which two serious weaknesses were pointed out as the causes of the League's past failures. Firstly, the League had a common objective but no unified approach or concrete plan for its realisation; secondly, there were many men of genuine ability and sincerity, but the leadership of the League had failed to enlist their services, and consequently, within the League the lack of a concrete plan had given rise to deviation, separatist movements, internal disputes, and defection—the behaviour of such men as Chang Ping-lin, T'ao Ch'eng-chang, and Liu Kuang-han were examples. Outside the League, the absence of a genuine, efficient revolutionary organisation and leadership had led many able men to pursue individual courses of action, causing great wastage of talent for little result.

The declaration went on to assert that these phenomena bred incoherence and non-co-operation within the revolutionary movement, which, as history had frequently revealed, might eventually lead to struggles for power, while the absence of popular and efficient leadership caused men of lesser understanding to sacrifice their lives for nothing, thereby impairing the revolutionary movement itself. It was to remedy these weaknesses that the Central China Office was organised.[33]

Ostensibly the Central China Office was organised as a branch of the Chinese League. It even acknowledged its subordination to the virtually defunct head office in Tokyo, and recognised the South China Office as a friendly ally. But its pretension to central authority, simmering between the lines of its declaration, was unmistakable. No specific recognition was extended to the position of Sun Yat-sen. Instead, charges were brought against him and his followers for having failed to seek fundamental solutions to the weaknesses of the League, and for having resorted to superficial means and neglected essential groundwork for uprisings in the execution of party policies. 'This', the declaration read, 'was primarily responsible for the repeated failures of our party's uprisings, culminating in the most tragic defeat of last April!' Furthermore, the leaders in the south were blamed for shirking their responsibilities after the event.

One died of disappointment [so the declaration ran], one became downhearted, and one retired into comfortable seclusion.* No leader was to be found, and as a result, comrades scattered like wild birds and animals with all their hopes and zeal vanishing into thin air like bubbles.

Constitutionally, the Central China Office could not claim legality for its existence as a branch of the League as it did not recognise the authority of Sun Yat-sen as *Tsung-li*. The 1906 constitution stipulated that all regional offices should adhere to the constitution of the head office. All rules and regulations drawn up by them should be passed by the legislative department of the head office, and approved by the *Tsung-li* before implementation. But the Central China Office did neither. The argument that the contravention was an act of expediency is not convincing. True, the League's head office in Tokyo existed only in name, and it undoubtedly affected the attitude of the organisers of the Central China Office, but there was nothing to prevent them from consulting Sun Yat-sen if the latter's authority as *Tsung-li* were respected. No communication before or after its formation ever took place. The extent of insulation between them could be seen in the fact that, as late as the middle of July 1911, two weeks before the formal establishment of the Central China Office, Sun Yat-sen, in replying to the inquiry of a Japanese about revolutionaries operating in Shanghai, stated that he had no colleagues permanently residing there![34]

The constitution of the Central China Office, which was drawn up by Sung Chiao-jen, also contained stipulations directly contravening the 1906 constitution of the League. The most obvious of these was the article concerning the headship of the Central China Office. The 1906 constitution of the League stipulated that the head of the regional office was to be appointed by the *Tsung-li*, but the constitution of the Central China Office ruled that its headship was to be left vacant for the time being and would be filled by election according to the laws passed by the Central Executive Council.[35]

Prior to the election of a President, leadership was exercised collectively by five men who constituted the Central Executive Council and were also concurrently respective heads of five departments. They were to be elected annually by members of the Central China Office. The first batch of men elected to this committee and to the five departments consisted of the following:

---

* The first referred to Chao Sheng's death; the rest could mean any of three leaders, Huang Hsing, Hu Han-min, and Sun Yat-sen.

Sung Chiao-jen   (Secretariat)
Ch'en Ch'i-mei   (General Affairs)
Pang Tsu-i   (Finance)
T'an Jen-feng   (Communication)
Yang P'u-sheng   (Accounting)[36]

Since leadership was to be exercised conjointly by the above five men, they were of equal status. But one could not fail to see Sung Chiao-jen's dominating influence in the organisation. As head of the Secretariat whose duties were to counsel the committee and to draft laws and regulations, he seems to have taken the initiative in most organisational matters. The constitution of the Central China Office drafted by him consisted mostly of his own political ideals. A distinctive feature of the draft was that the aims of the organisation were stated to be 'the overthrow of the Manchu régime and the establishment of a democratic constitutional system of government'. This marked deviation from the triple aims of the League, namely nationalism, democracy, and social welfare of the people, was much criticised later, and became the source of Sung's political nickname, 'the Believer in Dual Principles of the People'.[37]

What were the causes of these constitutional deviations? Apart from its organisers' political ideals, two factors, the weaknesses of the former organisation, and the dictates of circumstance seem to be primarily responsible. Firstly, since the dispute over the leadership of the League, the office of *Tsung-li* had been discredited. The leaders of the Central China Office were sceptical of the wisdom of reintroducing it. The alternative was collective leadership. In their inaugural declaration it was stated clearly that the collective device was aimed to 'rectify the inclination towards partiality and to prevent the rise of tyranny'. To attain this end, the constitution of the Central China Office laid down that the Central Executive Council would follow a unanimity rule in the adoption and execution of policies. A further safeguard was that the members of the Central Executive Council were elected annually.[38]

Secondly, the change of the League's triple aims to two appears to be (at least partly) due to circumstances. The immediate aim of the Central China Office was to instigate revolution in the Yangtze provinces. To do so it needed the support of all anti-Manchu forces in the area. Some years previously a group of the League's adherents had organised the Mutual Advancement Society and changed one of the three principles of the League ostensibly to accommodate the uneducated members of the underworld. This society then had grown in size and influence. In order to enlist the co-operation of this and other similar societies in the region, a degree of flexibility in doctrine

was obviously desirable. In 1911 the cry for constitutional government had reached its highest pitch in China. No one could fail to
see the wide appealing power of the term.

Without a doubt these considerations had weighed heavily on
the mind of Sung Chiao-jen when he was drafting the constitution,
and made him lay down the 'overthrow of the Manchu régime and
the establishment of a democratic, constitutional system of government' as the primary targets of his organisation.

Sung Chiao-jen, as the drafter of the constitution of the Central
China Office, is often held responsible for these apparent shifts of
stand. He has been charged as a dual-principle partisan who recognised only nationalism and democracy as legitimate aims and relegated social welfare, the third principle of the League, to a place of
oblivion. That there was a smack of opportunism in Sung's policies
is undeniable. In any criticism of his action, however, one should
bear in mind the fact that Sung was primarily a revolutionary and
political activist whose immediate duty was to muster enough
strength and support to overthrow first a despotic and corrupt régime,
and then erect an alternative system of government in its place.

Besides, it may be noted that the belief in political change as a
prerequisite to solve China's basic problems, whether security,
economic or social, was never in doubt. It was this conviction, as
well as national sentiment, which led Sung Chiao-jen and his
generation to seek a quick political solution by means of armed
revolution. The aim to establish constitutional democracy, and the
exclusion of vague and ill-defined terms such as socialism from their
platform, had very practical results. As later events reveal, it eased
the way for China's conservative forces to come under their banner.

But the inroad of conservative forces into the revolutionary camp
had serious after-effects. They strengthened the party's anti-
Manchu effort, but thwarted its determination to advance the cause
further. The result is well known. The alien Manchu régime was
overthrown, but the revolutionaries found themselves relinquishing
leadership to a no less reactionary group.

Therefore, Sung Chiao-jen and his colleagues may be blamed for
lacking resolution, and for resorting to opportunism and expediency.
It was the price for seeking quick success. It was, however, a general
characteristic of the revolutionary movement of that time rather
than a question of personal weakness. Perhaps more emphasis
should be given to the positive contribution of Sung Chiao-jen and
his friends to China's revolution. The Chinese League had begun
disintegrating in 1907. Following the disastrous Canton uprising of
April 1911, its activities had virtually come to a standstill, and its

morale was at its lowest ebb. It was Sung Chiao-jen and his colleagues who stepped into the vacuum with their Central China Office, and gave a timely leadership and encouragement to the restless and intensifying revolutionary fervour of the Yangtze valley.

The Central China Office represented also the first attempt of the revolutionaries to centralise command over the widely scattered revolutionary forces of the region. Until then, each local or provincial unit acted on its own under only nominal leadership of the League.[39] The existence of the Central China Office, as one of its founding members pointed out, provided an important link between the revolutionary organisations of eight provinces (Kiangsu, Chekiang, Anhwei, Kiangsi, Hupeh, Hunan, Szech'uan, and Shensi) and was the pivot of the Wuchang uprising.[40] This fact points to another deviation of this office. It was not the same regional office envisaged in the 1906 constitution of the League. Its head office was in Shanghai instead of Hankow, and its operational area had extended to include the region originally designed for the Eastern China Office. Szech'uan and Shensi, of the West and North China Offices respectively, were also drawn into its orbit. Even Fukien of the South China Office was represented in Shanghai. Nation-wide support for the Central China Office was canvassed, and it was stated explicitly in its constitution that it 'is organised by its supporters among the members of the Chinese League'.[41] Its pretension to central leadership could not be over-emphasised.

The Central China Office operated basically according to a strategy advocated by Sung Chiao-jen a decade before. It aimed to secure Hupeh, which commanded vital land and water communication between the north and south. To safeguard its rear, as well as to ensure food provision and reinforcement, the control of Hunan and Szechuan was also its objective. To block the enemy's advance on Wuchang from north China, the revolutionaries planned to occupy Wu-sheng-kuan, an important pass controlling the entry of the Peking-Hankow railway from Honan to Hupeh, while simultaneous revolts were to take place in Shansi and Shensi, to interrupt communications with Peking. In order to control the lower Yangtze River, and to isolate the enemy's navy, Nanking was also to be seized immediately, in the event of uprisings. This plan of campaign was unfolded to Huang Hsing, a recognised military leader of the League, and received his hearty approval.[42]

Immediately after its establishment, the Central China Office took active steps to implement its plan. Key members were sent to organise, amalgamate, or advise various local revolutionary groups with the aim of extending its leadership and influence as far as possible.

Tseng Po-hsing returned to Hunan; Fan Hung-hsien went to Anhwei, and Chang Tzu went to Nanking. At least two persons were sent to Ichang, a strategic town on the border of Hupeh and Szechuan, to raise funds and to enlist supporters. Hsiung Yueh-shan was sent to Hong Kong, presumably on a mission to contact Huang Hsing; Wu Yung-san, a Szechuanese, assumed responsibility for his native province; Shensi was in the hands of Ching Wu-mo.[43]

To the key provinces of Hupeh and Hunan, which were to assume the role of initiating the uprising, a decision was made to send T'an Jen-feng, and later Sung Chiao-jen, who, in the words of T'an Jen-feng, possessed far better qualifications, ability, and influence than he.[44] The authority and influence of the Central China Office over the revolutionary forces in the provinces could be seen in the tone and confidence of the resolution of 7 October 1911, in which T'an Jen-feng referred to his proposed trip to Hunan and Hupeh as an act of maintaining the faith and confidence in the Central China Office of the revolutionaries in those provinces, and his trip to Nanking as a mission to 'deal' with Cheng Tsan-ch'eng, a member of the League, who was a liaison officer appointed by the Central Command of the South China Office. The necessity to 'deal' with him presumably arose out of Cheng's indisposition to co-operate with the Central China Office.

More conclusive evidence of the office's authority is the resolution on the time for the uprising. At the time of its establishment, there was unrest in Szechuan over the railway disputes. The revolutionary groups in Hupeh were inclined to start an uprising in response to this unrest, but, in the judgment of the leaders in Shanghai, the upheaval in Szechuan was subsiding and both Hunan and Nanking could not be relied on. Accordingly, it directed that the activities of the revolutionaries should be slowed down, and the plan for the uprising should be suspended until further developments.[45]

Parallel to organisational activities was a press campaign carried out by Sung Chiao-jen in his editorials in the *Independent People's Daily*. Both before and after the establishment of the Central China Office, Sung wrote profusely on national and international questions of the day, exposing the injustices and incompetence of the Manchu government, and external and internal problems resulting from these. The scholarliness, lucidity, and sound analysis which marked his writings were said to have won great popularity and made the *Independent People's Daily* one of the most influential publications in China on the eve of the 1911 revolution, thus contributing directly to accelerate the revolutionary movements in the Yangtze provinces.[46] The following is a specimen of his writing during this period:

It is a pity that the Szechuanese people only employ negative measures, and do not know the use of positive methods, causing the Manchu government to think that the people of Szechuan could be easily dealt with. They not only refuse to comply with the wish of the people but actually hand out repeated threats!

It is also lamentable that the people of Hunan, Hupeh, and Kwangtung are not standing by the Szechuanese, enabling the government to gloat over the latter's grievances, and to continue its much hated policies unabated. These shortcomings are indeed regrettable. If the people of Szechuan, through thorough observations, understand the causes underlying the rise and fall of governments, and the forces determining the changes of the world, they should not again concentrate on the trifling disputes about railways. They should proceed from negative to positive action, placing themselves at the head of four hundred million Hans, Manchus, Mongolians, Moslems, and Tibetans to march towards the goal of constructing a democratic and constitutional political system.

For the same end, the people of Hunan, Hupeh, Kwangtung, and other provinces should also rise simultaneously like whirlwinds and floods. When this happens, one may expect with good reason that the evil system of tyranny which has plagued East Asia for several thousand years will be swept clean, and together with it all bad practices such as the borrowing of foreign money and the deprivation of people's railway rights.[47]

It was the voice of revolution. Sung was appealing to the people to unite and rise against the incompetent Manchu government. Besides informing the nation of the real situation of China and the dangers it was facing, and fanning the people's hatred against injustices, corruption, and incompetence, Sung also wrote to communicate his political thoughts and beliefs to his colleagues. On 25 September 1911, ten days before the outbreak of the Wuchang uprising, Sung wrote an important editorial, setting out what he believed to be basic principles of action for successful revolutions. He recommended that, firstly, the revolutionary period should be as short as possible; secondly, the area selected for the initial uprising should be small but vital; thirdly, the revolutionaries should utilise what the old government relied on for maintaining its existence, i.e. they should first win over the government's armed forces to their side.[48]

Sung based his convictions on his observation of recent events in Portugal. Portugal was then a small European nation with vast overseas colonial possessions. A revolution against tyranny broke out in the capital at the end of 1910. With the help of the army and navy, the king and his government were overthrown overnight.

Immediately, order and stability were restored. Within several months, and before any threats of partition of her overseas possessions, as suggested by Germany, could materialise, a constitutional republican government was firmly established. Sung was very impressed, and regarded it as an excellent lesson for Chinese revolutionaries.

The policy of utilising government troops was not new, and had been tried out previously, notably in recent revolts in Canton. Moreover, more systematic infiltration of the army was then taking place in Hupeh and Hunan. Its effectiveness was revealed in the successful uprising in Wuchang on 10 October 1911. However, the revolutionaries' choice for their initial revolt of the seat of a provincial government in central China instead of the national capital, Peking, contributed to markedly different results. The Portuguese revolutionaries who began their uprising in the national capital, successfully ousted the reigning monarch and ensured the destruction of the former ruling classes (the nobility and the ecclesiastics). But their Chinese counterparts were less fortunate. They commanded the loyalty of only a small section of the nation's armed forces, and, starting their revolts a long way from the national capital, enabled reactionary forces to aggregate and grow into an opposing force, with the result that, although the revolutionaries secured the overthrow of the reigning dynasty, it was at the cost of seeing themselves engulfed by the residual forces of the passing régime.

EIGHT

The Revolution of 1911

AFTER THE proposal to introduce a Central China Office in 1910, Sung Chiao-jen, always cautious and methodical, prepared a three-year program for the revolutionaries. During this period there were to be no revolts, and the office was to make careful preparations in the Yangtze provinces, gradually extending its activities northward into Hupeh, the province of the national capital.[1] Obviously Sung still preferred a 'capital uprising' in accordance with his zonal concept, but, in consideration of the difficulties in instigating uprisings in the capital zone, the central provinces were chosen for initial activities.

Had Sung's suggestions been acceptable to his colleagues, a strong revolutionary organisation might have resulted from these preparations, and the extension of activities into Peking and its environs might have brought results similar to the contemporary republican revolution in Portugal. Sung's ideas were rejected, however, by Chao Sheng, who thought that great deeds should not be dilatory! The majority supported Chao, arguing that the emphasis in revolution was on sacrifice, not on immediate success. If care was emphasised, concern for gains and losses would be sharpened, and the courage and adventurous spirit of the revolutionaries dampened. Consequently, no time limits were set for preparations or uprisings, and the principal resolution of the meeting was a proposal by T'an Jen-feng to 'centralise' leadership and divide labour.[2]

When the Central China Office was formed, however, Sung's plans for a preparatory period won the day. In an attempt to prevent recklessness on the part of their scattered supporters, the leaders decided on 1913 as the year for 'grand revolution'.[3] Considering the magnitude of their task, which included the organisation of cadres, the subversion of the army, the transportation and accumulation of arms, and the raising of funds for these purposes, the time set was none too long.

No sooner was this decided, however, than it became apparent to the revolutionaries that the intensification of the peoples' opposition to the government, due to the scheme to nationalise railways, offered excellent opportunities for uprisings. They also realised that it might prove difficult to restrain colleagues in such trouble spots as Szechuan. As it was, subversive activities in the army in Wuchang had reached saturation point. The soldiers were clamouring for action, and the organisers showing signs of restlessness.

In September a special deputation was sent from Hupeh to Shanghai, requesting Sung and T'an to go to Wuchang. Sung and his colleagues were still cautious but flexible.[4] T'an was already on his way, and Sung about to follow, when the Wuchang uprising broke out on 10 October 1911. The revolt was a success, but the absence of a competent political tactician to guide it had profound effects on the subsequent course of revolution.

The outbreak of the Wuchang uprising came as a surprise, and its spectacular success was even more unexpected. The incident was discussed for years afterwards, but no one could agree on the causes of its success. Many, notably Sun Yat-sen, regarded it as accidental and a stroke of providence.[5] Sun maintained that, had the governor and the military commandant kept their heads and not taken to their heels, the city would not have fallen. This view tends to belittle the achievement of the well-organised revolutionary movement in Hupeh which dated back to the beginning of the century. To emphasise the latter fact, it is necessary to retrace the development of revolutionary movement in Wuchang since Sung Chiao-jen's departure.

The success of the Wuchang uprising was a natural outcome of Hupeh's peculiar development in the preceding decade or even decades, a fact receiving increasing recognition among historians.[6] Hupeh was the first province to introduce modern schools, both military and civil, and to develop a modern comprehensive educational system. It was also the first to send sizable groups of students to study in Japan and the West. Hupeh maintained the largest overseas student population ever sent abroad from a single province up to this time, and its students were among the first to take notice of Sun Yat-sen. The radical faction of the Mutual Encouragement Society, which was the first Chinese student organisation in Japan, included many Hupeh students, quite a few of whom lost their lives in the abortive revolt of the Independent Army in 1900. The revolutionary cries of the *Hupeh Student Circle*, the nationalistic sentiments expressed in the *Voice of China*, and the advertisement of the Alliance League all show the long and deep-seated revolutionary tradition in Hupeh.

Hupeh also led in the establishment of a modern army and the voluntary enlistment of educated men into the army. The latter phenomenon was hailed by a contemporary newspaper as an 'epoch-making' situation.[7] The formation of the Science Study Group, which extended membership to students, secret society members, and soldiers, not only opened up a new era in China's gentry-soldier relations, but also shaped the basic pattern of subsequent insurgent organisations, and laid a firm basis for the Wuchang uprising.

From the establishment of the Science Study Group in June 1904 to the Wuchang uprising, the revolutionary movement in Hupeh had gone through many vicissitudes. Following the dissolution of the Science Study Group for its connection with the China Resurgence Society's abortive Changsha revolt in October 1904, Hupeh revolutionaries went into a period of hibernation. Organised activities were resumed in February 1906, when the Society for the Daily Increase of Knowledge *(Jih-chih-hui)* was formally established under the protective umbrella of an American Episcopal Church, and immediately became an affiliated organisation of the Chinese League.[8]

Unfortunately, Kuo Yao-chieh, who had earlier helped Sung establish the magazine *Twentieth-Century China* in Japan, and for this connection was trusted and recommended by Sung Chiao-jen to the leaders of the society in Wuchang, ran into debt and betrayed the organisation to the Manchu authorities for a government reward. As a result nine leaders of the society were arrested, and their organisation was banned within one year of its formation.[9]

Revolutionary activities were continued by some members under different covers, however. Even the imprisoned leaders managed to form a secret organisation, the Iron and Blood Army of China *(Chung-hua t'ieh-hsueh-chun)*, and directions to followers outside continued to emanate from their prison cells.[10] The An-chun Prefecture Association for the Promotion of Public Good *(An-chun kung-i-she)*, later simply known as the New Association for the Promotion of Public Good, formed by educated and military men from districts in the An-lu Prefecture, stepped in to fill the vaccum, and acted as a liaison centre for members of the defunct society and other revolutionary bodies, until the formation of the Hupeh Soldiers' League, and was able to serve the cause with distinction because of its high social standing. The Hupeh Soldiers' League *(Hupeh Chun-tui t'ung-meng-hui)* was organised in July 1908 by the former members of the defunct society with the approval of Li Ya-tung, a leader arrested by the government and kept in the Han-yang gaol. At the time of formation, it had over four hundred members, and established a vernacular newspaper as its propaganda organ. After five months their activities once again attracted the attention of the government. Reorganisation became necessary, and the new establishment was given the name, Self-government Study Society *(Ch'un-chih hsueh-she)*.[11] The formation of this organisation coincided with a change of attitude in the Manchu government. Because of the failure of the use of force and coercion in stamping out revolutions, it was decided to adopt a more tolerant approach. Consequently the Self-government Study Society was able to carry out its activities with comparative ease for nearly two years, giving the revolutionary movement a firm foundation in Hupeh's New Army.

On 13 April 1910, in a protest against the rising price of rice and its continuing export from Hunan, a rice riot broke out in Changsha.[12] The Self-government Study Society planned to respond with an uprising in Hupeh, but was held back after the riot had been quelled by government forces. The advanced state of its preparations attracted the attention of the government, however. Its activities were watched and restricted, and its leaders were forced to flee. This ended its open existence and its mouthpiece, the *Commercial News (Shang-wu-pao)*, but its inner network was not affected. Within a few months its successor, the Military Studies Promotion Society *(Chen-wu hsueh-she)* was formed. Its recruiting activities were now concentrated on the soldiers in the New Army, and it succeeded in planting or recruiting a substantial number of men in five regiments.

In order to tighten security, only regimental representatives from each of the five regiments were admitted to the organisation's executive meetings. At an executive meeting on 11 October 1910, only one month after its establishment, a total membership of over 240 was recorded. To expand recruiting activities, a resolution was passed calling on each member to recruit at least one member per month. As a result, membership expanded rapidly over the next two to three months.

Accelerated subversion in the army, however, aroused the suspicion of a commanding officer, Li Yuan-hung, who took steps to purge his forces of subversive elements. Ironically, he became the leader of the Wuchang rebels almost a year later. He discharged from his Forty-first Regiment several leaders of the Society, including its Hunanese chairman. Leadership then fell on Chiang I-wu, another Hunanese, who came from Sung Chiao-jen's prefecture. However, Li Yuan-hung's action succeeded in interrupting the society's activities for two months that winter, during which time the morale of the revolutionaries was maintained chiefly by the *Great River Daily (Ta-chiang-pao)*, a newspaper established by its members.

When the atmosphere in Wuchang had returned to normal, the leaders of the Military Studies Promotion Society began to take steps to revitalise the organisation. To avoid suspicion the society decided to adopt a respectable and unobtrusive name, the Literary Society.

On 30 January 1911 the Literary Society was inaugurated by a group of soldiers, thus bringing into existence one of two organisations which were directly responsible for the successful Wuchang uprising. It consisted mainly of common soldiers in Hupeh's New Army, the only sizable and well-equipped army in China apart from the Peiyang group in North China. Its leadership was in the hands of a group of young intelligentsia, who, in their determination to overthrow the Manchu government, united with the common soldiers and converted them to their cause.[13] Here lies the essential difference between the Wuchang uprising and those before it. Other uprisings, mostly in the south, were instigated by leaders of the Sun-Huang group, and were largely dependent on a small number of party men as the main fighting force, with only subsidiary support from troops. These troops fought either for material gain, or on the orders of their commanding officers, who might be genuine revolutionaries or merely opportunists, giving or withholding support according to the prospects of success.

Wuchang was the only place where systematic infiltration of the entire modern army took place throughout the period of pre-Republican revolutionary movement. At the beginning of 1910 the Literary Society had more than 800 members; more than 90 per cent were soldiers and less than 3 per cent officers. With the enlistment of Chang Yu-k'un into the cavalry division in March 1910, every section of the New Army of Hupeh was covered by the revolutionaries. By May, membership of the society had swelled to more than 3,000, and by August 1911 it had reached 5,000.[14]

Another feature of Hupeh's revolutionary movement was the presence among the rank and file of revolutionaries from other provinces, especially Hunan. Not a few ambitious men with revolutionary leanings were attracted to Wuchang from other provinces because of its strategic importance, its improved treatment of soldiers in the New Army, and its strong revolutionary undercurrents. The close association of Hupeh and Hunan in the revolutionary movement dated back at least to 1904, when Sung Chiao-jen and Hu Ying helped to found Hupeh's first revolutionary organisation, the Science Study Group. Hunanese, such as Hu Ying, continued to assume important roles in leadership. The last three revolutionary societies in this particular (and perhaps the main stream of Hupeh's) revolutionary movement, were all headed by Hunanese.[15] The roles of Chiang-I-wu, president of the Literary Society, and Liu Yao-cheng, head of the society's Disciplinary Department, were particularly significant to subsequent events.

At the time of the China Resurgence Society, when Sung was preparing a revolt in the prefecture of Ch'ang-te, Chiang I-wu was a student in a teachers' training school in Ch'ang-te, and he apparently shared Sung's activities.[16] Following the collapse of the revolt and Sung's escape to Japan, Chiang was expelled from his school.

Liu Yao-cheng also came from Sung's prefecture, and actually shared with Sung the responsibility for starting uprisings in west Hunan in 1904. After Sung's escape to Japan, he also went into hiding until 1905, when he joined Ma Fu-i's revolt. When this revolt failed, he went to Japan and joined the Chinese League on Sung's recommendation. He returned to China in the spring of 1906 to work for the revolution in the Yangtze provinces. In 1909 he went to Shanghai, and was engaged in the publication of a journal with Chiang I-wu. Later he was invited to Hankow to edit the *Commercial News (Shang-wu-pao)*. It was here that he became directly associated with Hupeh's revolutionary movement.[17]

Both Liu and Chiang joined the New Army, and played an active role in Hupeh's revolutionary movement from the time of the Self-government Study Society to the formation of the Literary Society. This close association between Sung, Chiang, and Liu, and Sung's past association with Hupeh's revolutionaries, undoubtedly prepared the way for their co-operation in 1911. Sung was confident of their support for the leadership of his Central China Office and for its Yangtze operations. They were also responsible for the all-out support of the Literary Society for Sung's Nationalist Party in 1912.

The other organisation which shared the honour of initiating the Wuchang uprising was the Mutual Advancement Society. Throughout 1908 it took active steps to organise the secret societies of the Yangtze provinces for revolution. Its Hupeh branch was established by Sun Wu and others in early 1909.[18]

Sun Wu was typical of the majority of revolutionaries of this period. A brief examination of his activities in this period will illustrate the complicated relationships between the various insurgent groups, the revolutionaries' attitude towards their tasks, and shed much light on the general character of the 1911 revolution.

Sun Wu was a native of Hupeh and a graduate of the Hupeh Military School. After graduation he served in the army in both

Hunan and Hupeh, and was involved in the plot of the Independent Army in 1900 and that of the Science Study Group in 1904. In 1905 he went to Japan to receive naval training, but soon became involved in the movement against Japan's attempt to impose stricter control over Chinese students. Returning to Wuchang, he was soon on the run once more, for taking part in the activities of the Society for the Daily Increase of Knowledge. He took refuge in Manchuria, where he travelled from place to place conferring with Sung Chiao-jen, Wu Lu-chen, and others on plans for instigating uprisings.[19] Later he went south with the idea of joining Huang Hsing's Yunnan uprising. By the time he reached Hong Kong, however, the Yunnan uprising had collapsed. Finding no further immediate action, he went again to Japan, where he joined the Mutual Advancement Society and was put in charge of military affairs. Towards the end of 1908 he was put in charge of recruiting men for the Hupeh branch, and accordingly returned to that province to carry out his responsibilities.

During April 1909 offices of the Mutual Advancement Society were set up in Hankow and Wuchang. Within a few months the secret societies of the Yangtze provinces were gradually drawn together under the leadership of the society. Sun Wu, a soldier by training, naturally also sought to establish connections with revolutionary-inclined elements in the army. A closer association between the Mutual Advancement Society and the Self-government Study Society was soon established, and Sun Wu even persuaded some members of the latter to join the Mutual Advancement Society. However, in the late autumn of 1909 Sun Wu's activities were apprehended by the government, and he once more left for the south.

Now, for the first time, he assumed the name of Wu. He went to Hong Kong, joined the Chinese League, and then returned to Hupeh the following summer. By this time the Mutual Advancement Society had made great strides within the army and the secret societies. It was further strengthened by a number of members who returned from Tokyo that winter. It was arranged that future uprisings should be simultaneous, and shadow-governors were named to take charge of various provinces.[20]

In early 1911, when T'an Jen-feng visited Hunan and Hupeh to secure support for the Canton uprising in April, he met Chu Cheng, a member of the Chinese League and also a foundation member of the Mutual Advancement Society, and Sun Wu. T'an left with them $800 from the fund given to him by the South China Office.[21]

Sun Wu's life bore characteristics common to most revolutionaries of this period. The overthrow of the Manchus was their primary objective, and they rallied together to attain this end. Different organisations existed according to regional, social, and occupational divisions rather than ideological differences which were only vaguely felt, and were generally relegated to second place. This feature made possible the amalgamation of various organisations to form the Chinese League, but also undermined its solidarity after its formation.

When the co-operation between the Literary Society and the Mutual Advancement Society was first proposed, it was significant that the objection raised by the leader of the former organisation was one of social distinctions and not ideological differences:

> We are lowly soldiers and they are either gentlemen clad in Western-style clothes or Mandarins in flowing robes and wide-sleeved jackets with superior wisdom and high reputations. They will never condescend to look at us and we cannot have anything to gain by hanging around them. You must be careful not to fall into their trap.[22]

This feature also explained the practice of multi-party membership and the complicated interwoven relationships between the various revolutionary groups. The absence of a well-defined ideology other than that of nationalism gave flexibility to their choice of allegiance. Prior to the overthrow of the Manchus, this flexibility was a source of strength. After the revolution, the sudden fulfilment of their nationalistic ideal left a vacuum which was impossible to fill at short notice. The various organisations fell apart and resettled with different centres of gravity. But, in this pre-revolutionary situation, Sun Wu and his like were instrumental in bringing together the Literary Society and the Mutual Advancement Society on the eve of the Wuchang uprising, and in facilitating the extension of influence and leadership of Sung Chiao-jen's Central China Office.

The close association which had developed between the Mutual Advancement Society and the Self-government Study Society during 1909 was interrupted by government action against both societies. All contacts between them were cut, and the latter society was not anxious to renew its ties, because of class differences which might cause friction.[23]

Following T'an Jen-feng's visit to Wuchang in early 1911, on behalf of the South China Office, to obtain support for the imminent Canton uprising, the Mutual Advancement Society accelerated its activities within the New Army.This encroachment on the main recruiting ground of the Literary Society inevitably led to friction between them. Leaders contemplated amalgamation, but social differences continued to be an obstacle. It appears that, since the betrayal of the Society For the Daily Increase of Knowledge by a returned student from Japan, members of succeeding organisations became a little apprehensive of the reliability of overseas students. This attitude accounted partly for their policy of recruiting only soldiers below officer rank.[24]

After the failure of the Canton uprising, hopes for success in the south vanished, and the revolutionaries of Hupeh and Hunan decided to assume the initiative. Protests against the nationalisation of railways were already looming large, and the urgency of the situation required the co-operation of the two societies in Wuchang. The first *rapprochement* was made in May, with both parties promising joint action. On 1 June, co-operation was formally proposed and approved by both societies. But the basis for co-operation had yet to be agreed upon. After several months of preparation, the two societies gathered together for a joint meeting in mid-September 1911, and decided to establish a joint command. They agreed to suspend the use of their former names, and the leaders renounced their offices. Members were to be known simply as revolutionaries, in order to delimit organisational boundaries. Chiang I-wu and Wang Hsien-chang of the Literary Society were elected Chief and Deputy Commanders respectively, with Sun Wu of the Mutual Advancement Society as Chief-of-Staff. No one was willing to assume the headship of the revolutionary government, however, so it was decided to request the presence of Huang Hsing, Sung Chiao-jen, and T'an Jen-feng in Wuchang. Chu Cheng and Yang Yu-ju left Wuchang on 16 September on this mission. They arrived in Shanghai on 25 September, and immediately visited Sung Chiao-jen, Ch'en Ch'i-mei, and T'an Jen-feng to present their request.[25]

According to T'an Jen-feng, the Central China Office had been kept informed of developments in Wuchang by one P'eng Shou-sung, who worked as an adviser to Tuan Fang, and whose residence in Hankow was used by party members as an operational centre. It appears that, before the arrival of Chu Cheng and Yang Yu-ju, T'an had already received a telegram from Hupeh urging him to go to Wuchang. Accordingly, a meeting of the Central Executive Council of the Central China Office was held to consider this request on 20 September. T'an was sick at the time and, in order that he might enter hospital for treatment, Sung offered to go in his place. Sung was to leave Shanghai on 11 October.

Following the arrival of Chu and Yang, a full meeting, attended by representatives of all member provinces of the Central China Office, was convened. Pleased with the preparations in Hupeh as reported by Chu and Yang, the meeting decided on simultaneous uprisings in Wuchang, Nanking, and Shanghai, to be followed by similar ones in other member provinces. Special dispatches were sent to inform Huang Hsing in Hong Kong of the latest developments in the Yangtze area, and to invite him to return to take charge of the situation. Sung Chiao-jen and T'an Jen-feng were also preparing to go to Hankow together.

Unfortunately, Hu Ying, who was still in prison, misjudged the situation and sent a student, Ts'en Wei-sheng, to stop Sung.[26] Hu Ying and Sung were close friends, and because of their close association in the past Sung was inclined to trust his judgment. He hesitated. T'an Jen-feng, believing that the situation was urgent, urged Sung on his way. After a meeting on 3 October, Sung consented to leave after the Moon Festival (6 October). But two considerations delayed him; firstly, Yu Yu-jen was away from Shanghai and Sung was reluctant to leave his responsibilities to the *Independent People's Daily* until Yu returned to take charge; secondly, Sung wished to ascertain first Huang Hsing's movements and his opinion. Apparently he had not overcome the doubts raised by Hu Ying's letter.

Doubts on the readiness of the revolutionaries for an all-out uprising were reflected in a motion at a special meeting of the Central Executive Council on 7 October. The motion read:

> The disturbances in Szechuan are quietening down, and Hunan and Nanking are not reliable. In view of these circumstances, arrangements for revolts should naturally be slowed down. Please decide on the length of postponement and the criterion by which a situation may be judged as ripe for uprisings.

The relevant resolution read, 'It shall be determined according to developments'.[27]

It was clear that leaders in Shanghai did not think the situation in the Yangtze region ripe for an uprising. They were cautious, and their attitude, as it turned out, coincided with Huang Hsing's suggestion that they should wait until late October.[28]

T'an Jen-feng, however, disagreed with the majority. He alone believed in the urgency of the situation in Wuchang, and declared at the meeting that he would go to Hupeh and Hunan next day in order to retain the confidence of the affiliated organisations. He also hoped that Sung Chiao-jen, whose reputation and ability were superior to his, would follow within a short time. Sung promised to follow, and T'an left next day, 'with his medicine', as he had not yet recovered from his illness.[29]

T'an arrived in Nanking on 8 October, where he informed the revolutionaries of the situation in Hupeh, and asked them to respond in the event of uprisings occurring there. T'an and Chu Cheng then

continued on their journey and reached Kiukiang where they heard
news of the Wuchang uprising.[30]

It happened that, while leaders in Shanghai were discussing the
situation, many revolutionaries in the army in Hupeh were being
transferred from Wuchang to the Hunan-Szechuan border. According to a participant in the uprising, the troop movements worried
the revolutionaries in Wuchang, not because they might not have
enough strength to take the city, but because they might not have
enough soldiers to hold it afterwards. The leaders thought it necessary
to act quickly, and on 24 September decided to stage the revolt on
the night of 6 October, the occasion of China's Moon Festival which
was traditionally associated with the rebellions that led to the down-
fall of the Yuan dynasty in China. Word was sent to the revolutionaries in Hunan imploring them to revolt at the same time.[31]

During the next few days the atmosphere in Wuchang was tense.
Rumours of imminent revolts were circulating. Forces loyal to the
Manchus, chiefly military police, patrol and defence troops, and gun
boats, were put on the alert. This condition, coupled with the fact that
Chu Cheng and Yang Yu-ju had not yet returned from their mission,
and that both Huang Hsing in Hong Kong and Chiao Ta-feng in
Hunan requested postponement, forced the Hupeh leaders to postpone the uprising. At least three other tentative dates (9, 11, and
16 October) for an uprising had been suggested, but evidence suggests
that no decision was made on this matter, owing to the fluidity of the
situation. Plans for the uprising remained unchanged. The various
army leaders had been given detailed instructions regarding their
specific responsibilities for attacking routes and targets. They only
awaited the signal to go ahead. As Li Lien-fang points out, no date
was set for the revolt, but everyone felt its proximity. The time was
left open so that advantage could be taken of the government's most
unguarded moment.[32]

The revolutionaries did not succeed in their plan for a surprise
attack, however. A premature bomb explosion on 9 October in their
hideout in the Russian Concession in Hankow exposed their intentions and deprived them of their initiative. Sun Wu was wounded in
the explosion. On hearing of the accident, Chiang I-wu, who had
returned that morning from his outpost in Yueh-chou for a special
meeting, decided to start the uprising at midnight. He only just
managed to escape the closing arms of the police, thanks to his
pigtail, peasant outfit, and dull countenance.[33] Three other leaders
were captured and executed; among them was Liu Yao-cheng, one
of the most important political and military brains of the Wuchang
revolution. His death was an irretrievable loss, and one historian,

also a participant in the revolt, remarked that Liu's death affected the course of revolution more than the delay of Sung Chiao-jen and T'an Jen-feng, or the escape of Chiang I-wu and Liu Kung.[34]

In the absence of top-ranking leaders, the responsibility of carrying out Chiang I-Wu's orders for uprising, issued on 9 October at 5 p.m., fell on the soldiers themselves. The revolt was originally scheduled for midnight, but the strict curfew imposed on the city prevented the orders from reaching their destined hands in time. On 10 October executions and arrests caused a great disturbance. It was rumoured that a revolutionary membership register had fallen into the hands of the government, and mass arrests were imminent.[35] Hupeh's revolutionary movement had reached the point of no return. The course confronting them was to rise and fight for their ideals and a chance of survival, or lay down their arms and be destroyed. They fought, and to everyone's surprise they proved completely successful.

According to one considered opinion, there were eighteen battalions, numbering about 9,000 men, in Wuchang at the time. Of these eighteen battalions only three were loyal to the government. The rest, heavily infiltrated by the revolutionaries, had no will to resist the rebels. The numerical ratio between revolutionaries and forces loyal to the Manchus was about three to five. However, the 3,000 revolutionary soldiers, being units of the New Army, were well trained and better equipped than the loyalists, a conglomeration of police, office guards, armed firemen, patrol and defence troops, and three battalions of the New Army.[36] Besides being a superior fighting force, the revolutionaries were fighting for their very lives. Though leaderless and without a centralised command, they were able to follow the well-laid plans to carry out co-ordinated attacks on government positions. After an all-night battle, they succeeded in holding Wuchang on 11 October, and on the following day Hankow and Hanyang also fell into their hands. Within a week the loyalists were driven seven miles outside the city, and within a month thirteen provinces declared their independence. In diplomacy, the revolutionaries also scored a decisive victory when, on 18 October, the foreign consular body at Hankow adopted a policy of neutrality and accorded the revolutionaries the status of a belligerent party in a civil war.[37]

Despite initial successes, however, the position of Wuchang's revolutionaries was not secure. When Sung Chiao-jen and Huang Hsing arrived on 29 October, only four provincial cities had risen in response,* and Wuchang was confronted with government reinforce-

---

* Changsha of Hunan and Sian of Shensi fell to the revolutionaries on 22 October 1911, Kiukiang of Kiangsi the next day, and T'ai-yüan of Shansi on 29 October.

ments from the north. Sung expressed his concern for the military situation in Wuchang in a letter to the Central China Office in Shanghai on 31 October:

I safely arrived in Hupeh the day before yesterday; the situation here is tense, and I sincerely hope that other places will respond. I hear that the ammunition deal in Shanghai has not come off. I wonder whether other channels have been explored? I beg you to do your best to secure them. Please also keep me informed of the situations in Shanghai, Nanking and North Anhwei. Changsha, Kiukiang, Ichang, and Yueh-chou have definitely fallen into our hands. At present our only worry is the opposing Peiyang army. Has Mr Po [Po Wen-wei] left? If action has been taken in North Anhwei, a force should enter Honan to threaten the northern army. Otherwise, I fear, the army of Hupeh fighting difficult battles alone will find it hard to maintain its ground. . . .[38]

Two days later, on 2 November, Hankow fell back into the hands of the enemies, and Sung again wrote to his colleagues in Shanghai, requesting that they contact a certain Japanese merchant about the purchase and transport of fifty to seventy thousand 6·5 millimetre guns (1897 or 1904 models), and urging them to take action in Nanking and Anhwei. He wrote, 'Telegrams arrived today reporting the successful recovery of Yunnan and Shansi. We certainly cannot face others if Nanking and Anhwei still take no action. I beg you to act quickly. . . .'[39] These letters not only reveal the situation in Wuchang, but also provide a first-hand account of the role of the Central China Office and Sung himself in this revolution.

Sung Chiao-jen was ill in bed when the Wuchang uprising took place. The news of successes in Wuchang was said to have cured him immediately.[40] The original plan of campaign long ago conceived by members of the Central China Office headquarters and later adopted by a meeting of its provincial representatives in Shanghai on 26 September 1911, was to secure three bases, Wuchang, Nanking, and Shanghai, for initial uprisings. Five days after the Wuchang uprising, Sung Chiao-jen reaffirmed this strategic concept openly in his daily newspaper, emphasising the strategic significance of Wuchang and Nanking, both vital centres for attack on north China as well as for the defence of southeast China against the north.[41] In Sung's opinion Nanking would not be difficult to take, since there were in the New Army in Nanking a substantial number of revolutionary sympathisers and former followers of such revolutionaries as Chao Sheng, Ni Ying-tien, Lin Shu-ch'ing, and Po Wen-wei. They needed only a revolutionary leader who could command the loyalty and confidence of the troops in Nanking. Accordingly he invited

Po Wen-wei, an old associate of the New Army in Nanking, to return from Manchuria to take charge of Nanking's military operations. At the same time he wired Huang Hsing to come to his aid.[42]

Huang Hsing arrived in Shanghai on 24 October and entered into an all-night discussion with Sung. There is no record of the substance of their discussion, but, judging by their subsequent activities, we may conclude that it probably centred on Wuchang and Nanking and which city was to have their first attention. For military considerations Sung wanted Nanking secured as soon as possible in order to protect Wuchang and southeast China against onslaughts from the north. It is also possible that he looked at the capture of Nanking from a political standpoint. The absence of revolutionary leaders from Wuchang at the time of the uprising had caused leadership to fall on a non-revolutionary man, Li Yuan-hung. The capture of Nanking would balance the position and compensate for the loss of initiative and leadership in Wuchang. Huang Hsing probably agreed with Sung's ideas, but disagreed with his approach. Militarily the defence of Wuchang was more urgent and important than the capture of Nanking. Besides, the latter task could best be left to men who had closer connections with the region. Those who had closer associations with Hupeh should go to Wuchang, where they could rely on the co-operation of local men and obtain assistance and reinforcements from Hunan. Hung's argument was readily appreciated by Sung Chiao-jen. It would enable them to regain leadership. Huang, primarily a military man, needed the political skill of Sung Chiao-jen to reshape the political situation in Wuchang. Therefore Sung left Shanghai with Huang Hsing for Wuchang, leaving the task of capturing Nanking to Po Wen-wei and Fan Kuang-ch'i.[43]

On arrival in Wuchang on 29 October, they found the military situation worse than expected. For two days Hankow had come under the strong attacks of some northern army units. Huang Hsing immediately went to the front, and Sung wrote to urge his friends to take Nanking. If Wuchang's military front appeared precarious, its political front was solidly entrenched and difficult to alter. The absence of recognised leaders at the initial stage of the uprising had forced the revolutionaries to abandon their original plan to organise a Hupeh revolutionary government with bona fide revolutionaries filling the key posts.* Instead, the most important post in the Hupeh

---

* Apparently the headship of Hupeh's military government was originally reserved for either Huang Hsing or Sung Chiao-jen. When 6 October 1911 was decided as the date for uprising, the personnel of its provisional government included Liu Kung as President, Sun Wu and Chiang I-wu as Commander-in-Chief and Deputy Commander-in-Chief, and Sung Chiao-jen as Foreign Minister. See Yang, *Hsien-chu-chi*, pp. 48-52, 71 and *KMWH*, Vol. IV, pp. 465-6.

military government was forced upon a non-revolutionary and an ex-Manchu officer, Brigadier Li Yuan-hung. By the time Sung arrived in Wuchang, Li Yuan-hung's position as Hupeh's Military Governor was so well established that his attempt to supersede him met with strong objections.

Sung's attempt to reshape the revolutionary government in Wuchang took place at a secret meeting on the night of 2 November, following the fall of Hankow to the Manchu forces. A group of revolutionary leaders, including Sung Chiao-jen, Chu Cheng, and T'ien T'ung, met with high officials of Hupeh's military government to discuss the official title and position under which Huang Hsing was to assume responsibility. According to three eye-witness accounts[44] which differ slightly in detail, two titles were suggested by what Li Lien-fang, the Chief Secretary of Li Yuan-hung's military government, referred to as 'the new arrivals from the Chinese League'. Both titles, 'Governor-General of Hunan and Hupeh' and 'Commander-in-Chief of the southern people's Army', were obviously designed to put Huang's authority over that of Li Yuan-hung. The pretext was that, in view of the lack of co-ordination and discipline among the troops in Hankow and the imminent arrival of reinforcements from Hunan for the defence of Wuchang, Huang Hsing should be given a wider authority to control and lead all forces coming from seceding provinces. However, members of the Hupeh military government feared that a change might upset the existing equilibrium. They wanted Huang Hsing to remain subordinate to the military government.

The main difference between the three accounts is in the description of the manner in which the meeting was held. According to Li Lien-fang, the meeting was held by moonlight in the courtyard of a former provincial advisory council building. Thirty to forty people stood in a circle, discussions were calm and casual, and, in view of the pressing war situation, no one pursued the subject and no heated argument took place.

According to Ts'ao Ya-po, the meeting was summoned by Chu Cheng. His proposal to make Huang Hsing Governor-General of Hunan and Hupeh was enthusiastically received by some members, but rejected strongly by Wu Chao-lin, an army officer and a former member of the Society For the Daily Increase of Knowledge, who kept aloof from revolutionary activities from the time of the collapse of that society until after the Wuchang uprising. Like Li Yuan-hung he had been forced to join the revolution, and had risen in rank under the revolutionary government. He objected for three reasons: firstly, if Li Yuan-hung was not a revolutionary in the beginning, he had now fully committed himself to the cause and had won the support of non-revolutionary as well as revolutionary men from all circles in Hupeh; any change affecting his position might lead to friction and split the revolutionary camp. Secondly, foreign relations of the revolutionary government had been conducted in his name; his sudden replacement might shake the confidence of foreign powers in the stability of the revolutionary government. Lastly, Huang Hsing was a well known revolutionary; if he, in his present capacity as Commander-in-Chief, could lead the revolutionary forces to victory, more important posts would be awaiting him when the central government was formed. There was no need for him to contest a local appointment.

A heated argument ensued. Supporters of Huang Hsing argued that Huang Hsing's new position would not affect Li Yuan-hung, just as the election of a national president at some future time would not affect the position of provincial governors. Besides, precedents of changing governors were not lacking in recent events—notably in Kiangsi, where Ma Yu-pao replaced Wu Chieh-chang as Governor. Wu Chao-lin pleaded caution, however, and reminded them of the special position occupied by Wuchang in being the first to rise successfully against the Manchus, and the international status it had acquired through recognition as a belligerent party by the foreign powers. Seeing that no agreement could be reached on this proposal, Sung Chiao-jen halted the discussion before passions became uncontrollable.

Yang Yu-ju's account agreed substantially with Ts'ao's. It is interesting to note the names he gave for the contending groups, and the way he classified them. Among the group in favour of Chu Cheng's proposal were Sung Chiao-jen and Tien T'ung, who were new arrivals from the Chinese League, and Chiang I-wu and Yang Wang-p'eng, who were slightly affected by regional prejudices. Among those against the proposal were Liu Kung, Sun Wu, Ts'ai Chi-min, Wu Hsing-han, Wu Chao-lin, and Yang himself, all of whom were initiators of the Wuchang uprising. It is also interesting to note that after the revolution, from the second group of men came some of the leading dissidents who impaired the unity of the revolutionary camp by forming a separate party, the People's Society (*Min-she*).

Apparently Sung Chiao-jen did not express his own opinion until the end of the discussion. As an astute and cautious politician, he seems to have kept himself in the background to observe and assess the trend of opinions. However, he recognised the danger of prolonging the discussion, and put an end to it with a careful explanation of the motive behind the proposal:

> This subject is raised in order to obtain a consensus of your opinions. It is raised not because of prejudice but because it appears to some colleagues that Huang Hsing's long standing in the revolutionary movement and his great prestige may serve as good propaganda, and enhance chances for the speedy fulfilment of our aims. We have only just arrived in Hupeh, and are not familiar with local conditions. Since it may cause friction, we will drop the subject.[45]

Therefore the effort to supersede Li Yuan-hung failed. Huang Hsing was put under Li and the military government of Hupeh, and assumed the position of Wartime Commander-in-Chief of the People's Army.

There is another account, by Ts'ai Chi-ou, who was also a participant in the Wuchang uprising, but it is not clear whether he was also present at this secret meeting. His description of the meeting coincides with the last two accounts, except that he named Sung Chiao-jen, T'ien T'ung, Chu Cheng, and Hu Ying among the originators who used Chu Cheng to introduce the proposal.[46] Ts'ai's account is probably the correct one. Sung Chiao-jen was the master-mind behind this political move, although Chu Cheng, a native of Hupeh, was asked to introduce it in order to avoid the suspicion of regional prejudice. Chu Cheng, however, made no mention of this in his writings, nor did he make any specific reference to this secret meeting. Chu was the chief author of the Regulations for the Organisation of Provincial Military Government *(Tutu-fu tsu-chih t'iao-li)* according to which the government of Hupeh was organised. To avoid suspicion he submitted them as an original draft from the Chinese League, and they were adopted on 17 October and led to a reshuffle of personnel in Li's government.[47]

Chu later recalled that at the time he had already realised the undesirability of entrusting too much power to non-revolutionary army officers, and insisted that revolutionaries be put in charge of military administration, particularly the department of military supply. When the question of Huang Hsing's appointment to the post of Wartime Commander-in-Chief of the People's Army under the Military Governor of Hupeh was discussed, however, Chu supported this proposal as consistent with the established framework of Hupeh's military government. He also suggested that, to demonstrate the importance of Huang Hsing's new post and to enhance his prestige, a solemn and impressive ceremony should be held for Huang Hsing to receive authority from the Military Governor—such as the ceremony held when Han Hsin was made a General by the first Emperor of the Han dynasty.[48]

It is probable that these apparently contradictory accounts refer to different stages of the same problem. Chu Cheng probably agreed with Sung Chiao-jen's plan to put Huang Hsing above Li Yuan-hung at first. After the secret meeting, however, Chu assessed the opposition, and proposed a second alternative by which Huang Hsing might gain effective control over Hupeh's army. He suggested that Huang Hsing be formally installed in public by the military governor. A curious feature of the Chinese revolution was the respect for legality. This incongruous feature led Kita Ikki, a Japanese who sympathised with the Chinese cause of revolution, to criticise some of the leaders as confusing revolution with war, and tying their own hands with conventional morality at the risk of losing their objectives.[49]

Kita Ikki was a close friend of Sung Chiao-jen, and joined him in Wuchang at this time. According to his writing, Sung recognised the formation of a central government as his first and foremost task on arrival in Wuchang. He wanted to establish, with Hunan and Hupeh as initial units, a central authority in accordance with the League's 'Plan for Revolution' laid down in 1907 and amended by himself in Hong Kong before the Canton uprising of 27 April 1911. Sung apparently hoped to establish authority while revolutionary spirits were still high. But he could not secure Huang Hsing's agreement to this. Huang Hsing wanted to establish himself with victories in the battle field before he could bring himself to participate in the formation of a supreme revolutionary authority. This delay had unfortunate consequences.

Huang's acceptance of a commandership under Li Yuan-hung confirmed his subordinate status within Hupeh's government structure, and impeded him subsequently from assuming positions higher than Li. The loss of Hankow, though not his fault, cost him his prestige. As one scholar points out, putting the question of personnel before the establishment of a system of government inevitably caused suspicion and ill-feeling. Sung Chiao-jen had to suspend his plans in order to preserve unity and harmony in the revolutionary camp.[50] Later, following the loss of Hanyang, Huang Hsing found himself in a pitiful position. Hupeh's leaders did not respect him because of his defeat in the defence of Hanyang, and he himself did not feel he should stay on to defend Wuchang.

It is not known whether Huang Hsing ever regretted not having accepted Sung's ideas earlier. Later events prove that not only Huang Hsing, but all revolutionaries, had to pay dearly for leaving Li Yuan-hung in control of Hupeh. Li and many of his associates were not only non-revolutionary, but opportunistic, with strong attachments to the old society. It was said that Li Yuan-hung was actually unwilling to head the revolutionary government of Hupeh until he came to an understanding with a high Manchu official* that while the revolution lasted, Li was to protect this official's life and property, and if the revolution failed, the official would in turn use his influence in the Manchu court to guarantee Li's safety.[51] Two years later, when, following Sung's assassination and the dispute over foreign loans, war broke out between the revolutionaries and Yuan Shih-k'ai, Li Yuan-hung sided with Yuan, thus depriving the revolutionaries of their stronghold against the north.

Following the loss of Hankow, Hanyang came under attack. Even Wuchang, on the other side of the Yangtze, was threatened by Manchu troops with their long-range guns. As the noise of enemy fire shook the city, Sung Chiao-jen resolved to leave Wuchang. A representative of Fan Kuang-ch'i, one of the two men entrusted by Sung with the capture of Nanking, arrived with the news that the revolutionaries in the lower Yangtze were planning a joint assault on Nanking with a combined force from Kiangsu and Chekiang. There was friction between these army units, and the good offices of Sung Chiao-jen were required to mediate.[52]

Sung's foremost consideration, however, was the formation of a central government which would put the revolutionaries in firm control of the revolution. The Hupeh leaders had made his plans to form a central government inoperative in Hupeh. He wanted a place where he could utilise his political talents to consolidate the gains of the revolution. This view coincided with that of colleagues in Shanghai who wanted to see the hegemony of the Chinese League in the revolution established, and, accordingly, planned to control the lower Yangtze region.[53] There were also strategic considerations. Nanking was vital, not only for the defence of Wuchang, but also for the defence of the entire region south of the Yangtze. Sung's motives for leaving Wuchang were expressed in a conversation with Kita Ikki:

> As has happened in the past, we have come here because Huang Hsing would not listen to me. Old T'an [T'an Jen-feng] was already here and it was hardly necessary for another two to come. I wished to use the New Army in Nanking to secure control of the provinces south of the Yangtze so that the hopes of controlling China may be fulfilled. But Huang Hsing would not listen. Instead he dragged me with him to this place and put our party under the orders of

---

* This official was said to be K'o Feng-shih, whose official title was 'Minister-plenipotentiary for the Collection of Opium Tax in Eight Provinces'.

Li Yuan-hung. Yesterday a representative arrived from Nanking for me. I intend to go down to the lower Yangtze to secure its control irrespective of Huang Hsing's success or failure here. If Nanking could be obtained, Hankow could easily be recovered.[54]

On the evening of 13 November 1911, having left a note of farewell for Huang Hsing at the Hanyang front, Sung boarded a Japanese ship in Hankow and sailed down the Yangtze with Kita Ikki.[55] As they passed through Nanking, they found the city heavily guarded by the Marine Defence Battalion of the 'pig-tail general', Chang Hsun, a reactionary whose attachment to the old order was so strong that he not only fought the revolutionaries with determination in 1911 but attempted twice to restore monarchy to China after the establishment of the republic.*

Since the dispatch of the messenger to Sung, the best chance of capturing Nanking had been lost. The ruler of Nanking, realising the unreliability of the New Army, had partially disarmed them and moved them forty miles outside the city. Defence of the city was then entrusted to Chang Hsun's loyal Marine Defence Battalion. Under such a man there was no room for revolutionaries to operate in Nanking. He searched the city, and had young men killed for no more reason than having had their queues cut or wearing modern school uniforms.[56] The New Army, angry and indignant, tried to take Nanking on 8 and 9 November, but failed because of shortage of ammunition. It was said that each soldier had only three bullets to use in this attack.[57]

As Sung approached Nanking the 'yellow flags of the Manchu government flew proudly in the wind'. He managed to get into the city, but found most revolutionary organisations destroyed. There seemed nothing he could do there, so he left for Chen-chiang, which had fallen to the revolutionaries on 8 November following the successful rising in Shanghai on 4 November. He arrived in Chen-chiang on 16 November,[58] and found that various revolutionary army units from Shanghai, Chekiang, and other parts of Kiangsu were gathering for a decisive assault on Nanking. But before they could begin the attack, differences occurred within the armies over the appointment, to the position of Commander-in-Chief of the joint forces, of Hsu Shao-chen, who was originally Commander of the New Army units at Nanking and led the first unsuccessful attack on that city. Under the circumstances, Sung's arrival was timely. He was at once invited to mediate between the dissenting leaders. Sung apparently did not think the dispute serious enough to warrant his

---

* Chang Hsün supported Yüan Shih-k'ai's attempt to make himself Emperor in 1916, and tried to put P'u-yi back on his throne in 1917.

stay, however. He entrusted mediation to one of his close colleagues, and left to tour Shanghai, Soochow, and Hangchow, with the intention of forming a provisional government.

As he had expected, events connected with Nanking went smoothly. The military leaders had enough sense to put aside their squabbles to meet a more urgent task. Telegrams from Wuchang indicated the imminent fall of Hanyang: the revolutionaries must capture Nanking to offset its loss. Hanyang fell to the Manchu forces on 27 November. Four days later, the revolutionaries took Nanking, which not only stabilised the overall position of the rebels but heightened the prestige of the Shanghai revolutionaries. Sung's first goal was accomplished. It remained for him to bring his provisional government into existence.

Before he could do this, however, he was faced with the thorny dispute over the military governorship of Kiangsu. This dispute was partly the result of the unsolved leadership dispute between the military leaders before the fall of Nanking. There were three main contenders for the position, Ch'eng Te-ch'uan, Hsu Shao-chen, and Lin Shu-ch'ing. Ch'eng was formerly Governor of Kiangsu at Soochow. On 5 November he declared independence from Peking, and was elected Governor by both the leading gentry and the military leaders of Kiangsu. Hsu Shao-chen was the commander of the New Army at Nanking. During the assault on Nanking he assumed the post of Commander-in-Chief of the combined forces of Kiangsu, Chekiang and other units. Lin Shu-ch'ing, on the other hand, was an old revolutionary, and an army officer under Hsu. He initiated the uprising in Chen-chiang, and was elected as its Military Governor. Chen-chiang later became the base for the attack on Nanking, and Lin, being directly responsible for the taking of Nanking, and on the spot when the city fell, was proclaimed Military Governor of Nanking.

The contentions between them and their supporters occurring in a strategic city posed a serious threat to the cause of revolution. With the Wuchang experience still fresh in their minds, the revolutionaries in Shanghai, and in particular Sung Chiao-jen, were fully aware of the danger. Sung remarked to a friend, 'As we don't know when a [provisional] government will be formed, we should pay particular attention to the question of the governorship of Kiangsu'.[59]

Sung went to Nanking on 3 December, and, as a result of his discussions with his colleagues, Ch'eng Te-ch'uan was made Governor of Kiangsu; Lin was to lead the northern expeditionary forces, while Hsu was to command the relief force to Wuchang.[60]

In view of Sung's anxiety over having a non-revolutionary at the head of the revolutionary government in Hupeh, the choice of

Ch'eng Te-ch'uan, also a former official of the Manchu government, as the Military Governor of Kiangsu needs explanation. In 1911 China was ripe for revolution. Apart from the revolutionaries there were other forces, such as the constitutionalists and local gentry leaders, who hoped for the destruction of the Manchu government for their own separate reasons. The revolutionaries, aware of their own meagre strength and inadequate preparation, were only too keen to rally all anti-Manchu forces, irrespective of differences in origin, motives, and ideologies, in order to hasten the fall of the Manchus. The revolutionary leaders had a number of objectives in this revolution, but the foremost in their minds then was nationalism, particularly anti-Manchuism. This facilitated the inclusion of non-revolutionaries into their ranks.

Ch'eng Te-ch'uan had very wide support among the gentry of Kiangsu. As a result of his interest in new ideas and reform, and above all, of his initiative in the Soochow revolt, he was more acceptable to the revolutionaries than Li Yuan-hung, who was forced to assume leadership.

In Nanking, as in Wuchang, respect was shown for legality. Thus Ch'eng, who was the Governor of Kiangsu on the eve of the Wuchang uprising, and the first to declare independence for Kiangsu, was favoured.[61] Sung's chief consideration in supporting Ch'eng Te-chuan for the governorship was probably the money and men which Ch'eng might be able to supply for the revolution, however. This seems clear in his conversation with Lin Shu-ch'ing, who was one of the contenders for the same office. He said, 'If Hsueh-lou [Ch'eng Te-ch'uan] assumes the governorship of Kiangsu, he would be able to provide all military supplies for your northern expeditionary force, and free you from all such impediment'.[62]

However, later events revealed that the appointment of Ch'eng Te-ch'uan to the governorship of Kiangsu was as serious a mistake as that of Li Yuan-hung to Hupeh. In the struggle against Yuan Shih-k'ai, both of them sided with Yuan. The faults probably lay in the whole revolutinary movement rather than in the mistaken action of any individual, however. The ripening revolutionary situation in China in 1911 was not matched by adequate preparation by the revolutionaries. As a result, the latter had to rely heavily on the co-operaton of other heterogeneous forces for the completion of their revolutionary task, and in the prcoess their own position was weakened.

The capture of Nanking by the revolutionaries marked the beginning of a new phase in the revolution of 1911. Two significant events took place. Firstly, the capture of Nanking, under the more or less direct leadership of Sung Chiao-jen and other members of the Central China Office of the Chinese League, and, of course, the capture of Shanghai by the same leaders, enhanced their prestige and gave them greater right to speak for the anti-Manchu camp. The loss of Hanyang to the Manchu forces, on the other hand, put Wuchang in an awkward military situation, and weakened its position as a revolutionary centre. The result was the shift of leadership from Wuchang to Nanking, and the formation of the Nanking provisional government, which gave the anti-Manchu camp some form of unity.

Secondly, on the day of the fall of Nanking to the revolutionaries, a truce of three days between the opposing forces was arranged, marking the beginning of negotiations that led to the abdication of the Manchu Emperor, the establishment of the Republic of China, and the acceptance of Yuan Shih-k'ai by the revolutionaries as the Provisional President to replace Sun Yat-sen. This period, which began with events leading to the formation of the Nanking provisional government and to the assumption of the provisional presidency by Yuan Shih-k'ai in Peking, coincides with the short official life of Sung Chiao-jen. He, acting first as Chief of the Legislative Bureau in Nanking, and then as Minister for Agriculture and Forestry in the first cabinet of the Republican government in Peking, continued to play a leading but ineffectual role in both party and national affairs. This phase of his life, though lasting only about six months, gave him practical experience in government as well as a great deal of frutration and disappointment, which together pushed him to the next and final stage of his life, that of a political party organiser and democratic martyr.

Thus the fall of Nanking to the revolutionaries marked the end of an epoch and the beginning of another in the history of China. As for Sung Chiao-jen, it meant the end of his conspiratorial life and the commencement of an official political career in which he sought to reconstruct China on a new basis. His first act in this new role was the formation of the Nanking provisional government.

NINE

The Nanking Provisional Government

AN ANONYMOUS fortune-teller in Tokyo once told Sung Chiao-jen that he would have thirty years of peace during which to serve as China's Prime Minister.[1] This prediction never came true, but his detection of Sung's political aspirations was correct. Sung looked upon himself not only as a revolutionary, but also as a nation-builder who would reconstruct a new China on the debris of revolution.[2] Sung's political talent was well recognised by his colleagues. In early 1911, before the Canton uprising on 27 April, he was entrusted with the drafting of rules and regulations in preparation for the formation of a revolutionary government.[3] Following the successful uprisings in Wuchang and other parts of China, Sung immediately turned to the problem of government.

Quite apart from his personal inclinations, his urge to form a central government stemmed from two chief considerations: internal unity and external relations. Firstly, the spontaneous nature of the revolts made the organisation of a central authority imperative. A variety of men, conservatives, opportunists, and revolutionaries, had taken part in this revolution for different reasons. The situation of the anti-Manchu camp has been succinctly described in the following manner:

The medley of provincial leaders who declared for 'independence' were in fact sitting on the fence and watching in which direction the wind would blow. The governor of Shantung, for instance, having declared for 'independence', telegraphed a 'memorial' to the throne to explain his action, and promised to withdraw the declaration as soon as the situation became more stable. The Viceroy of Manchuria, Chao Erh-hsun, although refusing to declare for independence, set up a Peace Maintenance Society which operated side by side with the local government. The Governor of Anhwei, Chu Chia-pao, disbanded the revolutionary troops in his province, announced independence, and then, three days later, ran away. In Kiangsi, there were three different military governors in a hundred days; in Szechwan, two independent governments; in Kiangsu, thirteen military governors; and in Hunan and Kweichow, confused struggles among local warlords. The revolution was a sham; the independence of the provinces a farce.[4]

These were the circumstances facing revolutionaries like Sung Chiao-jen who realised that if they, the genuine revolutionaries, ever wished to lead the revolution to victory, they should take the initiative in organising a central government and firmly place leadership in their own hands.

Secondly, foreign relations required the attention of a unified authority. In the modern history of China, foreign relations constituted a major problem which vexed the minds of Chinese statesmen and students. Foreign intervention posed a dilemma which haunted the revolutionaries, and was a major argument of the reformers in opposing revolution. In his search for an answer to the problem of foreign relations in China's revolution, Sung had spent many studious hours on the history of revolution, carefully collating the factors of success and failure.[5] In 1911, shortly before the Wuchang uprising, Sung found what he thought to be the right answer, and declared emphatically, 'a national revolution, not accorded with the recognition of foreign nations, cannot succeed'.[6]

Sung based his statement on his observation of the success of Portugal's recent republican revolution, and the contrast provided by the failure of similar undertakings in the Philippines and the Boer Republic of South Africa, which led him to conclude that the crucial factor was the attitude of the foreign powers.[7]

Naturally, acting on this conviction, Sung considered the winning of recognition and friendship of foreign powers as one of the most urgent tasks at the outbreak of revolution. Four days after the Wuchang uprising we see Sung Chiao-jen putting forward what he considered to be the essential bases for recognition by foreign nations: firstly, that the revolutionaries exercise full control over a region; secondly, that an efficient administrative system be established; thirdly, that methods of warfare conform with the conventional practices of modern nations.[8] The intention of this argument is clear. The first and third requirements had been met. It only remained for a government to be formed. With this end in view, Sung accompanied Huang Hsing to Wuchang, and took steps to realise his scheme. In consultation with local leaders, Sung drafted a constitution for the government of Hupeh, which, as Li Lien-fang, a contemporary Chinese historian and revolutionary, has noted, was 'full of democratic spirit' and 'a harbinger of Chinese republican constitutionalism'.[9]

Parallel to these activities, Sung urged the formation of a central authority. The first step in this direction was a telegram sent out of Hupeh in the name of the Hupeh military government and its Governor, Li Yuan-hung, on 7 November 1911, consulting the opinion of other anti-Manchu forces.[10] Two days later another was sent, requesting the various anti-Manchu provinces to send fully empowered delegates to Wuchang for the purpose of organising a central government.[11]

By this time the formation of a central authority dominated the mind of every leader of the anti-Manchu camp. It seems that it was not only important for the cause of revolution. From the personal point of view, no one, either an individual or a group, would wish to see such an organisation formed without his participation. The initiative of Wuchang in calling for delegates was matched by that of the Governors of Chekiang and Kiangsu, who cabled the Governor of Shanghai their suggestion that each province should send two persons, one representing the existing provincial military government, and the other the former provincial advisory council and others.[12] This was followed by a telegram from the Governor of Chen-chiang, suggesting that Shanghai be the centre of the proposed meeting but that representatives should be sent by existing provincial and regional Military Governors.[13] Thereupon, the Governor of Shanghai cabled fourteen Military Governors on 13 November 1911, inviting them to send representatives.[14]

One noteworthy point was the inclusion of the Governor of Hupeh among those who favoured Shanghai for the proposed meeting. It appears that although Wuchang was the first to issue invitations, its messages were delayed by disruptions in communication, so that they arrived at their destinations considerably later than Shanghai's call.[15] Obviously, Shanghai included Wuchang among its supporters to give its own request additional weight. In fact Wuchang immediately cabled its objections, insisting that delegates should meet in Wuchang.[16] At this juncture Sung Chiao-jen left Wuchang.[17] His departure, occurring amidst Wuchang's call for delegates and immediately after Shanghai's telegram calling for the same, is a highly significant act. He had given up Wuchang in preference for Shanghai for the formation of a central government. On 15 November 1911 the representatives of three Military Governors (Shanghai, Soochow, and Fukien) conferred and established the United Assembly of Representatives of Provincial Military Governments *(Ko-sheng tu-tu-fu tai-piao lien-ho-hui)*.[18] The next day Sung was seen in Chen-chiang, conferring with its Military Governor about the planned attack on Nanking by the joint forces of Kiangsu and Chekiang.[19]

As he considered the fall of Nanking a certainty, and the disagreements between the military leaders of the joint forces only minor difficulties, he left for Shanghai to deal with the more urgent task of forming a government.[20]

In Shanghai he represented the military government of Hunan at the United Assembly of Representatives of the Provincial Military Governments. On 20 November he and others representing seven military governments cabled Wuchang, offering their recognition of the Hupeh military government as the central revolutionary government of the Chinese Republic.[21] In the light of the struggle for leadership between Shanghai and Wuchang, and the attitude held by Sung Chiao-jen hitherto, the action to accord Wuchang this recognition is a puzzle which has never been fully explained. It appears to have been an emergency measure. The anti-Manchu camp was badly in need of an authorised spokesman to deal with foreign nations, and to give itself an appearance of unity. Wuchang had the advantage of being the initiator in this revolution, and, as such, had been the focus of attention of foreign nations as well as of the Manchu government. For these reasons it must have seemed expedient to the leaders in Shanghai to grant Wuchang a leading position until a more permanent and popular authority could be constituted.

It should be pointed out that the leaders in Shanghai did not simply delegate all powers to Wuchang. Accompanying the recognition was the request for the appointment of Wu T'ing-fang and Wen Tsung-yao, both residents of Shanghai at this time, to take charge of foreign relations which were considered by Sung and other revolutionaries a most important aspect of their revolutionary wars. This was secured without difficulty, and represented a substantial gain by the Shanghai group in their bid for leadership. This recognition also enhanced Wuchang's pretension to central leadership, however, so that, when representatives arrived from Wuchang to plead for the transfer of the provincial representative body to Wuchang, the Shanghai group was obliged to cancel its resolution of 17 November in order to comply with their request.[22] Shanghai retained only one representative from each province, ostensibly for the purpose of keeping contact with his native province, but without doubt also to keep some measure of influence in Shanghai. Sung Chiao-jen was among the representatives who stayed behind in Shanghai, perhaps partly because Huang Hsing and T'an Jen-feng were already there, and partly because of his unfruitful efforts during his last stay in Wuchang, and his knowledge of the perilous military situation there.[23]

Whatever reason he might have had for not going with the main provincial delegates to Wuchang, later events reveal that his absence from the group which framed a set of laws to govern the formation of the provisional government was decidedly a mistake. The 'structural outline of the Provisional Government of the Republic of China' *(Chung-hua min-kuo lin-shih cheng-fu tsu-chih ta-kang)*, drawn up without his participation, failed to embrace some of his important political and organisational principles. His attempt to revise it later met strong opposition, and incurred the hostility of its makers, a fact gravely affecting his subsequent political activities during the period of the Nanking provisional government.[24]

It may be contended, however, that Sung had foreseen the fall of Hanyang and calculated that the delegates, harassed by the deteriorating military situation, would not be able to accomplish their task in Wuchang. If this were the case, he was only partially correct. By the time the provincial delegates reached Wuchang, Hanyang had fallen to the Manchu forces, so that they had to hold their meetings in the British concession in Hankow for safety. The first session was held on 30 November under the chairmanship of T'an Jen-feng. On the following day the delegates resolved to formulate laws for the formation of the provisional government, and appointed a committee of three to draft this document. Scarcely twenty-four hours later, a document of twenty-one articles, entitled the 'Structural Outline of the Provisional Government of the Republic of China', was drawn up, presented to the provincial delegates, and adopted. Such hasty composition of the articles meant that the document inevitably contained many loopholes. The haste could only be excused by reference to the transitional character of the document, and the urgent need for a central authority.

When a copy of it reached Shanghai, however, Sung found it too inadequate even for temporary purposes, and commented that it was only a draft, subject to revision in accordance with public opinion after the formation of the provisional government.[25] Unfortunately, this well-meaning suggestion was taken in the wrong light. The delegates, particularly those who drafted the document, resented Sung's criticism, and turned against him in all his subsequent activities.

Following the fall of Hanyang, Sung and his colleages immediately took advantage of the situation to shift leadership back into their hands. Of course, besides the leadership question, there was also genuine concern for the early establishment of a central government. On 1 December 1911, the provincial representatives remaining in Shanghai, headed by Sung Chiao-jen, cabled various provincial advisory councils, calling for the return of the provincial delegates to Shanghai to complete the task of organising a provincial government. This cable contained the following words, 'According to the report of an inside informant, the defeat of Hanyang is due to disunity in both administrative and military authorities'.[26] It was plainly an expression by Sung and his Shanghai colleagues of their disapproval of the leadership in Wuchang.

The capture of Nanking on 2 December strengthened their hand. Without consulting the delegates in Wuchang, those in Shanghai, supported by the Military Governors of Shanghai, Chekiang, and Kiangsu, resolved that Nanking was to be the seat of the provisional government, and Huang Hsing and Li Yuan-hung were to be Generalissimo and Vice-Generalissimo respectively, to conduct governmental affairs before the formation of the provisional government.[27] This blunt move to shift leadership away from Wuchang was naturally distasteful to Li Yuan-hung and his followers. But, since Hanyang had fallen into enemy hands and Wuchang was facing grave military threats, they were not in a position to challenge immediately Shanghai's decision. The delegates in Wuchang did not object to the choice of Nanking for the provisional government. In fact they had decided quite separately, at about the same time, 4 December 1911, to move to Nanking within seven days to elect a provisional president.[28] They could not concur on the creation of new offices, however, on the grounds that their colleagues in Shanghai had exceeded their function, which should have been confined to liaison and communication.[29] Consequently, Li Yuan-hung cabled on 8 December to voice his objection to Shanghai's 'extraordinary' resolution, and asked for its abrogation to avoid confusion.[30] The following comment of a conservative representative from Shantung sheds light on the nature and methods of the Shanghai revolutionary leaders' manoeuvre and the criticism they met:

> The election [of Huang Hsing and Li Yuan-hung] was entirely the work of Sung Chiao-jen and Ch'en Ch'i-mei who, fearing that Wuchang might become the real central government to the detriment of the Chinese League, stirred up a section of the delegates to stage this farce. They acted out of loyalty for the Chinese League, but unfortunately the opposite result was achieved. The prestige of the League suffered a severe setback as a result.[31]

According to this conservative member, Sung Chiao-jen and Ch'en Ch'i-mei committed three blunders in their action. Firstly, the delegates in Shanghai and those in Wuchang were in fact one body. Sung and Ch'en carried the group in Shanghai with them, but purposely failed to consult the opinion of those in Wuchang. Secondly, the participation of the Governors of Kiangsu, Chekiang, and Shanghai at the meetings of the provincial representative body was unconstitutional, improper, and offensive to the other provincial governors. Thirdly, the presence of a number of unauthorised persons, such as Chang Ping-lin, Chang Chia-shih, Ts'ai Yuan-p'ei, and others, at the provincial delegates' meeting cast doubts on the real nature of the delegates' business.[32] These charges were not entirely accurate, but nevertheless reveal the chaos of the revolutionaries in conducting their business, the price of haste, inexperience, and unpreparedness. The revolution occurred too soon.

In the face of this opposition from Wuchang, the resolution of the delegates in Shanghai would have been shelved for good but for an unexpected event which interrupted the election of a Provisional President. On 14 December 1911 the provincial government delegates from seventeen provinces met in Nanking and resolved that the election of the Provisional President was to take place two days later. But, on the following day, a Chekiang representative arrived from Wuchang with a message reporting on the progress of negotiations with Yuan Shih-kai's emissaries and the possibility of Yuan's support for the establishment of a republic.[33]

One of the first resolutions of the delegates when they met in Wuchang was to elect Yuan Shih-k'ai to the provisional presidency if he supported the revolution.[34] The delegates accordingly postponed the scheduled election to await further developments. In the meantime, to provide the anti-Manchu camp with the much needed central authority, they ratified Shanghai's resolution for establishing the offices of Generalissimo and Vice-Generalissimo, and also its election of Huang Hsing and Li Yuan-hung to these respective offices. They also amended the related laws to enable the officeholders to exercise the powers of the Provisional President before his election.

Unfortunately, opposition came from unexpected quarters. The army leaders of Kiangsu and Chekiang opposed it on the grounds that they did not wish to serve under the leadership of a defeated General, namely Huang Hsing. They wanted Li Yuan-hung to be the Generalissimo.[35] This intervention by the Kiangsu-Chekiang militarists in a purely political decision, the first case of interference in politics by soldiers, has been subject to various interpretations. One source regards it as an expression of the haughtiness of the soldiers who captured Nanking.[36] Another implies that the militarists did not wish to see any actual control over them.[37] However, the view of a Kiangsi representative who witnessed the event in Nanking, that the generalissimo issue was mainly a struggle between Hunan and Hupeh representatives, and that the soldiers of Chekiang and Kiangsu were merely pawns in the game, was probably correct.[38] This incident reveals the sagacity of Sung Chiao-jen in trying to include the soldiers in political decisions a little earlier. Unfortunately, the militarists at that time declared that they had no wish to interfere in political matters.[39] Had he been successful in inducing their participation, perhaps this act of army intervention would not have happened.

However, as a result of the militarists' objection, the delegates decided to resort to another expedient. This time they simply reversed the positions of the two chosen generals in accordance with a naive practice which has been figuratively described as 'changing water but not the medicine'. Li Yuan-hung was to assume the generalissimoship. But, as he was concurrently Military Governor of Hupeh, and could not possibly leave Wuchang for Nanking, he was to delegate his power to Huang Hsing, the Vice-Generalissimo. Accordingly, the laws governing the formation of the provisional government were amended once more so that Huang Hsing in his latter capacity could exercise exactly the same authority.[40] This readiness of the delegates to change their opinions revealed from the start a serious weakness in China's representative institutions, and earned for them the criticism of being a body deficient in sound purpose and firm revolutionary principles.[41] Since the delegates in Nanking were either appointed by the 'independent' provincial military governments, or elected by former provincial advisory councils, the revolutionaries exercised little influence over them. Neither could resolution be of much use in the face of the militarists' objection. The following words of a provincial representative who witnessed this event reveal the helplessness of the delegates:

> Looking back at the chaos of the time, and the childish solution to the controversy of the generalissimoships as if we were playing a game of chess, it was indeed laughable. Yet, had we not done so, disasters probably would have followed immediately. The extreme intricacy of the situation was far beyond the imagination of outsiders.[42]

The politicians, including revolutionary leaders, having no loyal army of their own, had no choice but to bow to the wishes of the militarists. Besides, public opinion pressed strongly for the early establishment of a central authority, which was likened to 'a raincloud after a long drought'.[43]

The expedient failed to solve the problem, however. The supporters of Huang Hsing were so angered by the changes that they

threatened to shoot some representatives from the not yet independent northern provinces of Chihli and Honan, whom they suspected
as the reactionary agents behind this sinister move to sabotage the
cause of revolution.[44] Li Yuan-hung at first refused the offer, but
accepted it after second thoughts.[45] But Huang Hsing was in no mood
to serve under Li. Probably partly feeling humiliated, and partly
influenced by Sung and other supporters, he insisted that Li should
take up the appointment in Nanking personally. This was undoubtedly a move calculated in the knowledge that the latter could not leave
Wuchang, the source of his power and influence.

Things were thus deadlocked, and Sung found himself in a very
uneasy situation. He was attacked by Li Yuan-hung's supporters for
being the chief opponent of Wuchang's leadership, and for having
masterminded the schemes which led to the present deadlock. His
own colleagues were also dissatisfied with him for allegedly conceding
to the demand of the militarists and the conservative elements.[46]
Things were made worse for him by Chang Ping-lin's 'declaration'
in the press that Sung was the most suitable and talented man for
the premiership.[47] It at once aroused suspicions in all quarters that
all of Sung's political moves were directed towards personal advancement, thus marring his chance of putting his political vision and
ability to use.[48]

The Li-Huang deadlock and Sung's fall in prestige directly
contributed to the emergence of Sun Yat-sen in China's political
scene. At the time of the Wuchang uprising, Sun was in the midst of
an American tour. When the news reached him, he immediately left
for Europe, where he hoped to gain support for the revolutionaries,
or, failing that, to secure the neutrality of the European powers.[49]
While he was in Paris, news of the convening of provincial delegates
in Shanghai for the purpose of organising a provisional government
reached him. He accordingly cabled Shanghai, undoubtedly, among
other things, to keep himself in the limelight.[50] This was responded
to two days later by the Governor of Soochow, who cabled various
provincial Military Governors, suggesting that Sun Yat-sen be
invited to return to form the provisional government.[51]

The reception to this proposal is obscure. The only available clue
is a telegram from the Governor of Hunan to Hupeh, suggesting that
Sun be appointed as Minister Plenipotentiary for the purpose of
seeking the recognition of the foreign nations.[52] It seems that at this
stage nobody particularly desired his return. It is probable that Sun
was still regarded by the leaders in China less as a politican and
statesman than as a seasoned diplomat and fund-raiser whose knowledge of foreign nations could be best used in the latter capacities.[53]

However, Sun Yat-sen's arrival in Shanghai on Christmas Day of 1911 was most timely. The revolutionary leaders in Shanghai found in him a good solution to their dilemma. In the interest of revolution, Sung Chiao-jen was also prepared to forget the differences between them.[54] At a welcome feast for Sun Yat-sen on 26 December, the decision to support Sun for the provisional presidency was arrived at between Sung Chiao-jen, Huang Hsing, and Ch'en Ch'i-mei, who, after a secret consultation, agreed to use all their influence to bear on the delegates for this end.[55] Consequently, Sun was elected Provisional President by an overwhelming majority on 29 December. On that day forty-five representatives from seventeen provinces gathered in Nanking to elect a Provisional President from three candidates. On the basis of one vote for each province Sun received sixteen out of seventeen, the remaining one vote going to Huang Hsing, while the third candidate, Li Yuan-hung, received nothing. The fact that Li Yuan-hung failed to obtain any votes at this election was a triumph of the Chinese League and a personal victory for Sung Chiao-jen, but it was also a badly timed snub for Li Yuan-hung and his supporters.

Sun Yat-sen would have been elected unanimously but for T'an Jen-feng, who, on behalf of the delegates from Hunan, cast his vote in favour of Huang Hsing. In view of T'an's past associations with Sun, his vote seems understandable. But apparently T'an acted from broader considerations. Firstly, in his view Li Yuan-hung, having borne the leadership of the initial uprising, should be retained for the transitional period so that his authority in Hupeh might be transferred to the revolutionaries. Secondly, he did not think Sun sufficiently familiar with internal conditions. In fact T'an asserted that before Sun's arrival in Shanghai the majority of provincial representatives agreed with his views, for 60 per cent of them were in favour of electing Li Yuan-hung to the provisional presidency, about 30 per cent in favour of Huang Hsing, and Sun Yat-sen was a very poor third in their preferences.[56] If T'an were to be believed, the swiftness with which this national representative body changed its mind in dealing with matters of such national importance is indeed astonishing.

On New Year's Day 1912 Sun Yat-sen was formally sworn in as Provisional President. For the time being the question of leadership was settled. But there remained the tussle over the revision of the 'Structural Outline of the Provisional Government of the Republic of China'. The champion of revision was Sung Chiao-jen, who thought the 'Outline' too inadequate even for a provisional purpose. In his opinion, the 'Outline' had omitted a number of vital points essential for the organisation of a democratic government. For example, it failed to state the power and obligation of the people, a vital feature of democracy; it also failed to define the power for initiating legislation, and the presidential power respecting the appointment and dismissal of civil officials below the rank of departmental heads. On the other hand, it laid down the structural divisions of the administration, which seriously impaired the elasticity of the executive to meet changing needs.[57]

Probably in support of Sung's move to revise the 'Outline', the *Independent People's Daily*, on the eve of Sun's arrival in Shanghai, published a criticism by two foreign legal experts, who commented that the two major weaknesses of the 'Structural Outline' were firstly, the fixing of the ministerial divisions, and secondly, the failure to provide a chief for the purpose of co-ordinating the policies of the various ministries. They suggested that, in order to remedy these weaknesses, the administration should be left entirely to the President, and a premiership should be instituted to spare the head of state any actual responsibility.[58] These were points for revision closest to Sung's heart. In the following week, he was seen fighting hard to get the 'Outline' amended along those lines, and in particular he pressed for the adoption of the principle of cabinet government. In addition to his conviction on the definite superiority of the cabinet system of government based on the British model, he had probably also considered the possible outcome of the current north-south peace negotiations, which, if successful, would put Yuan in the presidency.

These constitutional issues were first raised at a meeting of the revolutionary party's inner circle in Shanghai, after a decision to elect Sun Yat-sen to the provisional presidency had been made.[59] The meeting seems to have endorsed all Sung's amendments to the 'Outline' except one, namely the adoption of the system of responsible cabinet government. The latter was opposed by Sun Yat-sen, the Provisional President-elect, who was not willing to see the executive power taken out of his hands. To him, the cabinet system of government was devised to spare the head of state under normal conditions from direct involvement in the daily politics of the nation, a practice quite unsuited to the time of emergency. He argued that, during a revolution, it was absurd to restrict the authority of a person who assumed the presidency by popular vote and enjoyed the full confidence of the people. He was not disposed to play the role of a seemingly saintly but in fact completely useless figurehead. He could not be tied to the opinion of others, especially if the latter appeared likely to damage the cause of revolution.[60]

With regard to the outcome of this meeting, there were two conflicting accounts. According to Hsu Hsueh-er, Sung's biographer and personal friend, Sung managed to win over Sun and others to his views, and accordingly was invited to be Premier, but he refused. Instead, he persuaded Huang Hsing, who had already declined it once, to accept the post. Having settled this issue within the revolutionary party hierarchy, Sung and Huang went to Nanking for the purpose of revising the 'Outline'; unfortunately, the provincial delegates, ignorant of the decision reached in Shanghai, rejected the amendments. However, Hu Han-min, who was present at this meeting, wrote that the majority supported Sun Yat-sen's insistence on the retention of the presidential system.[61]

Probably neither account is entirely accurate. In the light of the amendments to the 'Outline' effected later, and the storm of opposition to Sung Chiao-jen arising from these amendments, it seems that suspension rather than outright rejection of Sung's idea took place at the meeting, and a final decision was deferred to a further meeting with the provincial delegates in Nanking on the night of 27 December. The following is an account of an eye-witness at the later meeting:

> On 27 December, a special train carrying Huang Hsing arrived in Nanking . . . That evening he attended a meeting of the provincial representatives, which was held at the Kiangsu Provincial Advisory Council building. He put forth three motions: (1) the new republic was to adopt the solar calendar system; (2) the new régime was to be known as the Republic of China; (3) the presidential system of government was to be adopted. After some discussion, the first two motions were combined into one, and passed unanimously . . . As for the third proposal, concerning the choice between presidential and cabinet system of government, Tun-ch'u [Sung Chiao-jen] still insisted on adopting the latter system. After a lengthy discussion . . . the majority favoured the presidential system, and it was adopted accordingly. Tun-ch'u then moved that, since the structural Outline of the Provisional Government had been adopted, the election of the provisional president be held in two days' time [29 December], and that all preparations for this purpose be left to the Representative Assembly. All concurred with this motion.[62]

On 31 December, two days after Sun Yat-sen was elected to the provisional presidency, Huang Hsing reappeared in Nanking. This time he was sent by Sun to explain to the provincial delegates the necessity to revise the 'Structural Outline'.[63] The origin of this revision was not clear. At least partly it was promoted by the need to accommodate the claims of various leaders to positions in the government.[64] Whatever the cause of the revision might have been, its importance was that Sung Chiao-jen immediately moved to amend the 'Outline'.

The main points of Sung's revision were three: firstly, a vice-presidency was to be created; secondly, the system of administration, and the appointment and dismissal of civil and military officials, were to be left to the discretion of the President, except for the appointment of cabinet ministers, which was subject to the approval of the Provincial Representative Assembly; thirdly, the cabinet ministers (replacing the name of members of the administrative or executive departments laid down in section three of the 'Outline') were to be made responsible for administrative policies and were required to counter-sign all presidential proclamations respecting law and order.[65]

The new amendments contained essentially Sung Chiao-jen's original proposal, a responsible cabinet. The only difference was the omission of a Premier. The delegates sat late that night, and passed amendments containing points one and two mentioned above before adjourning their meeting to 2 January 1912.

When they met again, the validity of the amendments passed at the previous meeting was challenged by the delegates of five provinces* on the grounds that such important questions should not be dealt with at night; the delegates, exhausted after a long day's work, were not in full possession of their mental vigilance, and therefore were not in a fit state to consider matters of a serious nature.[66]

The truth is that, in the interval of one day, suspicion and jealousy had been aroused. Some members who for some reasons seemed naturally averse to Sung Chiao-jen, suddenly realised the implication of the second and third amendments, and connected them with the alleged aspiration of Sung Chiao-jen for the premiership. They saw the amendments as another of Sung Chiao-jen's clever manoeuvres to fulfil his private political ambition. Although the amendments contained no provision for a Premier, the suspicious representatives were satisfied that, under the new amendments, it was within the President's power to create one. Sung Chiao-jen might in the course of time prevail on the President to create such an office for him. Sung at once became the target of personal attacks; this was an extremely unhealthy political phenomenon, for, instead of the merits of the legislation in question, personal relations became the dominant factor in making political decisions.[67]

It was significant that the most vehement opposition to the amendments came from Ma Chun-wu, a representative from Kwangsi who was also one of three drafters of the 'Outline'. He

* Kiangsu, Anhwei, Chekiang, Kwangsi, and Fukien.

seemed determined to take vengeance on Sung for the latter's public criticism of the 'Outline' in the press. Ma was also an ardent supporter of Sun Yat-sen. He was present at the meeting in Shanghai during which Sung fought for the adoption of the cabinet system. He seems to have been convinced of Sung's personal ambitions in the manoeuvre, and determined to prevent their consummation. The result was a reappraisal of the amendments passed by the previous meeting. The power of the President respecting the creation of new offices, such as the appointment of cabinet ministers and diplomats, was made subject to the approval of the Provincial Representative Assembly.[68] To quote Li Chien-nung, a well-known Chinese historian, the important point of the reappraisal was that a vice-presidency and cabinet ministerial chairs were added, but cabinet responsibility was removed, in other words, Sung's ideas were successfully quashed. The same historian justifiably lamented, 'to determine the organisation of a governmental system in the spirit of likes and dislikes for an individual, which featured the representative body of this time, is an extremely unhealthy state of mind'.[69]

The prejudice of the representative body against Sung Chiao-jen continued after the episode of revision, and crippled his political activities. Neither Sun Yat-sen nor Huang Hsing, whose prestige was high among the representatives, appeared anxious to back Sung. Consequently his appointment to the cabinet as Minister for the Interior was also opposed by the assembly, and had to be withdrawn. Neither was his suggestion that all cabinet posts should be filled with genuine revolutionaries accepted.[70] Of the nine ministers appointed by Sun Yat-sen, only three were revolutionaries. The rest were former bureaucrats of the Manchu court, and at least five of them held lukewarm attitudes towards the provisional government. Some never took up their posts. Those who did, stayed only briefly in Nanking, and then moved to live permanently in Shanghai's International Settlement.[71]

Thus, with the formation of the Nanking provisional government, the heterogeneous nature of the revolution of 1911 was increasingly apparent. Sung disagreed entirely with the set-up of the Nanking provisional government, but, having incurred the wrath of the representative body, he was in no position to take effective measures. To compensate him for his loss of a ministerial post, as well as to utilise his legal training, he was appointed Attorney-General of the Legislative Bureau. Sung's attitude towards this state of affairs could be seen from his conversation with some of his colleagues who, feeling the injustice of the treatment meted out to him, visited him. He said to them:

To be a minister or not is of no importance. I have always favoured the cabinet system of government, especially one based on a party system. Now the government is a mixed bag of incongruous elements, the cabinet posts are no longer worthy objects of pursuit. At this infant stage of our republic, no one but members of our party could carry out bold reforms courageously, and no one but we are worthy to tackle the subject of politics. The former bureaucrats were non-committal and timid. We can hardly expect to discuss revolution and republicanism with them. If we do, it will be simply a waste of effort. However, since the government has appointed me to head the legislative bureau, I am going to carry out my share of responsibility so that no one can accuse me of shirking my duties out of anger.[72]

Sung was true to his word. In his capacity as Attorney-General he laboured hard to put the law of the Nanking provisional government in order, and contributed much to the legislation of the young republic.[73] Prejudice against Sung Chiao-jen persisted among the representatives, however. Its seriousness could be seen in the fact that, when he was asked to draft a provisional constitution, he was obliged to decline, with the suggestion that it would be best handled by the representative body itself.[74]

Sung Chiao-jen's aim in hastening the organisation of a central institution for the anti-Manchu camp was to create an authority firmly invested in the hands of the revolutionaries, so that the heterogeneous forces involved might be welded together to fulfil the objectives of the revolution. After three months of unceasing effort, this authority at last came into existence. But it was not what he had envisaged. The revolutionaries were not strong enough to shape the form of government according to their own ideal, not to mention the fact that they themselves were divided on the system of government they should adopt. The dissenting and incoherent features of the Nanking provisional government were in fact manifestations of the incongruous nature of the anti-Manchu camp. Clearly China's revolution of 1911 was not the result of a uniform revolutionary movement such as the communist movement of recent time or even that of the Nationalists under Chiang Kai-shek. A number of forces of different origins and motives were involved. The conservative officials acted out of despair with, rather than hatred of, the Manchu government; the local gentry rose because some of their vested interests had been threatened by the Peking régime; and opportunists threw in their lot to get what they could out of it.

The revolution of 1911 has been likened to a great landslide set in motion by the movement of a small pebble.[75] The pebble, then, was the revolutionary movement of Sung and his colleagues, while the sliding mass symbolises the spontaneous forces involved in the risings. Once the landslide began, the pebble was in no position to control or guide its direction. Sung's achievement was perhaps his success in keeping himself and his colleagues on top of the moving mass. If they could not control the course of development, they could at least see where they were being carried to. The mass headed for the plain of north China, engulfing the last remnants of the Manchu dynasty in its course, and then, as a spent force, subsided at the feet of Yuan Shih-k'ai.

TEN

The Transfer to Peking

THE NANKING provisional government had taken Sung and his friends eighty days to establish. Within nearly as many days of its formation, it passed under the control of Yuan Shih-k'ai. What were the causes of this phenomenon? Writing in 1921, J. O. P. Bland, an influential 'old China hand', explained it as the lack of principles on the part of the revolutionary leaders, whom he regarded as self-seekers 'more concerned for the furthering of their private ambitions than for the application of Republican principles'.[1]

On the other hand, Li Chien-nung, undoubtedly influenced by Sun Yat-sen's view and later party opinion, concludes that it was due to the revolutionaries' disregard of the Chinese League's plan of revolution.[2]

These views are, of course, gross generalisations, which not only disregard the circumstances giving rise to these events but also leave no room for the separation of the sheep from the goats. Broadly, three factors may be brought to account: the internal conditions of the anti-Manchu camp, the manoeuvres of Yuan Shih-k'ai, and the fear of foreign intervention.

Some attention has already been drawn to the incoherent nature of the forces involved on the side of the revolutionaries. It was this incoherence which made the revolutionaries' plan of revolution inoperative, and caused Sung to seek alternative means of maintaining unity. Unfortunately, the provisional government he helped to bring into existence fell short of this role. It became more a focus of regional and personal differences than a source of unity and strength. The most urgent problem confronting the newly formed provisional government was finance, but attempts to solve it were effectively blocked by dissenting factions, consisting mainly of conservative and non-revolutionary elements. The provisional government tried to raise foreign loans on the security of the China Merchants' Steam Navigation Company and the Kiangsu railways. It also planned to concede joint-control rights of the Hanyehping

Mining Company to Japan in return for financial assistance, but this was opposed by Chang Ch'ien, the Minister for Industry, the government of Hupeh, and its representatives in the National Assembly, and had to be called off. A Russian loan of £1 million was also opposed by representatives from Hupeh and Kiangsu, and, according to Ch'en Chin-t'ao, then Minister for Finance in the Nanking government, it nearly had disastrous results.[3] There were, of course, very plausible reasons for opposing foreign loans, but mere opposition offered no effective solution to the provisional government's dire financial difficulties.

It is highly significant that the main opposition to foreign loans came from the Yangtze provinces of Chekiang, Kiangsu, and Hupeh, particularly the latter two provinces, the heads of which were originally non-revolutionaries, and the industrial and commercial assets within their boundaries were involved in the loans. Provincialism and conservative reaction began to emerge in the anti-Manchu camp. It was also in these provinces that some revolutionaries, having failed to obtain the desired positions for themselves in the Nanking provisional government, began to ally themselves with conservative elements to oppose the revolutionary leadership in Nanking. Chang Ping-lin and Sun Wu were cases in point. Chang's opposition to Sun Yat-sen dated back to earlier days in Tokyo. After the Wuchang uprising he sided with the non-revolutionary camp. Sun Wu was said to have coveted the post of Vice-Minister for the Army, and, failing to obtain it, supported Li Yuan-hung and used him to oppose the policies of the Nanking provisional government. He was also said to have instigated the opposition of Hupeh and its representatives to Nanking's plan for raising loans.[4]

The inability of the provisional government to raise money naturally hampered its leadership and the execution of its policies, which in turn weakened its resistance to Yuan Shih-k'ai's overtures for peace, quite apart from the fact that, from the beginning of the uprising, the anti-Manchu forces, including most revolutionary leaders, aimed for a quick end to the fighting and perpetuated an inclination to take the easiest course.[5]

Yuan Shih-k'ai (1859-1916) was a powerful official of the late Ch'ing dynasty. He rose to prominence after 1895 for his role in founding a modern army in north China, which, being loyal to him personally, was the mainstay of his political prominence. For this progressive gesture in 1902 in joining Chang Chih-tung, Viceroy of Hunan and Hupeh, to memorialise the Manchu throne on the subject of abolishing the traditional examinations and modernising education and his stand against the Boxer uprisings two years earlier, his international prestige was high.

After the death of the Empress Dowager Tz'u-hsi in 1908, however, he fell out of royal favour, and was dismissed from all his offices. He would have met harsher persecution still but for the intervention of the British and American ministers, who 'demanded and obtained from the Manchu court an assurance for his safe-conduct to his home in Honan'.[6]

Bearing in mind Yuan Shih-k'ai's life and experience prior to 1911, his subsequent betrayal of the Manchu cause can be easily understood. Apart from personal ambition, there was his unpleasant memory of his relationship with the Manchu court. Therefore, right from the outset, when he was recalled from retirement to quell the rebels, he did not intend to save a régime which had once disgraced him, and was inclined to take advantage of the situation to do the best for himself. His problem was how to make both sides voluntarily and willingly relinquish authority in his favour, and spare himself the onus of being a bully or usurper, either of which in the Chinese concept of morality would subject him to moral sanction.[7] The strategy he adopted was threefold: attack, halt, and intimidate. He attacked to demonstrate his strength, halted to let negotiations begin, and threatened in various ways, including the resumption of hostilities with the anti-Manchu camp on the one hand, and resignation from the Manchu court on the other, to force both sides to make way for him.

However, despite his display of force and intimidation, and the Manchu court's complete reliance on him for support, he probably would not have succeeded in cudgelling the two factions into submission but for a third factor, the fear of foreign intervention, and his successful exploitation of this fear.

On the eve of the revolution in 1911, there was talk in the foreign press, particularly in Japan, of possible foreign intervention in the event of revolution in China.[8] When approached on this question, Sung Chiao-jen was said to have held the opinion that, in view of the trend of thought in the modern world, the diplomatic attitude of the powers in the international scene, and the necessity of political reform, China had little to fear from foreign intervention. He optimistically declared that, should China really opt for revolution, not only would there be no intervention by foreign powers, but the latter would be glad to help it succeed.[9] Subsequent events show that Sung's observation was only partially correct.

Officially the foreign powers observed neutrality, but this only indirectly assisted the revolutionaries. Behind their apparent unanimity on the policy of neutrality, the powers were basically divided in attitudes towards the contending factions and towards China as a whole. Each had its pros and cons in accordance with its own national interests and, if one is prepared to grant the policy-makers of respective nations the benefit of the doubt, perhaps also that of the world. Their interplay contributed substantially to the rise of Yuan Shih-k'ai to power at the expense of both the Manchus and the revolutionaries. Thus John Gilbert Reid, an American Consul in China at the time of the revolution, made the following analysis of the attitudes of the powers in this period. In the midst of rapid changes, 'two facts stood out: the powers permitted the dynasty's abdication and the imperial system's overthrow, and they backed Yuan Shih-k'ai to head a new so-called republic'. The reason as he explained it was that the British trading interests in the Yangtze region, combined with the personal friendship of the British Minister, John N. Jordan, for Yuan Shih-k'ai, and his hostility towards the Manchu dynasty, called for peace and compromise at the expense of the Manchu dynasty; France, with its economic interests in south China, its Indo-chinese colonies bordering revolutionary territory, and its republican sentiments, also called for an early compromise at the Manchu's expense; Germany preferred retention of the dynasty under a constitutional monarchy, but was not free to support its view; Japan favoured the retention of the dynasty over which it hoped to exercise major influences, but it dared not undertake separate action without the consent of the other powers and for fear of losing its trade in revolutionary-controlled territory; Russia welcomed the disintegration of authority and wished to prevent a strong neighbour from emerging; while the United States preferred concerted action to separate intervention by any one power, and its trade interests and republican sentiments favoured a compromise.[10]

The same scholar also explained why Yuan was preferred by the powers. It was because they could bargain with him to recognise the status quo in exchange for political recognition and foreign loans; and such an arrangement would not interfere with autonomous Tibet, Turkestan, and outer Mongolia, nor with the special position of Russia and Japan in Manchuria, nor with the consortium's financial control plans for China.[11] To this it should be added that Yuan, with his powerful army, appeared to be the only strong man who could command the obedience of all China, and maintain peace.[12] Yuan himself, of course, played a major role in gaining power. The friendship of the British Minister stood him in good stead. The *Chinese Mail* of Hong Kong reported on 15 January 1912, the British Minister's consent to the request of Yuan's generals to use his influence on the Hongkong and Shanghai Banking Corporation to release the saving deposits of the Manchu nobles for military use. This news seems a little far-fetched, but nevertheless reflects accurately the side with which the British Minister's sympathy lay.

In addition, Yuan sought and received the sympathy and support of such men as G. E. Morrison, an Australian and an influential correspondent of *The Times*, who, besides shaping British public opinion in Yuan's favour, also offered advice on how to deal with the Manchus and the revolutionaries. According to Morrison's own account, he had helped to solve Yuan's financial problem by providing his faction with a plan showing where the palace treasure was kept. Apparently the idea of getting the chambers of commerce of Shanghai and Hong Kong to petition the abdication of the Manchu Emperor also came from Morrison. Another foreigner who helped to bring about the abdication of the Manchu emperor was Dr John Gilbert Reid, then an American Consul in Nanking, who, in January 1912, visited the capital and brought to bear upon the distracted Manchu court all possible evidence he could adduce in favour of the policy of abdication.[13] These gestures of foreign support, even if they were unofficial and private in character, undoubtedly emboldened Yuan to seek supreme power by every means.

It has been said that the truce [which began on the fall of Nanking to the revolutionaries, 2 December 1911] and the ensuing peace were a foregone conclusion.[14] The actual peace negotiations between Yuan and the revolutionaries, which began in Wuchang, continued in Shanghai, and finished up by telegraphic exchanges between Peking, Nanking, and Shanghai in January and February 1912, need not be dealt with here except in so far as they involved Sung Chiao-jen.

According to a report in the Japanese press, Sung was present at the first meeting between the Wuchang military government and Yuan Shih-k'ai's emissaries on 11 November 1911. On this occasion, Sung was said to be the chief spokesman for the revolutionaries. He rejected outright Yuan's offer of peace on the basis of constitutional monarchy, on the grounds that monarchy, constitutional or despotic, was fundamentally incompatible with the revolutionaries' goals, and, that, since the Manchu régime was in a state of virtual isolation, and its collapse was a matter of time, the revolutionaries were not interested in compromise. The question of making Yuan Shih-k'ai President, if the latter supported the revolution, was also said to have been raised by Yuan's emissaries, but Sung was non-committal. He reminded them that, as the presidency was to be filled according to the wish of the people no promise made by a few in advance could be binding. He advised that Yuan should first prove his sincerity and establish his popularity by taking Honan and Hopeh for the revolutionaries; then his future would be assured.[15] At this stage Sung and other members of the Hupeh military government were not in a compromising mood, especially when Yuan's real intention was not yet ascertained. Sung strongly suspected that Yuan was making an empty gesture to divide the revolutionary camp.[16]

This meeting in Wuchang seems to be the only occasion in which Sung took a direct part in the peace negotiations with Yuan. Thereafter he left Wuchang for the lower Yangtze region, to attend to the capture of Nanking and the task of forming a provisional government, while negotiations were entrusted to special delegates who through both open and secret channels of contact managed to work out a compromise.[17]

Having considered the circumstances which favoured Yuan Shih-k'ai's rise to power, attention should now turn to the devices with which the revolutionaries hoped to preserve the fruits of their labour against the possible treachery by a non-revolutionary head of state. Apparently they had no illusions about Yuan Shih-ka'i. Sung Chiao-jen, in a letter to Li Hsieh-ho, the Military Governor of Woo-sung, described him as an 'uneducated man of despicable conduct',[18] and the *Independent People's Daily* of 24 January 1912 warned the nation of the possibility of Yuan Shih-k'ai one day 'changing democracy to monarchy'.[19]

Generally speaking, two precautions were taken, the adoption of a provisional constitution, and the relocation of the national capital.

The adoption by the National Assembly, formerly the provincial Representative Assembly, at Nanking, of a provisional constitution embracing the principle of responsible cabinet government was a personal triumph for Sung Chiao-jen, who had fought so hard previously for its adoption without success. However, the motives which lay behind its adoption differed. If Sung had aspirations to head the cabinet, he also believed sincerely in the superiority of the cabinet system. But the National Assembly took matters of personal politics into consideration in their decision on the issue of cabinet government. Just as cabinet government was thrown out previously by the National Assembly because of the likelihood of Sung Chiao-jen becoming the Premier, it was now adopted because a different person was assuming the presidency. From beginning to end, the personnel factor loomed large in China's politics in this period. Institutions were made to suit a particular individual rather than vice versa—an extremely unhealthy political phenomenon.[20]

The choice of Nanking as the capital of the new republic seems to have been primarily Sun Yat-sen's idea. There were good reasons for this choice. It aimed to take Yuan Shih-k'ai away from his stronghold, to make him more submissive to the control of the Provisional Assembly at Nanking, and to give the young republican government a more conducive environment in which to take root. In terms of internal politics, it was a sound suggestion. But in terms of external and overall strategic consideration, Nanking was not regarded as a suitable location for a national capital. To a majority of the leaders in Nanking, particularly to Sung Chiao-jen, who had been to Manchuria and possessed intimate knowledge of the economic and strategic value of the land and foreign intrigues in the region, the removal of the capital southward was tantamount to abandonment of the territory north of the Great Wall.[21] National interests overrode internal political considerations. It is not surprising that, when the question of the capital was first raised in the National Assembly at Nanking, the majority of provincial representatives voted for Peking.[22] This resolution was reversed only after Huang Hsing had threatened to invoke party discipline against all members of the Chinese League in the National Assembly.[23] Incidentally, Huang Hsing's threat to send military police to discipline dissenting members of the National Assembly, even though the latter were also members of the Chinese League, reveals the shaky position of democracy. When even professed republicans like Huang Hsing were ready to sacrifice the lofty principle of popular wish in order to carry through the government's policy, how could Yuan Shih-k'ai, a complete product of the old order, be expected to respect democratic practices?

Sun Yat-sen and Huang Hsing were able to coax the Nanking Provisional Assembly round to their way of thinking on the issue of the capital, but they failed to move Yuan Shih-k'ai, the key figure in question. He was unwilling to depart from Peking, knowing that his power and influence would be curtailed if he did. His stay in Peking was supported by at least two sections of public opinion; the militarists, who were loyal to Yuan personally; and the foreign legations, which argued in favour of Peking on the grounds of the expense and inconvenience involved in the removal of the capital, as well as the consideration that such a removal contravened China's obligations to foreign powers under the Boxer Protocol.[24] Undoubtedly, internal disagreements in Nanking on this subject also reached Yuan's ears and strengthened his stand.[25] When Nanking insisted on this point, and sent a special delegation of nine men, including Sung Chiao-jen, to escort Yuan to Nanking, Yuan's army in Peking rioted. The property of local residents was pillaged and burned. Sung and other members of the special delegation were driven to seek refuge in a Japanese home.[26] The origin of this mutiny, whether it was caused purely by social tension and instability, or, as often alleged, it was an instigated affair directly or indirectly involving Yuan, is still far from clear. At the time few other than members of the revolutionary camp believed that Yuan had anything to do with it. If Yuan had done it, he had done it extremely well, for not even a journalistic wizard and China hand like G. E. Morrison seems to have suspected it. Apparently few outside the revolutionary camp entertained seriously the idea of Yuan leaving Peking. Under the circumstances, for him to have brought about the mutiny and shattered his reputation throughout the world does seem to be 'as unreasonable as to employ a steel hammer to crush a gooseberry'.[27] But could it be precisely here that Yuan's evil genius lay?

Whatever the cause of the mutiny, the effect is well known. It settled the question of the capital in favour of Peking. Some members in Nanking still objected to this solution, and talked of sending troops to Peking to subjugate the unruly elements and to escort Yuan south. Sung received a black eye from a rash member when he opposed this drastic step. Nevertheless, his counsel prevailed. The proposal to send troops to Peking was impractical. Peking was a long way away from Nanking, and the intervening territories were mostly under the control of Yuan's troops. The dispatch of troops from Nanking could only mean one thing, the resumption of war, and it would earn for Nanking no good will either in China or overseas.[28]

Having failed to take Yuan out of Peking, an alternative safeguard was taken by Nanking. The revolutionaries demanded and obtained from Yuan the appointment of Huang Hsing as the Resident General for Nanking, whose duties were to take charge of civil and military administration of the south during the transitional period. Had Huang Hsing been able to hold this position, the balance of power between the north and the south created by the revolution would have continued and afforded a strong deterrent to any attempt on Yuan's part to betray the republic.[29] Unfortunately, Huang Hsing's position was untenable on two counts. Firstly, public opinion favoured centralisation and unity, not decentralisation and division. Secondly, Huang Hsing was unable to find sufficient money for his administration and the maintenance of the army under his command. Yuan withheld all financial assistance from him. Huang Hsing was expected to disband his army. He was to smooth the transfer of authority to Peking, not to withhold it. Therefore it was not surprising that Huang Hsing was obliged to relinquish his post after only a little more than two months in office, and, together with this, the revolutionaries' means for ensuring respect for democracy and republicanism also disappeared.[30]

Only one instrument was now left to the revolutionaries—the implementation of the provisional constitution, particularly its principle of responsible cabinet government. As Sung Chiao-jen was the chief promoter of cabinet government, and one who had learnt the art of politics,[31] the revolutionaries looked to him for the establishment and preservation of democracy. His political stature had grown. Sun Yat-sen recommended him to Yuan Shih-k'ai, and spoke of him as one who possessed ability worthy of a place in the new cabinet.[32] When T'ang Shao-yi, the newly appointed Prime Minister, named Sung for the post of Minister for Agriculture and Forestry, the National Assembly in Nanking accepted him wholeheartedly.[33]

Yuan Shih-k'ai was sworn in as Provisional President of the Republic of China on 10 March 1912. Two days later the provisional constitution was passed by the National Assembly and formally adopted. Both T'ang Shao-yi, who was appointed by Yuan Shih-k'ai as Prime Minister, and members of his cabinet were approved by the National Assembly at the end of March. On 1 April Sun Yat-sen formally relinquished his post. The National Assembly, having voted once again for Peking as the national capital, authorised its own transfer and adjourned.

The first goal of the revolutionaries—the overthrow of the incompetent alien Manchu government—was fulfilled, but the fight for the establishment of democracy, their second goal, had only just begun. The next scene was mainly a struggle between Yuan Shih-k'ai and the revolutionaries for the control of government, a struggle carried out in the form of presidential power versus cabinet and parliamentary authority, and complicated by party politics. In the struggle, the National Assembly was torn into two parts, a pro-president and a pro-cabinet faction, or more exactly, an anti-revolutionary and a revolutionary group. Sung Chiao-jen stood in the forefront of the revolutionary party in this struggle. He provided most of the inspiration, organisational skill, political strategy, leadership, and ideals for the revolutionary faction.

ELEVEN

Cabinet Versus President

ACCORDING TO the provisional constitution of the Republic of China proclaimed in March 1912,[1] the powers of government were to be exercised by four bodies: the Senate, the President, the cabinet, and the judiciary. The power of the Senate acting as the nation's legislature, and that of the judiciary as the guardian of law, seem to have been well defined. The source of confusion lay in the executive. The power of the executive was from the start a bone of contention between the President and the cabinet, and the adoption of a system of responsible cabinet under the provisional constitution was a victory for Sung Chiao-jen's idea, as we have seen (Chapter 10). Unfortunately the cabinet, formed under the dual approval of the President and the contending factions in the Senate, was the weak and finally unsuccessful product of conflicting forces. Its failure marked the end of China's first experiment in democracy.

As early as February 1912 the constitutionalists already turned their minds to post-revolutionary politics, and contemplated giving Yuan their support. Writing to Yuan Shih-k'ai, Provisional President of China in early 1912, Liang Ch'i-ch'ao, a former leading reformer and constitutional monarchist, pointed out that Yuan's political success depended on his handling of two important elements in the politics of the new republic—finance and political parties. With regard to the latter, he observed that people who were active in politics in the republic came from three groups, the former constitutionalists, the ex-bureaucrats, and the former revolutionaries.[2] In other words political strife in China after 1911 was basically a continuation of the pre-revolutionary pattern, but with one important difference. The revolutionaries had given up armed struggle against the central authority. They participated in government and sought to advance democracy by constitutional means. The Manchu régime had disappeared. In its place were Yuan Shih-k'ai and his northern military clique, formerly the mainstay of the Manchu monarchy. Yuan Shih-k'ai's faction and the revolutionaries, formerly diametrically opposed to each other, were now jointly controlling the apparatus of government, with the constitutionalists between them as an unpredictable third force. For historical reasons, however, the constitutionalists were closer to Yuan Shih-k'ai than to the revolutionaries. They sided with Yuan in the latter's opposition to the revolutionaries, for no other reason than to reduce the power and influence of the revolutionaries and to extend their own.

The immediate conflict between them arose over the control of the government. Yuan Shih-k'ai, a thoroughbred bureaucrat of former times, was no great believer in democracy, and wished to concentrate power in his own hands. The revolutionaries, suspicious of Yuan Shih-k'ai's intentions, were determined to prevent tyranny by implementing the provisional constitution of the new republic.

Their battle was fought out on two fronts: in the legislature for control, and in the executive over the principle and practice of cabinet government. These were the two tasks to which Sung Chiao-jen dedicated himself after the transfer of the republican government to Peking. He was at the forefront of the fight to consolidate the infant republic and its democratic institutions. In subsequent months his political fame quickly soared to national heights.

Political parties in China were a twentieth-century innovation. The first open political party was the Comrades' Association for Petitioning for a Parliament *(Kuo-hui ch'ing-yuan t'ung-chih-hui)*.[3] When the National Advisory Assembly *(Tzu-cheng-yuan)* was formed, the unofficial members, elected from the Provincial Advisory Council *(Tzu-i-chu)*, were mostly members of this party. They joined together to form the Friends of the Constitution *(Hsien-yu-hui)*. It was also referred to as the People's Party, to differentiate it from the two government parties, the Society for the Realisation of Constitutional Government *(Hsien-cheng shih-chin-hui)* and the Nineteen-eleven Club *(Hsin-hai ch'u-lo-pu)*, both being organisations of the official members in the National Advisory Assembly, and composed entirely of bureaucrats.

During the revolution the majority of constitutionalists sided with the revolutionaries, while the bureaucrats went through a period of hibernation. In the post-revolutionary era the strength of both the constitutionalists and the bureaucrats, apart from necessary adjustments to new conditions, remained intact, and their re-emergence was greatly facilitated by two factors, the rise of Yuan Shih-k'ai and the centrifugal tendency of the revolutionary party. Following the ascendancy of Yuan Shih-k'ai to the provisional presidency of the republic, the conservative forces naturally gravitated towards him. The former bureaucrats clustered around him to gain their second lease of life and prominence; the constitutionalists also rallied to support him, for no other reason than that of extending their own influence at the expense of the revolutionaries.[4] Yuan was, of course, glad to enlist the aid of the constitutionalists and the former bureaucrats, and even purposely fostered their emergence. In the face of a common opponent, their interests were mutual.

Factional conflicts within the revolutionary movement have already been described. For a time during the revolution the tension of war enabled them to paper over their differences. But when their goal of overthrowing the Manchus was near fulfilment, and the military pressure was reduced, old discrepancies re-emerged. The infiltration into their ranks by non-revolutionary elements during the revolution increased friction and quickened the process of their disintegration. Thus we see Liu K'uei-i, a revolutionary veteran of ten years standing, taking the lead in promoting the dissolution of all pre-republican political organisations including the revolutionary party, so that the political party system under the republic might be constructed anew and all parties placed on an equal footing.[5] Before long a Joint Association of the Chinese Republic *(Chung-hua min-kuo lien-ho-hui)*, with the aim of uniting China and assisting the establishment of a 'perfect republican government', was proposed. Among its means for the fulfilment of this aim were active assistance to the central and provincial government's military needs, and censure of organisations which were in the way of the republic.[6]

This Joint Association was a constitutionalist-inspired organisation with Chang Ping-lin, another prominent revolutionary figure, as its chief spokesman. Chang's role in the anti-Sun brawl within the Chinese League has already been noted. It is not surprising that after the revolution he was easily drawn into the constitutionalist camp. His animosity towards Sun Yat-sen continued, and he urged, on behalf of the constitutionalists, the dissolution of existing revolutionary organisations. He demanded, in effect, that they should voluntarily relinquish their hard-won hegemony in the post-revolutionary era.[7]

Talk of this kind threatened the leadership of the revolutionaries in the republic and the continuing existence of their organisation. Because Sung Chiao-jen's Central China Office had, since the disintegration of the Chinese League, practically assumed full leadership in the revolutionary camp, it naturally suffered most. It was in an effort to salvage this situation that Sung turned to support Sun, and fostered a reunion of all factions under the banner of the former league and Sun Yat-sen's leadership.

Shortly after Sun's arrival in Shanghai on 25 December 1911, a meeting was held by the revolutionaries to discuss the revival and reorganisation of the defunct Chinese League headquarters. On 2 January 1912 an announcement in the name of the defunct head office of the League appeared in a Chinese newspaper in Shanghai, stating the need to consolidate the position of the revolutionaries with a grand reunification of all factions under the League. It also hit back at talks of dissolution, and pointed out the danger if such suggestions were allowed to prevail.

> The revolution is still far from completion, since the arch-enemy is still fighting back like a cornered tiger. Even if the revolution is over it does not mean the end of responsibility for the revolutionary party . . . The responsibility of our party does not terminate with the fulfilment of nationalism, but with that of democracy and the social welfare of the people.[8]

In this document, the revolutionaries further sought to clear themselves of charges that they intended to subject China to a one-party dictatorship. They declared that, after the establishment of the republic and the restoration of order and stability, they would call for a party congress to draft a new constitution and reorganise their party into 'the greatest political party in China'.

This represented the view of the democrats in the revolutionary faction, particularly that of Sung Chiao-jen, who regarded the democratisation of China's governmental machine as a prerequisite for the regeneration of China. Had there been no pressures from the constitutionalists and the breakaway group of the party who challenged the leadership of his organisation, it is probable that Sung would not have been so readily inclined towards reunion with the southern revolutionary faction and towards support for Sun Yat-sen in the formation of the provisional government at this time. Thus the same document which is said to be Sung's work, and therefore represent his opinion, runs that: 'the reorganisation of our society and the union of our party is due to consideration of matters of an extremely urgent nature which bind us to our task despite the strain of differences between us'. It is probable that 'society' refers to Sung's Central China Office, and 'party' refers to the almost defunct Chinese League as a whole, and that the reunion of former factions was found necessary to meet an exigent situation.

As a result of this meeting in Shanghai, the foundation for the re-amalgamation of the factions within the Chinese League was laid. On 22 January 1912, after the establishment of the provisional government in Nanking, a formal meeting, attended by over two thousand members representing eighteen provinces, was opened in

Nanking.[9] At this meeting, two major decisions were taken. Firstly, at the suggestion of the Cantonese faction, the aims of the Chinese League were changed to the following, as expressed in its new oath: 'To overthrow the Manchu régime; to consolidate the republic, and to promote the welfare of the people'. Secondly, the Chinese League was to come out of its secret shell to become an overt political party.

According to Hu Han-min the first decision was arrived at without opposition, but opinions were sharply divided on the second. Some, including Hu Han-min himself, held that the aims of revolution were still far from fulfilment, and the future of the young republic was not certain. In their view the League should retain its original revolutionary and secret character, and should not put too much emphasis on legitimate political activities. Others contended that the military stage of the revolution was over, and hence the League should be transformed into a formal political party to participate in national politics in a constitutional manner, and, on behalf of the people, supervise the government.[10]

The argument against changing the nature of the Chinese League was not without some validity. Subsequent events tended to prove the correctness of the stand against change. Had this suggestion been followed, however, the Chinese League would have been flouting the trend of public opinion. It is doubtful whether in these circumstances the League would have fared any better. Hu Han-min, who regarded Sung as the leader of the League's right-wing group, as opposed to the more radical elements, and therefore held him to be chiefly responsible for changing the Chinese League into a normal political party, conceded that the reorganisation of the League was a natural development. For, as he explained, the League was composed of educated men, and was supported by a class of 'have nots', consisting of members of secret societies and destitute peasants as well as labourers and members of the bourgeois class among the overseas Chinese. Generally, party members did not realise the need for thoroughness in revolution. A lessening of pressure immediately gave rise to centrifugal tendencies which were a marked characteristic of the educated and the bourgeoisie. Hu further pointed out that the Chinese League was the only revolutionary political party in China at this time, but its organisation was imperfect. The party could not direct its members as the body does its limbs. There were good members who, sincere in their beliefs, were able to inspire others through their sacrifices, but they were individual efforts rather than the influence of the party. The educated looked upon freedom and equality as general ethical demands, and hence only a loosely knit organisation like the Chinese League could accommodate them. But even the League was not free from criticism for being over-rigid and dictatorial.[11] Hu seems to be criticising the weaknesses of the organisation and its members generally. But in effect Sung was the target of his attack, since he held Sung to be the leader of the right-wing group which voted for change.

A further significance of this meeting was the election of a member from each province to the party's highest executive body, the Council of Review *(P'ing-i-pu)*, and the election of Wang Ching-wei instead of Sun Yat-sen to be the head of the party. Sun, being the Provisional President of the republic, was considered unsuitable to run party affairs.[12] Wang, however, never took office. Though a well-known revolutionary, he had no real political capital. Besides, his acceptance would have appeared to challenge the leadership of Sun Yat-sen, who was very much his senior in the revolutionary movement, and who was also his fellow-provincial, who possessed the loyalty of a large number of Cantonese revolutionaries. Therefore, party affairs were mainly run by the Council of Review, a body closer to Sung's democratic concept of collective leadership than to Sun Yat-sen's idea of concentrating the party's authority in one leader, a strong indication of the diminution of Sun's authority and leadership in the party.

Following the abdication of the Manchu monarch in February 1912, and the resignation of Sun Yat-sen from the provisional presidency in favour of Yuan Shih-k'ai, the Chinese League convened another congress to carry out its pledge of January to change itself into an open political party. On 3 March 1912 it passed a new constitution, and adopted as its principal political goals the consolidation of the Republic of China and the realisation of the principle of social welfare. A nine-point political platform was also adopted. It included the unification of administration and promotion of local government; racial assimilation; state socialism; compulsory education; equality of the sexes; conscription; reorganisation of finance and a unified fiscal system; international equality; and attention to problems of migration and the opening up of waste lands.[13]

An important change in the reorganised Chinese League was the structure of the party's hierarchy. The prominent positions of President and Vice-Presidents were given to Sun Yat-sen, Huang Hsing, and Li Yuan-hung respectively, but the actual responsibility for the discharge of party affairs was vested in an executive body of ten men, of whom Sung Chiao-jen was one. The party's five administrative departments were also headed by men from this executive body. The were Wang Ching-wei (General Affairs), Sung Chiao-jen

(Political Affairs), Chang Chi (Public Relations), Li Chao-fu (Documents), and Chu Cheng (Finance).[14]

It can be seen that the reorganised Chinese League strongly resembled the Central China Office in organisation and power structure, suggesting the continuing and rising influence of Sung Chiao-jen and his central China group. At this time, when the Chinese League was striving to become the greatest political party in China, Sung's assumption of the leadership of the Political Affairs Department was of particular significance. The functions of this department were stated in the constitution as 'to study all political problems, draft political proposals, and co-operate with those members serving in government and parliament in order to effect a uniform opinion'.[15]

It is easy to see where the main source of the Chinese League's political power lay at this time. Sung's assumption of this office made him in fact, if not in name, the key man and the chief motivating force of the reorganised Chinese League.[16] It was an important victory for Sung Chiao-jen, and marked the beginning of widespread confidence in him among the members of the Chinese League. The assertion that the reorganisation of the Chinese League marked a major stride towards the fulfilment of Sung's political aspiration is no exaggeration.[17]

At about the same time as the Chinese League was organised into an open political party, a host of other political parties also came into existence. These parties were formed by either dissidents of the Chinese League, notably Chang Ping-lin and his Chekiang-Kiangsu-based Joint Association of the Republic of China and Sun Wu and his Hupeh-centred People's Society, or former constitutionalists and ex-bureaucrats, or their combinations. An example of the last category was the amalgamation of Chang Ping-lin's Joint Association and the bureaucrats led by Chang Ch'ien, Ch'eng Te-ch'uan, Hsiung Hsi-ling, and other members of the Preparatory Public Association for Constitutional Government *(Yu-pei li-hsien kung-hui)* to form the United Party *(T'ung-i-tang)* in April. Later the United Party amalgamated with Sun Wu's People's Society and other off-shoots of the constitutionalists to form the Republican Party *(Kung-ho-tang)*, with Li Yuan-hung as its President.[18] The other constitutionalists were at first divided into five separate parties, and each held its own until the autumn of 1912, when they finally decided on amalgamation to form the Democratic Party *(Min-chu-tang)*.

The history of China's political parties in this period is a story of frequent division and fusion between them. In this process one

distinctive feature can be recognised—the insurmountable difference between the revolutionary and the originally non-revolutionary camp. Despite numerous frequent fragmentations in both camps, subsequent fusions rarely embraced units of the opposing groups. The diagram facing p. 158, showing the development of China's political parties in this period, illustrates this point.

This permanent and unbridgeable gulf between the opposing camps was a factor of great importance, as it contributed substantially to the course of subsequent political development. The immediate political issues of the day were the consolidation of the republican institutions and the prevention of tyranny, which appeared likely to recur in the person of Yuan Shih-k'ai, the President, whose bureaucratic origin and military power made him the most unreliable and unconvincing supporter of democracy. The revolutionaries, led by Sung Chiao-jen, sought to achieve the end of consolidation by asserting parliamentary supremacy and the principle and practices of responsible cabinet government. The constitutionalists also professed to strive for this end. But, conscious of their origin, aggressively jealous of the revolutionary party, and deeply entrenched in their pro-government tradition, they were obliged to diverge from the policy of their opponents.

The revolutionaries sought to limit the power of the President; the constitutionalists rallied to enhance his position. The former wanted strict observance of the republican constitution, but the latter were ready to overlook it if it helped the President to curb the aspirations of the revolutionary party. If the revolutionaries demanded responsible cabinet government on party lines, the constitutionalists readily echoed the President's emphasis on talent irrespective of party membership. In short, they followed a policy of obstruction, doing all they could to block the aspirations of the revolutionary party, which, if attained, might give the opposition party political hegemony. Past enmity blurred their vision and made sagacious analysis of existing political issues impossible. They preferred to risk presidential domination than to see the rise of their traditional opponents.

This is not to say that, besides their somewhat obstinate opposition to the revolutionary party, the constitutionalists had no political objectives. Some of their leaders recognised possible difficulties with Yuan Shih-k'ai, who, in the words of one constitutionalist leader, 'was cunning and crafty, and not easy to work with'.[19] They also knew, however, that to be pro-Yuan was really their only alternative to a pro-revolutionary policy, since neutrality was dismissed as impracticable. They saw in their pro-Yuan policy a chance to gain power and influence in the nation. Their choice was also partly determined by inherent tradition. Enlightened despotism was first propounded by Liang Ch'i-ch'ao in 1906 as a necessary transitional stage towards full constitutional government. It was now revived by him in his offer of advice to Yuan Shih-k'ai.

The whole policy of the constitutionalists was summed up in Liang Ch'i-ch'ao's letter to Yuan Shih-k'ai on 23 February 1912, in which he advised Yuan to utilise a political party composed of former constitutionalists and the milder elements of the former revolutionary faction to oppose the radical revolutionaries.[20] It seems to have foreshadowed not only the political phenomenon which characterised the politics of the young republic, but also the process of amalgamation of some revolutionary and constitutionalist factions to form successively the United Party, the Republican and the Democratic Parties, and finally the Progressive Party *(Chin-pu-tang)*.

It is against this background that Sung Chiao-jen's political role in this period is to be seen. He was a minister in the first cabinet of the unified republic, and later a political party builder and democratic fighter.

The first cabinet of the Republican government in Peking consisted of a Premier and ten ministers. Apart from the Premier, T'ang Shao-yi, who seems to have attained a neutral position, and Shih Chao-chi, a professional diplomat who was related to T'ang Shao-yi and appointed by him to fill the vacant post of Minister for Communication, the rest were products of the north-south compromise. They represented three factions, the ex-bureaucrats headed by Yuan Shih-k'ai and his other followers, the Chinese League, and the Republican Party. The distribution of posts reflected the strength of respective parties. The key posts of Army, Navy, Interior, and Foreign Affairs went to Yuan's henchmen. The Chinese League had a major share of the lesser posts of Education, Judiciary, Agriculture and Forestry, Industry and Commerce. Hsiung Hsi-ling of the Republican Party was given the post of Finance, largely because of a deadlock between Yuan Shih-k'ai and the Chinese League. But Hsiung was no neutral man. Later events revealed that he sided with Yuan, and the cabinet floundered over his bickering and uncooperative attitude.[21] It was a coalition government in which the revolutionaries played at best second fiddle.[22]

In view of Sung's strong opinion about the undesirability of a coalition government, his participation in T'ang's cabinet, assuming a post he was ill-fitted for, needs an explanation. The following was Sung's answer:

> I have participated in this cabinet and assumed this post of Agriculture and Forestry. At a time like this, when the establish-

ment of fundamentals for law and government is the most urgent concern, it has never been my desire to undertake responsibilities of a dilatory nature. However, I thought at first that, as a member of the cabinet, I was also one who shaped the nation's policy. Perhaps there was a chance of putting my political conviction into practice. For this reason I joined the cabinet.[23]

Thus the hope of putting his political beliefs into practice through actual participation in the nation's policy-making body was Sung's reason for joining the republic's first cabinet. Moreover, two other factors must also have influenced his decision—his appraisal of the political realities at this time, and his duty to the revolutionary party. Firstly, as the republic was the result of a compromise between two major factions, it was natural that its government should be a coalition. The revolutionaries had even less choice than at the time when the Nanking provisional government was formed. Secondly, as has already been pointed out, the inclusion of the principle of cabinet government in the provisional constitution of the Republic of China was a victory for Sung Chiao-jen. It was logical that Sung should take his place in this system which he had fought so hard to achieve. Undoubtedly his colleagues and supporters also expected him to implement and strengthen this system from within.

In Peking this cabinet was widely known as the 'T'ang-Sung Cabinet', and Sung was regarded as the mastermind behind the Premier's manipulations to assert the cabinet's authority.[24] It was probably a speculation or rumour with malicious intent. Nevertheless it was sufficiently indicative of the role Sung was expected or suspected to have assumed as a cabinet minister. Friends and foes alike expected him to be the chief guardian of the principles of cabinet government and the principal architect of cabinet policies.

Unfortunately, this cabinet was not destined to achieve greatness. It was precluded from all chance of success at the outset by four factors: internal disharmony, conflicts with the President, bickering in the divided legislature, and difficulties in finance and foreign relations.

The first three factors were actually interrelated, and could be taken as one problem. Sung had foreseen the difficulties of coalition, but failed to comprehend their extent and their insoluble nature. This incomprehension was evident in his expressed hope of realising his political dream through this mixed cabinet. The function of the cabinet was to exercise the power of government for the President.[25] For this reason, all factions wanted to have their fingers in this cabinet pie. The revolutionaries participated in order to ensure the proper working of the cabinet, which was their only check on the power of the President. Yuan Shih-k'ai put his men in the cabinet to safeguard his own authority. The Republicans joined in on the side of Yuan because they did not wish to see domination by the Chinese League, and they were too weak by themselves to pursue an independent course.

Therefore there were two fundamentally incompatible groups of men in control of the nation's highest executive and policy-formulating body. As they were diametrically opposed to each other in aims, interests, and sincerity, it was no wonder that no policy emanated from this body. The cabinet meetings were either confined to petty or routine matters, which caused Sung Chiao-jen to complain bitterly, or had to face boycott by Yuan's men who, acting in their master's interests, did not wish to see any effective policies or solutions take shape in the cabinet.[26] Yuan Shih-k'ai wanted a cabinet to carry out his wishes, not one to make decisions for him. It was already a near miracle that he allowed the first cabinet to come into existence. His initial forebearance could only be due to the fact that he needed time to consolidate his position. Besides, it paid him to be diplomatic by giving in a little to the revolutionaries, and he undoubtedly felt that he could trust T'ang, the Premier, to manipulate it for him. When T'ang proved to be disobedient, he decided to discard the cabinet.[27]

The extent of non-co-operation and obstruction by Yuan's men in the cabinet can best be illustrated by the words of Sung Chiao-jen, who complained about the lack of unity and the handicap of party prejudice in the cabinet. He wrote in July 1912:

Since I entered the cabinet, nearly three months had gone by. But no major policies were in sight. At our daily meeting, only routine matters were discussed. No thoughts had ever been given to methods of separating the civil and military administration, nor had there been any suggestion on procedures to centralise administration. There were talks of repatriating the soldiers but there was no offer of plans to take over control of the provincial armies. There were also talks of reorganising finance, but no one knew what to do when the emergency loan from the Six-Power Consortium was used up. The prevailing attitude was to pass time by delay and procrastination, a sign of deficiency in unity, ideals, and spirit required for the formulation and execution of major policies. Although Premier T'ang has the wish to lead and guide, and all the ministers desired reform and progress, their approach was individualistic, and their pursuits were handicapped by the lack of co-ordination, rendering administration completely devoid of system and orderliness. Adding to these the divergent factional prejudices and personal ambitions, the hope for harmony and co-operation was hard to fulfil indeed.[28]

The pro-Yuan faction's non-co-operation, and even deliberately obstructive policy, could further be illustrated by the way Sung Chiao-jen's effort to effect a basic governmental policy was thwarted. Sung believed that in the twentieth century China could maintain its existence only if it could achieve national unity and an effective and highly centralised government. Accordingly, on 28 May 1912, worried by the harsh conditions of foreign loans and feeling indignant over the meanness of foreign powers, Sung spoke at a cabinet meeting on the dangers facing China and the need to arrive at a definite policy to solve her difficulties. According to Sung, all members of the cabinet were moved by his appeal, and asked him to draw up a policy for consideration on the following day. He sat up all night to draw up the policy. He diagnosed that China's basic difficulties stemmed from two primary sources, weak central government and chaotic finance. Hence he suggested that immediate measures should be taken to consolidate the central government's authority and to straighten up the country's finance. To achieve the first, he proposed separating the civil and military administration, and placing both military and civil financial administration under the control of the central government. For the second goal, he suggested the organisation of a central bank, the unification of currency notes and their production, the reorganisation of the existing revenue system, the introduction of new taxes, and the reduction of army personnel.[29]

Sung's policy, aiming to strengthen the hands of the central government and to reduce China's reliance on foreign loans, might not have been a sufficient cure for China's trouble. But had his plan been accepted and implemented, the infant republic would at least have been given a chance of restoring stability, and its first cabinet the credit of having made this effort. Unfortunately it died a premature death. It was sabotaged by the Republican Party's Minister of Finance, who handed in his resignation at the inopportune moment when the cabinet met to discuss Sung's proposal.

The story of Hsiung Hsi-ling's resignation, coming at the vital moment when the cabinet was arriving at a definite policy to solve China's problems, has never been properly told. Ostensibly it was due to difficulties in loan negotiations. But there is other evidence which casts doubt on this simple explanation. There were reports of uncordial relations between him and the Premier, and of close friendship between him and Liang Shih-yi, Yuan's henchman. The following is one of these reports:

Liang Shi-yi and Hsiung Hsi-ling entered the *Han-lin** in the same year, during the former Ch'ing dynasty. The contact between the

---

* Han-lin-yüan, the Imperial College of Literature at Peking.

President and the cabinet ministers was mainly maintained through him [Liang]. Therefore, he is still an important figure in the political circle today. Liang was a strong supporter of Hsiung Hsi-ling for the post [of Finance], and exerted all his influence to get Hsiung to accept this post. One day he said to Hsiung, 'The fact that you have not appointed a Deputy Finance Minister all this time is evidence of your unwillingness to assume this office. Whatever it may be, the Deputy Finance Minister must be chosen. How about deciding it at your earliest convenience?' Thereupon Hsiung reluctantly produced a list of people he wished to appoint to his ministry . . . This Liang took and put away in his pocket. On 3 [June] he went to the cabinet. When he saw that Hsiung was present, he informed T'ang [the premier] of the list made by Hsiung. Before he could show it, Hsiung snatched it and said, 'I have now resigned, and these appointments may now be cancelled'.

Again,

Last Saturday [8 June] when all the cabinet ministers met at the presidential palace for a conference, arguments arose between them. Hsiung declared that he would resign after the loan agreement had been signed, and T'ang replied that, if the Finance Minister resigned, then he would ask the president to invite others to form a cabinet. It is not clear what Hsiung had said in between which caused the usually mild and serene scholar, Ts'ai Yuan-p'ei, to object in a loud voice. He said, 'The Finance Minister should not behave in this manner. If he is not satisfied with the present cabinet, he may form another Republican government'. He meant, of course, the formation of a government by the Republican Party.[30]

Clearly Hsiung was basically hostile towards the Premier and his Chinese League colleagues, and his resignation and absence from the cabinet at a decisive moment could not have been mere coincidence. It was aimed to hurt T'ang and frustrate Sung's effort. Both the President and the Finance Minister, and their factions, had good reason for preventing Sung's plan affecting finance and the control and usage of funds from being implemented by the cabinet. Nothing likely to fortify the position of the cabinet or to enhance the prestige of the Chinese League should ever be allowed to materialise.

The obstructive nature of Hsiung Hsi-ling's action was even more evident when it was connected to the events that followed. Immediately after his resignation, which caused the cabinet to postpone its decision on Sung's scheme, the Premier had to present the government's policy on the issues in question to the Senate. Since there was no decision by the cabinet, he had nothing to offer. This sparked off a barrage of criticism from the Senate, particularly from members of

Hsiung's Republican Party. Their attack on the cabinet was so vehement that the Premier was obliged to resign.

After mediation, in which the President was delighted to be more or less an arbiter between the disputing parties, the crisis was smoothed over. T'ang consented to carry on as Premier, and Hsiung also agreed to remain in his post, on the condition that some understanding with regard to loans should be arrived at between the factions before he resumed his duties. But the cabinet after this setback had lost even that little zeal which it had first shown towards Sung's suggestion. Several times he had tried to revive its interest in his proposal, but obtained no response. The ill effects of an incoherent cabinet were now apparent to him, and Sung Chiao-jen made up his mind to resign as soon as the government's loan negotiations with the foreign powers came to an end.[31] He did not have long to wait. The cabinet had barely survived this ordeal a fortnight when it capsized under a presidential storm. The Premier was virtually driven to resign by Yuan Shih-ka'i, who, having come to the conclusion that T'ang was no longer his obedient follower, deliberately infringed the Premier's constitutional right of endorsing all presidential actions by commissioning Wang Chih-hsiang, whom T'ang had committed to appoint to the governorship of Chihli, to a post in Nanking without the Premier's consent.[32]

Only the causes for the failure of the first cabinet have been described. It remains to narrate the cabinet's foreign relations to complete the picture.

Just as economics were from the very beginning a basic factor underlying China's foreign relations with European powers, the cabinet's contact with foreign nations centred on the question of finance. A century of maladministration, foreign exploitation, and intermittent warfare, both internal and external, had so disorganised China's economy that China had completely lost its financial independence by the first decade of this century. The Manchu government depended on foreign loans to meet its administrative costs. The new republic was no different. The only departure was the Premier's attempt to break the strangle-hold of the Four-Power Consortium's loan monopoly by borrowing from a Belgian bank, an institution of a non-consortium nation. This served to worsen relations not only between the first cabinet and the consortium nations but also within the cabinet, between the Premier and the Finance Minister, who preferred to appease the consortium powers. The Four-Power Consortium exercised pressure to block the Belgian loan, and demanded supervision of the Republic's budget and expenditure and the repatriation of soldiers as conditions for its own loans. These were, as one journalist explained, due partly to their lack of confidence in China's existing situation and partly to their hostility towards the Premier, whom they charged with responsibility for the Belgian loan, and with a breach of good faith.[33]

Negotiations with the consortium were broken off on 3 May 1912 over the supervision clause. At a cabinet meeting that followed, T'ang proposed the introduction of a compulsory national debt to meet the government's needs. Ts'ai Yuan-p'ei suggested two ways of dismissing the revolutionary army. One was to appeal to their dignity and disperse them without pay, and the other was to authorise them individually to raise subscriptions for themselves. Sung Chiao-jen rejected both as impractical, and advocated a reasonable accommodation of foreign demands in order to obtain the much needed funds. Sung's view won the support of the majority of ministers, and decided the issue. The Finance Minister was to take over negotiations from the Premier. He was known to have opposed the Belgian loan. With this background, he was confident that he could improve the cabinet's relations with the consortium. But the Premier took a dim view of his optimism, and thus sowed the seeds of discord between them.[34] Thereafter their friction increased, and extended into the Senate, where the pro-Hsiung Republican faction accused the Premier of obstructing loan negotiations, while the pro-premier members from the Chinese League counter-charged Hsiung and his supporters with conspiring to overthrow T'ang's cabinet. This state of affairs continued until T'ang and his cabinet offered to resign on 20 May.[35]

The weakness of the whole Republican set-up was thus exposed. Disagreements and quarrels in the cabinet and in the Senate, and the detached relationship between the cabinet and the National Assembly played straight into the hands of Yuan Shih-k'ai, the President who watched with delight the feuds between the nation's Legislature and the cabinet, and the discord between the political parties. Amidst accusations and counter-accusations, he saw his opportunity of rising above them all and making them dance to his tune. This goal was not far off. He first attained the position of mediator, and then that of arbiter.

A word should be said about the republic's Legislature, commonly known as the Senate. This body began its formal existence on 28 January 1912 under the Nanking provisional government. Under the 'Structural Outline of the Provisional Government of the Republic of China', it consisted of three representatives from each province. The method of producing them was left to the respective provincial governors. As a result, this body was a mixture of three elements:

members appointed by the provincial government, members representing provincial assemblies, and members directly or indirectly elected by the people. In such a gathering, naturally unity was lacking and friction was rife. Within one month of its establishment, members of Kiangsu and Hupeh resigned in protest against the loan policy of the Nanking provisional government, and there were talks of forming a rival Legislature in Hupeh, on the grounds that the Nanking Legislature was not an elected body.[36] The Senate survived this upheaval, but the weaknesses of this heterogeneous body were also fully exposed.

Generally the revolutionaries were able to retain a precarious hold over the Senate. This was evident in the national capital issue, in which Sun Yat-sen, with Huang Hsing's aid, was able to get his way with them. But that was the last time the revolutionaries managed to carry this body. Following the removal of the provisional government to Peking, the revolutionary party's influence waned. The increase of members on the eve of its transfer, from thirty-nine to more than a hundred, under the newly promulgated provisional constitution drastically altered the composition of the Senate to the disadvantage of the revolutionary party. The Republican Party, composed of former progressive bureaucrats, constitutionalists, and breakaways from the revolutionary camp, now held a slender majority over the Chinese League, each occupying just over forty seats. With the aid of a third party, the United Republican Party (*T'ung-i kung-ho-tang*), which was mainly composed of ex-League members and occupied twenty-five seats in the Senate, the Republicans could harass and obstruct the revolutionary party at will.[37] It was in this situation that the Chinese League lost both the chairmanship and the vice-chairmanship of the Senate to its political opponents.[38]

T'ang Shao-yi, the Premier, had become a member of the Chinese League shortly after his appointment by Yuan Shih-k'ai. It was a fatal mistake. Irrespective of his sincerity and intention to maintain harmony, he was identified as a member of the revolutionary mob, a target for opposition. It made things doubly difficult for him when he tried to assert the cabinet's authority, which was also identified as the League's policy. Not only did Yuan Shih-k'ai distrust him despite twenty-six years of close acquaintance, but the non-revolutionary elements also suspected him and did not wish to see him succeed.

The Premier was thus driven to resign. He slipped away from Peking to Tientsin on 15 June 1912, and never returned. His explanation to Liang Shih-yi, who went on Yuan Shih-k'ai's behalf to ask for T'ang's return to Peking, revealed the heart of the matter. He could not on account of personal friendship sacrifice principles in discharging national affairs.[39] Before this event, Sung Chiao-jen and his close colleagues in the cabinet had already made up their minds to resign from their posts. They were held back only by T'ang Shao-yi, who asked them to delay until current loan negotiations were completed. Now that T'ang had left, there was nothing for them to stay for. T'ang's resignation was formally accepted by the President on 26 June, and those of Sung Chiao-jen and his colleagues on 14 July.[40]

Immediately after T'ang left for Tientsin, rumours about the cause of his unannounced departure and speculations on his successor were rife. Amidst this confusion, a noteworthy point emerged. Sung Chiao-jen was once again the controversial figure, the target of malicious attack. The old charge that he wanted to be the Premier was revived by his political enemies. Moreover, it was accompanied by a new charge, that T'ang was squeezed out by Sung Chiao-jen, as were the other ministers from the Chinese League.[41]

Formerly Sung had not bothered to defend himself against such charges. Perhaps this was because it was then only suspicion among some members of his own party. But this time it was different. It was not only a deliberate attack by anti-Chinese League faction on himself, but also a calculated smear on his party. Therefore we find him replying in an open letter to the press, dismissing the absurdity of these charges and challenging his enemies to produce evidence to support their accusations. He further exhorted his adversaries to confine their criticism to political principle and practice, and not resort to personal attacks.[42]

An important feature of this crisis was the careful avoidance by all parties of the real issue, the President's breach of the provisional constitution. From Yuan's point of view, the resignations of T'ang Shao-yi, Sung Chiao-jen, and other cabinet ministers were merely due to unhappy personal relations. To him, their resignations were not even due to party strife.[43] To others, especially people unsympathetic towards the Chinese League—such as Chang Ping-lin, who wrote a strongly worded letter to denounce the resigning ministers—it was due to partisan squabbles and conflicting personal ambitions.[44] At the inter-parliamentary party conference on 21 June 1912, called to consider this crisis, discussions were also confined to views on future policies of the respective parties with regard to cabinet government and its composition.[45] Some, such as Sun Wu, who was formerly Sung's comrade in arms and now a member of the Republican Party, regarded the ministers' resignations as merely the result of frustration and anger, and accused Sung of shirking responsibility in face of difficulties, so that Sung found it necessary to reply in an open letter clarifying his stand.[46] But even Sung himself carefully avoided a direct attack on the President's unconstitutional action. This silence on the constitutional issue in Li Chien-nung's view was due to ignorance.[47] Yet, in the communiques of the Chinese League's Peking headquarters of 23 June and 1 July, Yuan's breach of the constitution, and its implications, were brought out clearly.[48] An acceptable explanation, then, is that Yuan Shih-k'ai with his powerful army was too strong to be challenged. This was an important consideration which had earlier led the revolutionaries to relinquish leadership in the republic in favour of Yuan. Now the same consideration caused all to turn a blind eye on this vital issue. Neither Sung nor Ts'ai Yuan-p'ei, who explained publicly their reasons for resignation, mentioned Yuan's violation of the constitution. They preferred to take a less provocative stand, that of advocating a party cabinet. This, in their view, was more in keeping with their party line and more within their power to achieve without throwing down the gauntlet to Yuan Shih-k'ai.[49] Accordingly, they communicated their decision to the other parties at an inter-parliamentary conference on 21 June. The Republicans chose to support a non-party cabinet policy. The United Republicans agreed with the Republicans, but rejected their opinion that the premiership ought to be left to a man of Yuan's choice.[50]

Their inter-parliamentary consultation produced no useful agreement or understanding, nor a suitable working basis for closer co-operation between the three parties. Accordingly, the Chinese League resolved to stay out of all future coalition governments, and communicated their resolution to the President. If the League had no doubt about the undesirability of coalition government, the President was convinced of its desirability, and made this clear to the Chinese League. He in fact stated that as long as he was President, he would not permit the appearance of a single-party cabinet.[51]

Thus Yuan left his opponents in no uncertainty as to his intentions. The gulf between him and Sung Chiao-jen began to widen. Among the parliamentary parties, the Republican and the United Republican basically agreed with Yuan's idea of a 'talent cabinet', that is, that talent should be the sole criterion for appointment to the cabinet since neither was strong enough to form a cabinet on its own. The Chinese League was left quite alone in its insistence on party cabinet government. Even within the League different shades of opinion were found. This was clear at its meeting on 28 June, called to make a definite decision on the issue in the light of the President's uncompromising tone. Liu K'uie-i led the opposition to the proposed stand on party cabinet government, on the grounds that, in consideration of the League's weak position in Peking, non-participation in future cabinets would so isolate the party from government affairs that it would impair rather than enhance the party's position. A heated debate ensued. It was only after Sung Chiao-jen expressed his implacable stand on the party cabinet platform and his intention to uphold it at the cost of his party membership that the League resolved on its adoption. The following were reported to be the words of Sung Chiao-jen at this meeting, and illustrate his determination on this issue:

> In the cabinet reshuffle, I have already made clear to the public my stand on the principle of one-party government, and that members of our party will not join any government containing members of other parties. Even now, if no other cabinet members from this party wish to resign, I will resign alone. If party members do not approve my stand, I may also on account of principle and integrity leave the party.[52]

Henceforth no League members were to join Yuan's coalition cabinet.

To close Sung's official career in the Republican government, a word should be said about him as Minister for Agriculture and Forestry. This portfolio was a new creation under the republic. In submitting the names of his cabinet ministers for the Senate's approval in Nanking, the Premier, T'ang Shao-yi, said of Sung Chiao-jen:

> Although Sung Chiao-jen is not a graduate of a specialised school for agriculture and forestry, he has high attainments in modern knowledge. Besides, he can devote himself to duties with zeal and humility.[53]

In view of his interest in geography and economics, it was also an apt choice, but Sung himself would have preferred responsibility of a more urgent nature, such as foreign affairs or finance.[54] Prior to his appointment to the cabinet, there was talk of sending him to Japan to smooth the somewhat strained relations with that country. Therefore, on hearing of his selection by T'ang Shao-yi for a ministerial post, he at once declined, and suggested that he be sent on a special mission to Japan to obtain the latter's recognition of the republic, and that after the mission he 'would return to devote his attention to party affairs and to give support to the government'.[55]

On T'ang's insistence, however, he accepted the appointment and proceeded to draft plans to develop and promote the nation's agriculture and forestry. He held that agriculture was the basis of China's economy, and thus the main goal of his ministry was to improve and increase its output. He believed that China's agriculture had reached a high level of development but, in comparison with that of Western nations, it was backward because of the lack of planning in former times. Therefore he held that the immediate task of his ministry was to formulate a policy and to establish an apparatus to put it into effect. To increase agricultural output he suggested three main methods: the opening up of unused land, the exploitation and conservation of forests, and irrigation. Sung suggested that the opening up of unused land in China's outlying regions should be left to private enterprise, with active aid and encouragement from the government.

To facilitate these undertakings Sung suggested the establishment of special institutions for rural education and special banks to finance rural development schemes. He planned to accomplish his objectives in three stages, within ten years. The first was to conduct a survey of the nation's land and forests, the second was to formulate a policy, and the third was to implement this policy.[56]

He did not, however, remain long enough in his ministerial post to carry out his plan. He took up the post in April and resigned in the following June. Nevertheless, within the short time he was in office, several institutions connected with his rural development plan were brought into existence. In Peking experimental stations for agriculture, forestry, and pastoral industry were established, lecture centres for agriculture were introduced, and experts in forestry were sent out to survey the forests of Manchuria. A system of administration for forestry, reclamation, and fisheries had also been drawn up.[57] Politically, the Ministry of Agriculture and Forestry was only of of secondary importance in the infant republic. But in practical terms it was most important. In subsequent years turbulent China could not give its agriculture the attention it needed, however. The fulfilment of Sung's idea for establishing a national agricultural bank had to wait another twenty years.*

---

* According to Chang Yü-lan, *Chung-kuo yin-hang fa-chan shih*, p. 89, the first rural bank appeared in 1915 in the vicinity of Peking. In 1918 a so-called Chinese Agricultural and Industrial Bank was formed, but it existed only in name. The first real rural bank was founded in 1928 in Kiangsu.

TWELVE

Struggle for Democracy

HAVING PERSUADED his colleagues to adopt his stand on responsible
party government, Sung naturally directed his attention to ways and
means of fulfilling this goal. The main opposition to this policy, as
has already been noted, came from the President. To overcome this
opposition, two courses were open to the Chinese League, the overthrow of the President by force, or the gaining of his submission by
constitutional means. Following the fall of the first cabinet, rumours
of an imminent second revolution were rife.[1] In view of the circumstances under which the Chinese League accepted Yuan as President,
however, the use of force against him was out of the question. It was
logical that the second alternative must be pursued.

To compel the President to submit to the principle of party government by constitutional means meant in fact that the Chinese League
should seek to control the nation's highest representative body, the
Legislature, which, through its various checks on the President, as
empowered under the provisional constitution and undoubtedly also
under the new constitution after its completion, provided the only
possible means of harnessing the President to the Chinese League's
policies.

Therefore the control of the Legislature became the first objective
of the Chinese League. This could be achieved only if the League
could gain wider national support. To extend its influence, the
League could either expand its organisation in the hope that it could
gather sufficient influence in the nation to win the forthcoming
national election in January required under the provisional constitution,* or alternatively, it could seek the support of the already
existing political parties through amalgamation.

The second course was by far the more attractive to Sung Chiao-
jen, for the following reasons. Firstly, the first course offered no

---

* The Provisional Constitution of the Republic of China, Article 53, laid down
that a national parliamentary election was to be held within ten months of the
promulgation of the provisional constitution, i.e. by 11 January 1913.

certainty in results, whereas the second could score immediately. If the League managed to win over the minor parties, especially those such as the United Republican, which had already wielded some influence in the senate, not only would the prospects of winning the forthcoming election be good, but the League would have immediate control of the Senate. Secondly, amidst political instability and chaos, and quarrels between the numerous political parties which came into existence in the post-revolutionary era, Chinese public opinion had turned against the multi-party phenomenon. Students of politics who were familiar with British and American political practices wished to see the introduction of a bi-party system into the Chinese political scene. Thus Chang Shih-chao, a returned student from Britain, wrote on the need to destroy existing political parties to provide room for the rise of a bi-party system. He suggested that a political consultative congress should be called, in which all parties should participate to thrash out their basic differences, so that they might regroup into two opposing camps.[2]

Sung Chiao-jen had shown great interest in the British political system, and his thinking closely resembled that of Chang Shih-chao.[3] Therefore it was not surprising that he leapt at the first opportunity of amalgamation. He had good personal relationships with a number of political leaders in other parties. Hence it was within his capacity to bring about a *rapprochement* with their parties. A serious obstacle was that these parties were led by dissidents of the League. They were unlikely to return to the fold unless the League was willing to meet them halfway, by at least modifying some of the organisational features and aims they originally found displeasing. In short, amalgamation to form a new party rather than a simple absorption into the League was demanded by the other parties. The United Republicans had in fact advanced three conditions as the basis of amalgamation. They demanded that the name of the Chinese League should be changed, the principle of social welfare be removed, and the structure of the party be reorganised.[4]

These demands of the lesser parties constituted the main difficulties which Sung had to overcome. The Chinese League after the revoluton was thought of as the main founding party of the republic, and as such, it was felt, should be preserved for ever. This view was held by a strong section of the Chinese League, and was successfully sustained against pressure for its abolition during the time of the Nanking provisional government.[5] Even as late as July 1912, the idea of adopting a new name for the League to avoid public hostility and to facilitate the conduct of party affairs was rejected twice, first by the majority of the party's office-holders at their Peking headquarters, and later by the majority of members at a party congress on 21 July 1912.[6] The opposition to the change of name or platform was so strong that Sung Chiao-jen, who was elected by the congress to head the League's General Affairs Department, could only make a general statement, pointing out the current dangers facing China, and the need to build up a strong political party to save her.

> The ways to strengthen our party [Sung declared] are firstly, to do our best to line up with other parties which are willing to support our policy, and secondly, to pay great attention to the [coming] parliamentary election to make sure that our party members occupy the majority of seats.[7]

The threat of force which was used against the Senate by the President to secure the Senate's approval of his choice of Lu Cheng-hsiang as Premier, however, brought home the political reality in China to all parties except the pro-Yuan factions, and they realised that they must unite to secure victory in the coming election if the undemocratic and authoritarian tendency of the President, aided by the sectarian Republicans, was to be checked, and the principle of party government enforced.[8]

Seizing this opportunity, Sung Chiao-jen communicated to Sun Yat-sen and Huang Hsing the three conditions of the United Republican Party for amalgamation. They approved, and Sung immediately instructed Chang Yao-tseng to draft a new constitution.[9] On 5 August thirteen leaders, representing respectively the Chinese League, the United Republican Party, and the Nationalist Public Party *(Kuo-min kung-tang)*, met formally in Peking to find common grounds for amalgamation.

It was a meeting of great importance. Unfortunately it was not well recorded. Still, from the sketchy information available, the essence of the discussion at this meeting can be pieced together. It centred around two main aspects of the proposed amalgamation— the name of the new party so formed, and its basic political platform. On the first point, the Chinese League suggested 'Democratic Party', which was most probably Sung's choice. But the majority preferred 'Nationalist Party', for two reasons. Firstly, the Democrats of United States of America had not won an election for many years. Secondly, the name 'Nationalist' would serve to remind the nation that, under the Republican system of government, people were the masters and the new party had their welfare at heart.[10]

On the question of party platform, the Chinese League's proposal contained two lines of four characters each. They read 'the consolidation of the republic', and 'the preservation and promotion of the welfare of the people'. The representatives of the other two parties opposed the term 'welfare of the people', however, on the grounds that it had a narrow connotation which could be easily confused with the League's principle of social welfare. They proposed that it be changed to 'the consolidation of the republic' and 'the practice of equal citizenry'. The League's representative, Li Chao-fu, insisted on the inclusion of the word 'welfare' however, arguing that its removal from the new party's platform would offend the radical wing of the Chinese League and prevent the project of amalgamation from consummation. Finally a compromise was found. The fourth of the new party's five political planks was to be changed from 'the adoption of a socialistic policy' to 'the adoption of the people's social welfare policy'.*

The next point discussed at this meeting was the system of organisation. Here the League's proposal to adopt collective leadership met with unanimous approval. Under this system an elected committee of seven was to be formed. It was to be the party's highest executive body. After some discussion, an executive head was added to the committee, but, in order to prevent the concentration of power in one person, and to ensure equality within the executive committee, the executive head was to be chosen from the committee members by the members themselves. In other words it was the same system which Sung Chiao-jen had introduced for his Central China Office. The objective of the system also remained the same—to prevent the tyranny of a single man.

Seven names were submitted tentatively for the first executive committee. They were Sun Yat-sen, Huang Hsing, Ts'en Ch'un-hsuan, Ts'ai O, Wu Ching-lien, Chang Feng-hsiang, and Sung Chiao-jen.[11]

The foundation for amalgamation was thus laid. Thereafter things moved swiftly. Two other parties, the Nationalist Mutual Advancement Party *(Kuo-min kung-chin-hui)* and the Republican Party for Practical Advancement *(Kung-ho shih-chin-hui)*, which feared isolation, also sought amalgamation with the Chinese League and were accepted. Within five days after the meetings of 5 August, the respective negotiators reported to their own parties on the agreement reached. A meeting of the Chinese League was held in its Peking headquarters on 10 August to hear Sung Chiao-jen's report on the substance of negotiation, and the basic agreements for amalgamation. When it was requested that they endorse the agreement, an overwhelming majority voted in favour. Only five of the more than

---

* The other four political planks of the Nationalist Party were: maintain political unity, promote local government, carry out the policy of racial assimilation, and preserve international peace.

seventy leaders present opposed amalgamation. Consequently negotiations for amalgamation reached their final stage. The League elected four persons to meet the representatives of other interested parties to hammer out the final arrangement.[12]

On the following day a formal inter-party conference was presided over by Sung Chiao-jen. Sung informed the gathering of the League's approval of the proposed basis for amalgamation. The representatives of the other parties followed suit. Apart from a query by the Nationalist Mutual Advancement Party on the fourth political plank, the adoption of a social welfare policy, amalgamation became a fact. Subsequent discussions mainly centred on organisational matters. In this connection, a point of significance was the opposition to Sung Chiao-jen's idea of creating a sixth department of electioneering. It was rejected on the grounds that electioneering by political parties was held in low esteem in Chinese tradition. Yet winning the coming election was the central concern of the new party! As a compromise, electioneering was relegated to be a sub-function of the Department of Political Affairs, so that it would not be too 'obtrusive'.[13] This contradiction is an indication of the true state of China in 1912 and the difficulties in the way of democracy. It was essentially a problem of conflict between old and new, existing not only between individual personalities but also in the mental make-up of the majority of China's political leaders.

The new party was thus knocked into shape at this conference, which closed a successful day by appointing Sung Chiao-jen, Chang Yao-tseng of the Chinese League, and Yang Nan-sheng of the Nationalist Public Party to draft a declaration to announce the birth of the new party. On 13 August this declaration was issued to the world. It expressed the new party's intention to devote itself to the task of reconstruction under the republic, and its aspiration to become a nucleus of political power in the constitutional republic, and to help to bring about a bi-party system.[14] On the same day a communique was issued from Sung's Department of General Affairs of the Chinese League to all its regional branches, informing them of the League's amalgamation with other parties, and that 'from now on, ours will be the strongest of the republic's political parties [and] despite all its prowess, the Republican Party will not be able to challenge us!'[15]

On 25 August the Nationalist Party was formally established. Its inauguration was arranged to coincide with the visit of Sun Yat-sen and Huang Hsing, so that the new party could receive the blessing of these two revolutionary giants. Sun Yat-sen did not disappoint his colleagues. He attended the inaugural ceremony of the Nationalist

Party and addressed an audience of 2,000, praising its establishment and exhorting its members to strive for its fullest development.[16] After the endorsement of its constitution by the gathering, election to offices followed. In accordance with article eighteen of the new constitution, nine men were elected to its highest executive committee, and Sung Chiao-jen was one among them. In terms of votes scored, Sung came third in popularity, the highest number of votes being cast for Sun Yat-sen and Huang Hsing.[17] In terms of responsibility, however, Sung was undoubtedly the pivotal figure in the new party. Sun was elected on 3 September by the executive committee as its head, a position which made him *primus inter pares*, and he then delegated this position to Sung Chiao-jen. Obviously Sun's name still carried influence, but all actual responsibilities were Sung Chiao-jen's; it was Sung who was the moving spirit and the chief architect of the Nationalist Party. Outwardly, Sun abstained from office in order to concentrate his effort on the country's economic development, particularly on his scheme to build 100,000 miles of railways. But the new party's opponents charged that he was forced out of office by Sung Chiao-jen.[18] In view of Sun's personality and his past connections with the so-called 'moderate' wing of the revolutionary party, the truth was probably that Sun could see that the new party, brought into existence mainly by Sung Chiao-jen and his close associates, could be run without him. Besides, being only one of nine members of the executive committee, each with equal status, was probably not the kind of leadership he desired for himself. The explanation provided by his followers nowadays is that he fundamentally disagreed with the formation of the Nationalist Party, and tolerated it only because of the circumstances under which he found himself.[19]

The much criticised features of the new party were its concentration on the winning of seats in Parliament, its removal of the principle of social welfare from the party's aims, and the disappearance from its political planks of two important goals of the Chinese League— insistence on equality of the sexes and striving for international equality. It was held that the concentration on popularity and expansion led to an indiscriminate intake of members of doubtful allegiance and sincerity, thereby diluting the revolutionary spirit and causing degeneracy in the party. The removal of the demand for equality of the sexes was, it was said, a capitulation to the conservative forces, while the shift from 'striving for international equality' to one of 'maintaining international peace' was a retrograde step aimed to appease foreign nations.[20]

In short, the main criticism lay in the new party's departure from some of the primary goals of the League, and Sung Chiao-jen naturally became the target of the new party's critics. The fact was that in 1912 there was no other workable alternative except leaving Yuan Shih-k'ai in supreme control, which, as suggested by some historians, was what Sun Yat-sen wanted.[21] But this suggestion does not take into consideration China's national and international position in 1912. Externally, China ran into difficulties with Britain, Russia, and Japan over Tibet, Sinkiang, Mongolia, and Manchuria. Internally, China had acute financial problems awaiting solution. The performance of Yuan Shih-k'ai's government so far had not indicated any ability to solve these problems. In other words, besides the party's aim of preventing tyranny, which sprang from a deep-seated distrust of Yuan and the genuineness of his desire to establish democracy, it remained doubtful about the competence of Yuan's governing clique to meet China's exigencies. This was clearly expressed in Sung Chiao-jen's utterances, both before and after the new party's formation.[22]

Sun Yat-sen himself obviously appreciated the difficulties of the time and therefore gave the new party his support. He took part in its establishment, accepted a nominal post, and exhorted party members to work for its fullest development. He even took the trouble to write to the overseas branches of the League where his influence was strongest urging them to accept the change and the new leadership.[23] When the champions of equality for women fought for their cause, first by resorting to fisticuffs with Sung Chiao-jen, and later by petitioning Sun Yat-sen for his intervention, Sun defended the party by saying that, in view of the dangers confronting China, the consolidation of government should have first priority.[24] As for criticism of the party's departure from the basic aims of the League, the studied opinion of Chang Shih-chao, a non-party observer, sheds a different light on the situation. After consulting important leaders of the League such as Sun Yat-sen and Yang T'ing-tung, Chang came to the conclusion that neither the principle of social welfare nor the equality of men and women, both regarded as important principles of the League, could be called proper political planks of the League, for he claimed that Sun Yat-sen had told him at an interview that the principle of social welfare was a policy for the future rather than the present, while Yang T'ing-tung, a League member in the Senate, said that there was no unanimity of opinion within the League on the women's demand for equal political rights.[25]

Clearly these so-called political planks of the League, which were alleged to have been discarded by Sung Chiao-jen from the new party's platform, had ceased to be held in high esteem long before the formation of the Nationalist Party. In this respect Sung was a political realist. He distinguished the immediate from the distant, and in this sense the practical from the impractical. He demanded that

> When we promote a principle, we must examine the nature and function of this principle itself, and consider the existing conditions and other independent factors, and thereby determine the results it is likely to bring.[26]

It was this attitude which led Sung to accept deviations from some of the original goals of the League, and to write a little earlier an article on socialism in which he pleaded with his contemporaries to adopt a critical and cautious approach to the propagation of ideas of such a radical and unexplored nature.

Among the last words of T'ang Shao-yi in Tientsin before quitting the premiership were:

> Judging by the national trend of today, no one except Yuan Shih-k'ai can maintain unity in China. As for the government of China, nothing except the sincere co-operation of Hsiang-ch'eng [Yuan Shih-k'ai] with the Nationalist Party* is workable.[27]

These words reflected the trend of public opinion at this time. The result of the first notion was the assumption of the republic's provisional presidency by Yuan Shih-k'ai, and that of the second was the formation of the first coalition cabinet. Unfortunately, the key word, 'co-operation', meant different things to different factions. To Yuan Shih-ka'i, co-operation meant complete submission to his authority and leadership. To the revolutionaries it meant the adoption of the principle and practice of cabinet government. The fate of the first cabinet was thus predestined to fail.

Even within the Chinese League, there was no unanimity between its leaders as to the form and extent of co-operation with Yuan Shih-k'ai. To Sun Yat-sen, co-operation meant complete withdrawal of the League from politics, to concentrate on social and industrial development through education and enterprises in heavy industry and communications. He wanted his party to play a non-political role and to perform a separate auxiliary function complementary to the new state.[28] But Sung Chiao-jen advocated the opposite course of action. Co-operation to him meant cabinet government, which was to assume the full responsibility of government on behalf of the president and the nation's Legislature. Huang Hsing, on the other

---

* The Chinese League was intended. At the time T'ang Shao-yi was heard to have expressed this opinion, the Nationalist Party was not yet in existence.

hand, was of the opinion that a strong stable government could only result from men of talent, supported by a majority party. With this conviction, Huang Hsing tried to press everyone to join his party.[29]

The actual events demonstrated that Sun Yat-sen's idea of co-operation carried little weight either in the League or later in the Nationalist Party, a fact lamented by later partisans and some historians.[30] Sung's plan was endorsed and carried out, but failed in its first phase of operation. This gave Huang Hsing and Sun a chance to be heard. The result was the so-called 'Cabinet Party', a nickname for the Nationalist Party. This draws our attention back to the political development following the fall of the first cabinet.

The second cabinet was a non-party, 'talent-oriented' cabinet. It was led by Lu Cheng-hsiang, a seasoned diplomat who held the post of Foreign Minister in the first cabinet. Since a large part of his official career had been in the diplomatic service, and he had only just returned from Moscow, where he had remained throughout the revolution, he had attained a seemingly neutral position in China's domestic politics. Therefore his appointment was easily endorsed by all parties in the Senate. Unfortunately, he failed to live up to his reputation. He had no policy to offer to the nation. Instead, he shook the confidence of the senators in his maiden speech with an account of his past life, and his personal likes and dislikes. It was disastrous for his cabinet. The United Republicans joined with the Chinese League to withhold approval of his nominees to the cabinet. He succeeded in forming his cabinet only with the help of the President and his quasi-military bodies which threatened to use force against the Senate.[31] He did not succeed in assuming office, however, for the Senate followed up with an impeachment for his neglect of duty. Thereafter he probably realised that he had no hope of commanding the support of the Senate, and went on sick leave. The post of Premier was vacant for two months, during which time Yuan's henchman and Minister for the Interior, Chao Ping-chun, acted as Premier, and later assumed full premiership.* Chao's assumption of the premiership reflects a peculiar compromise of ideas between Sun, Huang, and Sung. On the one hand, the Nationalist Party refused to participate in a coalition; on the other, it prepared to support Yuan's men to the cabinet, and all but four ministers in Chao's cabinet were persuaded by Huang Hsing, with the consent of Yuan Shih-k'ai, to take out Nationalist Party membership. It was also a compromise, in appearance at least, between the President

---

* Lu Cheng-hsiang was appointed Premier on 29 June 1912. His cabinet ministers received the Senate's approval on 26 July, but on 27 the Senate moved for impeachment. Chao Ping-chun became Premier on 24 September.

and the party leaders, for, following Chao's appointment to the premiership, Yuan announced his eight-point agreement with Sun Yat-sen, Huang Hsing, and Li Yuan-hung, the eighth point being 'to make an all-out effort to harmonise party opinions and to maintain order as the basis for winning foreign recognition'.[32] Thus a cabinet composed purely of Yuan's men was dressed in Nationalist garb, winning for the Nationalist Party the nickname 'Cabinet Party' instead of fulfilling the party cabinet aim.

Sung Chiao-jen did not change his stand on party cabinet. This was obvious from his staunch opposition to bona fide members of his party joining a coalition cabinet, and from the denial by his followers in the Senate that Chao's cabinet was to be recognised as a Nationalist cabinet.[33] Why, then, did he acquiesce in Huang Hsing's activities, and in the party's acceptance of these nominal members? The answer probably lay somewhere in the analysis of a contemporary observer who listed three possible advantages of this policy to the Nationalists. Firstly, it would reconcile Yuan Shih-k'ai. Secondly, by making Chao's cabinet look like a party cabinet, it might ease the way for true party cabinet. Thirdly, it symbolised the president's capitulation to the principle of party cabinet, a nominal victory which might enhance the prestige of the Nationalists and affect the coming election in its favour.[34] Sung Chiao-jen's political objective lay in the future, not in the present, a stand he reaffirmed to his friends on 29 December 1912 with the words, 'Since we are not contesting the present. . . .'[35] The ardent promoter of the policy of extending membership to members of Chao's cabinet was Huang Hsing, but it is only fair to point out that it had the tacit consent of the whole Nationalist leadership. Even Sun Yat-sen, who later disclaimed responsibility for the party's policies of this period, declared in a speech in Shanghai that the cabinet was now a Nationalist cabinet, and exhorted his Nationalist audience to give all support to the government and Yuan Shih-k'ai.[36]

China's external conditions at this time also helped to shape the compromising attitude of the Nationalist leaders. Foreign powers had stepped up their pressures on China's outlying regions, particularly Mongolia and Tibet. Public opinion demanded stability and unity so that China could face the external problems. To the Nationalist leadership, it was obviously unwise to withhold support from Yuan's government before the election. This explains their co-operative attitude, as expressed in the eight-point agreement announced by the government in the name of Yuan Shih-k'ai, Sun Yat-sen, Huang Hsing, and Li Yuan-hung on 25 September.

Sung Chiao-jen was usually blamed for the indiscriminate intake of people into the revolutionary party. It was claimed that, following such an intake, the party was filled with incoherent and self-seeking elements, causing a dilution of the revolutionary spirit and the loss of political vision.[37] Since China had adopted democracy, however, it was natural for party leaders like Sung Chiao-jen to seek the widest support for their party, and through this support to realise their political goals. Hence it was not Sung's policy to deny membership to people who sought it. This attitude underlay the formation of the Nationalist Party, and also Sung's action in joining Huang Hsing in an effort to persuade the newly formed Democratic Party to amalgamate with the Nationalists.[38] The problem of the Nationalist leaders at this time lay not in the admission of new members but in ensuring their loyalty and support to the party's policies after admission. In the latter, Sung had apparently achieved a degree of effectiveness which could be seen from the uniform support for his party platform and the party's overwhelming victory over its rivals in the national election. After Sung's death the Nationalist Party quickly disintegrated into factions, exposing fully the weaknesses of its composition. How much of it was due to the quality of its rank and file, how much was due to weak leadership or the lack of leadership—these are questions not easily answered. At any rate, Yuan Shih-k'ai correctly recognised Sung Chiao-jen as his only opponent, and so caused his removal by assassination. Sung Chiao-jen seems to have been the only leader who could hold the Nationalist Party together. After his death, it swiftly disintegrated, and ceased to be the political force that had once filled Yuan Shih-k'ai with fear and apprehension.

In accordance with the provisional constitution, which required the establishment of a formally elected National Parliament within ten months of the promulgation of the Provisional Constitution, laws respecting the organisation of this Parliament and its election were promulgated in August by the Provisional President. It was stipulated that the National Parliament was to consist of two Houses, the Senate and the House of Representatives. The Senate was to be composed of members representing the provincial assemblies, the electoral committeees of Mongolia, Tibet, Sinkiang, the academics, and the overseas Chinese. Members to the House of Representatives were to be elected by popular vote. It was also decided that election to both Houses was to be completed by January 1913, and the first Parliament was to assemble in the following February.[39]

Since winning this election was the first political objective of the Nationalist Party, it was natural that Sung Chiao-jen should set his party machine in motion for this goal almost immediately after its formation. The result was startling. In the House of Representatives, the Nationalists was 269 seats as against the 154 seats of the other three parties. In the Senate, the Nationalists took up 123 seats as against the other three parties' 69.[40] The accuracy of these figures cannot be checked, and they are complicated by multi-party membership holders estimated to be 147 and 38 in respective Houses, and the failure to identify the independents, said to be 26 in the lower House and 44 in the Senate. Generally, however, the Nationalist had clearly emerged as the biggest single party, with an effective working majority in the new Parliament.

Details of the Nationalist Party's manoeuvres to win this election are not available. In the press there were charges and counter-charges of corruption, which revealed that some underhand practices by the rival parties probably existed. The following account of Sung Chiao-jen's part in the election in Hunan is indicative:

> After the promulgation of laws governing the organisation of the National Parliament and the election to its two Houses . . . on 10 August 1912, the Nationalist Party began to make preparations for the election in the various provinces to ensure victory. At this moment, Hung Ch'un-t'ai, the Attorney-General of Hunan, died. As it was thought by all that election had something to do with law, Sung Chiao-jen wanted me to return to Hunan to assume this office, so that I could, on the one hand, take charge of the election in Hunan, and thereby help the Nationalist Party, and on the other, reorganise the Hunan branch of the Chinese League into a branch of the Nationalist Party. At this time I was the editor of the *East Asia News** and also studying law and administration. Therefore I was reluctant to return to Hunan. It was only after I was repeatedly urged by Sung Chiao-jen that I complied . . . After my arrival in Changsha, I found that election came under the . . . Department of Civil Affairs . . . At that time the man in charge of this department was Liu Jen-hsi, who was not a member of the Nationalist Party. Therefore T'an Yen-k'ai, the Governor, thought of a way of removing him, and put me in his place. Thereafter I immediately started on arrangements for the election. I made myself the chief electoral superintendent, and dispatched five electoral officers to take charge of Hunan's five electorates. As a result, the Nationalists scored an overwhelming victory in this election in Hunan. For this election, Sung Chiao-jen also returned to Hunan to conduct campaigns for his party. His speeches won the approval and sympathy of all the people.[41]

However, Sung Chiao-jen's effort to manipulate the election in Hunan should not be taken to be the standard practice of the

---

* *Tung-ya hsin-wen.*

Nationalists. Sung was able to do what he did in Hunan because it happened to be his home province, and a stronghold of the revolutionaries. Out of twenty-one provinces plus Mongolia and Tibet, only eight provinces had Nationalist governors. Even in these eight provinces obviously under Nationalist control, the results of the election were not always overwhelmingly in favour of the Nationalist Party. According to available figures showing the distribution of senators between the parties, the Nationalists won clearly in only four provinces, was equalled by the others together in three, and lost convincingly in one. In the other thirteen provinces administered by non-Nationalist governors, the Nationalists won clearly only in one, managed to beat the Republicans in one, and trailed it in the rest.[42]

Despite these formidable odds, the Nationalists still outnumbered the Republicans by thirteen seats, to become the largest single party in the Senate, and obviously this was largely due to the votes in the non-Nationalist-dominated provinces, where they had no control over official apparatus for election. Bearing this in mind, the Nationalist victory was an impressive one. There seems ample justification for the claim that it was a clean election, not matched by later elections in China. The Nationalist win came as a surprise to friends and foes alike. Sun Yat-sen in Shanghai exclaimed that 'fairness lay in the hearts of the people', and that 'the political platform of the Nationalist Party meets the wish of the nation', while Liang Ch'i-ch'ao wrote dejectedly to his daughter, regretting his return to China.[43] However, the most surprised person was perhaps Yuan Shih-k'ai, who, seeing that the new Parliament was going to be dominated by the Nationalists, on the one hand resorted to bribery and corruption to secure support in the Parliament, and on the other prepared to strike his deadly blow against Sung Chiao-jen, whom he knew could be bought neither with money nor with rank. In an effort to win over the parliamentarians, Yuan ordered reception centres to be set up at major communication centres such as Shanghai, Hankow, Nanking, Tientsin, and Chengchow, to entertain transit parliamentarians *en route* to Peking. His men arranged accommodation and transport for them, and at the same time made detailed observations of their individual characters and habits. When they arrived in Peking, the entire entertainment world of this old capital was mustered to keep them amused.[44]

At the time when T'ang Shao-yi resigned from his premiership, Sung Chiao-jen had already expressed his wish to go home to see his ageing mother, wife, and children, whom he had not seen since he took refuge in Japan eight years before. This was one of his main reasons for asking to be relieved of his duties as Minister for Agriculture and Forestry. Political obligations and party affairs tied him down to Peking for a few more months, however. It was not until October that he managed to leave Peking for Hunan. Even this was not entirely a pleasure trip. In addition to paying his family a long overdue visit, he carried with him the duty of fighting an election campaign for his party.[45]

Sung Chiao-jen was away from Peking for two months, during which the solidarity of the Nationalist Party was put to the test by its political foes. Taking advantage of Sung's absence from Peking, the opponents of the Nationalist Party resorted to many ways and means to divide the Nationalists. While Sung was away, the anti-Nationalist camp was further strengthened by the return of Liang Ch'i-ch'ao to Peking on 20 October 1912. Only a short while before, Sung Chiao-jen did not deem China's political climate congenial to Liang Ch'i-ch'ao's return.[46] Now Liang's support was keenly sought by all parties, including the Nationalist. It enabled him to boast of his popularity as 'exceeding that of Sun and Huang many times over'. Even within the Nationalist Party, the attitude towards Liang was far from unanimous. Not a few of its leaders wished to see Liang join the inner ring of their party, if only to prevent him from becoming the tool of their political adversaries.[47]

The apparent popularity of Liang Ch'i-ch'ao, the confidence and enthusiasm his presence inspired among the opponents of the Nationalist Party, and the dissension within the Nationalist head-quarters with regard to the attitude of the party towards Liang, worried some of Sung's associates in Peking. Sung was repeatedly urged to return to take the helm. However, Sung had full confidence in the solidarity of his party. He did not regard the upheavals in Peking as anything more than 'ripples'. 'There are not many', he confided to his friends, 'who are sufficiently able to upset our position. Besides, the present trend cannot preclude what is to come'.[48]

Events justified Sung's optimism. The activities of his foes wrought no visible ill effects on the Nationalist Party. Despite rampant rumours of discord between Sung Chiao-jen, Huang Hsing, and Sun Yat-sen, there was in the rank and file of the Nationalist Party harmony and concerted effort to win the election. Even Hu Han-min, the Governor of Kwangtung, who earlier disagreed with Sung's policies, made financial contributions to the party's propaganda organs. In fact an unprecedented degree of unity was maintained within the revolutionary camp, much to the discomfiture of the opposition.[49]

A difficulty in narrating Sung's activities during the two months following his departure from Peking is the singular lack of information.

Despite reports from his friends that he returned to Hunan to conduct
election campaigns for his party, little was written of his movements
or speeches in the major newspapers. Of his activities in Hunan,
there are only two records of significance. One is Sung's own letter,
which contained a reference to his trip to Ch'ang-te on 27 December
to settle an electoral dispute in western Hunan.[50] The other is a
speech which he delivered to the members of his party in Changsha
on 8 January 1913.[51] Of them the second is of particular importance,
for in this speech Sung made a veiled attack on the government in
Peking. He spoke of China's recent revolution as uncompleted, and
suggested that this lack of thoroughness underlay all China's present
difficulties. He compared the establishment of the Republic to the
application of nutritious medicine to a wound not yet cleared of
poison. The result was that China was worse, not better.

In view of the Nationalist Party's recent policies which emphasised
the co-operation of old and new forces in government, Sung's speech
marked a major departure. Thereafter, Sung stepped up his attack
on the policies, or rather the lack of policies, of the government, and
the procrastination of those in power towards the problems of the
nation. On 10 February 1913, when the result of the election was
clearly in his party's favour, Sung was in Hankow, openly assailing
Yuan Shih-k'ai and his government for their mismanagement of
both domestic and external affairs. He charged that internally the
government had done nothing to solve the country's acute financial
problem except to borrow; in foreign affairs, the government had no
positive policy and had failed to solve the nation's dispute with Russia
over Mongolia, an issue for which he had seen the President and the
Premier earlier urging them to seek a quick settlement; but nothing
was done, and so it had led to the present difficulty with Russia over
Outer Mongolia's declaration of independence. Sung pointed out
the danger of inaction in the current situation. He explained to his
audience that China's existence hung in the balance of power between foreign nations in China; failure to check Russian influence
in Mongolia would upset this balance and lead to the partition and
extinction of China. Mounting British pressure on Tibet was a signal
of this danger.

> Now [he added] the formal Parliament will be established soon.
> According to a report, the Nationalist Party is winning the election.
> It is indeed a pleasing phenomenon. I have no doubt that in the
> coming Parliament, the Nationalists will constitute the majority.
> The salvation of China depends entirely on the members of our
> party.[52]

Sung Chiao-jen had dropped his first bombshell. Thereafter he was seen travelling through the major political centres* in central China, reiterating his attacks on the apathy and incompetence of the present leadership in the central government, and the past mistakes of the Chinese League in neglecting its natural function as the nation's opposition party. At the same time he made known his views on a number of controversial subjects pertaining to the government of China. He reaffirmed his party's preference for responsible party government rather than presidential or any other form of cabinet government. On the question of provincial government, he preferred election of provincial heads by the people rather than direct appointment by the central government, so that the wishes of the people could be given fullest expression. On the question of centralisation and decentralisation, he held that existing conditions in China should be the sole criteria. He suggested a division of power between the central and the provincial governments. For example, foreign affairs and defence should be the concern of the central government. A major portion of power affecting the judiciary, communication, and finance should also be vested with the central government. Other functions of government not of national importance might be left to the provincial administration.† He further suggested that in forming new institutions and policies, customs and traditional practices should be utilised to full advantage. He pointed out that provinces, not districts or counties, should become the basic units for local government, since traditionally the latter had only remote connections with the central government. On the question of formulating a permanent constitution for the republic, Sung stated that it was to be left to the first National Parliament.[53]

These pronouncements of Sung Chiao-jen made clear the stand of the Nationalist Party on two important issues of the day, the means by which the constitution of the republic was to be produced, and the political system this constitution was to adopt. Of these two, the more important was naturally the first, since the character of the constitution depended on the apparatus that made it. Hence it became the focal point of discussion and the object of struggle between the central government and the provincial administrations, between the pro-Yuan factions and the Nationalist Party, and above all between the President and the advocates of cabinet government—all this despite the stipulation in the provisional constitution that the

---

* Sung was in Kiukiang on 13 February, Shanghai on 15 February, Hangchow on 23 February, and Nanking on 8 March 1913.

† These were identical with Sun Yat-sen's ideas. See 'Sun hsien-sheng yu Kan-chi', *Min-li-pao*, 2 November, 1912, p. 7.

drafting of the nation's permanent constitution was to be the responsibility of the first formal Parliament.

Besides the stand of the Nationalists as expressed by Sung Chiao-jen, other opinions on the constitutional question may be grouped into two categories. Constitutionalists like Liang Ch'i-ch'ao favoured the formation of a drafting committee composed of delegates from the Provisional Parliament, provincial governors, political parties, and the President, with the finished draft having to receive the assent of Parliament. This had the support of eighteen provincial governors and three parties, Republican, United, and Democratic. The other was exclusively championed by Yuan Shih-k'ai's clique, which held that the constitution should come from the President and be promulgated by his authority.[54]

A strange phenomenon in this connection was the lack of agreement even within the Nationalist Party. No less than two distinguished Nationalist Governors, Hu Han-min of Kwangtung and Li Lieh-chun of Kiangsi, supported the call to form a constitution drafting committee composed of persons chosen by Provincial Governors, while the Nationalist Party organ opposed it vehemently.[55] Sung's views had the effect of internally tranquillising the stand of the party on this and other issues, and externally warning his political adversaries of his implacable stand on democracy and the rule of the majority. The latter undoubtedly contributed much to his enemies' decision to remove him from the political arena once and for all.

The immediate response of Yuan Shih-k'ai and his supporters was provoked not by Sung's political pronouncement but by his criticism of the central government's domestic and foreign policies. An anonymous reply refuting Sung's criticism and attacking his personal conduct, as well as his Nationalist Party, appeared in various newspapers. He was again accused of coveting the premiership, and China's existing difficulties with foreign powers were held as the legacies of the first cabinet. This provoked a sharp reply from Sung Chiao-jen, but, more importantly, he revealed that the author of this anonymous article had access to most confidential information, and therefore must be a member of the government's inner circle. In fact he hinted that if the article was not the work of the President or the Premier, then it was at least written with their connivance.[56] This represented the first head-on clash between Sung Chiao-jen and the President, and its intensity, as revealed by the unreserved use of abusive language in the government-inspired refutation, signalled the governing clique's more ruthless measures to come.

In addition to this clash, there were two other sources of friction between Sung and the central government. One was the movement by a section of the Nationalist Party to get the new Parliament to meet outside Peking, and the other was the rumour that the Nationalists favoured Li Yuan-hung as President. The first movement began in August 1912, after the promulgation of the Parliament Organisation Law by the President. It was a reaction to the threat of force which was employed by the government to secure the Senate's approval to Lu Cheng-hsiang's cabinet in July. The *Rights of the People (Min-ch'uan-pao)*, a Nationalist newspaper, took the lead in this movement. It suggested that in future the National Parliament should be convened at a place of its own choice so that its independence might be ensured.[57] When the results of the election became known, a body was organised in Shanghai to welcome the Parliament, with a view to securing the first sitting of the new Parliament in Shanghai, and then permanently establishing it in Nanking. This drew a sharp rebuke from one of Yuan Shih-k'ai's powerful generals, who, rattling his sabre, threatened to curb this subversion by force.[58]

Whether Sung Chiao-jen himself had ever intended to dispense with Yuan Shih-ka'i and replace him with Li Yuan-hung as President, if his party won the election, is a question which probably can never be answered with complete certainty. There is some evidence which suggests strongly that he did. Kita Ikki, who was one of Sung's close Japanese acquaintances, had no doubt of Sung's intention to assume the premiership himself, with a docile Li Yuan-hung as President. Chang Ping-lin, in his autobiographical annal, recorded that both he and Sung intended to back Li Yuan-hung for the presidency, and had separately approached Li on this question, and that Sung lost his life because of a leakage of his secret deal with Li. To strengthen Chang's assertion there was Li's telegram of April 1913, in which he admitted that 'someone' offered to make him President.[59]

Whatever the truth is, the fact that the Nationalist Party had made no clear indication of support for Yuan for the presidency, and that its party organs criticised severely the attitude that only Yuan was fit for that post, was sufficient to cause uneasiness in Peking and drive the governing clique to seek the removal of the source of threat. At the height of the quarrels that followed Sung's death, a badly written document intended for the foreign press was sent from government sources to one of China's foreign political advisers for correction. Part of it read:

Sung Chiao-jen was one of the revolutionists . . . He went to Wuchang and visited General Li to whom he said, 'We cannot make Yuan Shih-k'ai our willing tool. I will have the members of my party elect you as the permanent president'. He also demanded a million of dollars. In reply Li said, 'I have no such talent as Mr. Yuan and will never be a candidate for presidency. My personal property is only worth $10,000. Since the revolution one half of it has been spent. Even if I were to give you all there would not be of any use'. Seeing that Li could not be fooled Sung went to Shanghai and arranged with his party to nominate him to be the premier. This was consented by the members. But the followers of Huang Hsing strongly opposed it and made fierce struggles between themselves. For this reason Huang and Sung broke away their friendship.[60]

This forms part of a lengthy but unrefined piece of writing less concerned with truth than with smearing. Probably for this reason it does not seem to have found its way into any press, for the political adviser to whom it was sent was no other than G. E. Morrison, who, after examining a similar document from the Chinese government at about the same time, commented that he would not be a party to such diatribes, and diatribe this was. Its suppression probably worked out better for the government than its release, which, like the lady who protesteth too much, would have exposed sooner to the world the insincerity and naked hostility of the governing clique towards Sung Chiao-jen and his party, and the seriousness with which it regarded Sung's alleged political activities.

Briefly, for four reasons Sung's fate was sealed. His criticism of Yuan's government, the renewed effort of some of his followers to shift the seat of government away from Peking, the uncertainty of Yuan's position, and, lastly, Sung's firm stand on party government and his likelihood of succeeding, all together forced Yuan's hand. After his speech in Nanking on 9 March 1913, he returned to Shanghai, where he conferred with his party members as well as members of the new Parliament, who, before proceeding to Peking, gathered together in Shanghai to hear the policy of their chief, and to work out a definite course of action. As result of these meetings, Sung outlined a political platform with the idea of giving it definitive form in Peking under his own direction. On 20 March 1913 he was on his way to catch an evening train for Peking via Nanking when his assassin struck. Two days later he died of a wound in his abdomen.

THIRTEEN

Epilogue

THE RAILWAY station, Shanghai North, where Sung Chiao-jen was assassinated, was just outside the International Settlement boundary.[1] At any point on his journey to the station he would still have been in the International Settlement. But once he crossed into the station yard he was beyond the protection of the Settlement authorities. A crime committed within the Settlement came under the foreign-controlled Shanghai municipal police, but a crime committed on the station premises came under Chinese jurisdiction. The plotters of Sung's assassination apparently took this into consideration, and chose the station for their murder, in the hope of escaping involvement with the Settlement authorities. But, as it turned out, Sung's immediate murderers all resided in the Settlement. Following their discovery by Sung's friends, they were arrested and prosecuted by the Settlement authorities. Chinese authorities in Shanghai and in Peking tried to effect an extradition of the criminals for trial in Chinese courts, but did not succeed until after the case had been thoroughly investigated and evidence against the criminals established.[2]

Immediately after the shooting, Sung realised that he could not survive the injury he had received. He asked for a telegram to be sent to the President, part of which read:

> Ever since I have been exposed to the teachings of the sages, I have been strict with myself. Although I am not faultless, I have never made enemies on personal account. In shouldering the responsibility of reforming the bad Manchu government, I also carefully observed the principles of humanity and justice, and dared not for one moment harbour thoughts of personal gain. The foundation of the nation is not yet strong, and the lot of the people is not yet improved. I die with deep regret. I humbly hope that your Excellency will champion honesty, propagate justice, and promote democracy so that the Parliament can produce an everlasting constitution . . .[3]

Had Sung lived a few more days, he would have spared himself the trouble. Both his assassin, an ignorant ex-soldier, and the thug who directed the execution were caught within a few days. Through an employee of the telegraph office in Shanghai, evidence implicating the government, particularly Chao Ping-chun, the Premier, and his Secretary, Hung Shu-chu, was discovered. Yuan Shih-k'ai, of course, denied his government's complicity.[4] But apparently he knew in his own mind that his argument was not convincing, and was secretly preparing for a show-down with the revolutionaries. Once again he breached the provisional constitution, this time by contracting a large foreign loan without reference to Parliament. Ironically, this illegal 'reorganisation' loan of £25 million ($US125,000,000) was signed on 26 April 1913, the same day the Court of Justice in Shanghai published its findings on the Sung case.[5]

In contrast to Yuan Shih-k'ai's preparation for any eventuality that might arise out of Sung's death, there was no unanimity within the Nationalist Party on the course it should take. In Shanghai, the central party leadership of the Nationalist Party was divided into a militant faction advocating immediate military action against Yuan Shih-k'ai, and a legalist faction preferring to await for a legal outcome.[6] In Peking, the newly elected Nationalist parliamentarians assumed a strong position, but, without Sung's guiding hand, they became easy prey to Yuan's corrupting influence, and provided material for a vivid if exaggerated account of the political scene in this old capital, which was to entertain inhabitants at the other end of the Eurasian continent. The following appeared in *The Times* on 29 April 1913:

> The debate which took place in the Lower House on April 16 on the subject of the election of the Speaker (this was the first open test of the voting strength of parties) gave to the Nationalists an apparently effective majority of forty-seven votes. It left them for the moment literally in possession of the field, for so soon as Yuan's incensed supporters perceived that their attempt to secure a secret ballot had failed, they left the House in a body. The Nationalist victory was, however, brief and barren, for lobbying in Peking is an art more primitive perhaps, but certainly more persuasive, than anything which exists in Europe or America. Fear, favour and affection, the timely word of the *tazen* in power, are powerful arguments with most of the youthful delegates who profess to represent the southern central provinces. There is something in the atmosphere of the capital, as many Europeans have learned, which conduces to uniformity and acquiescence. It is therefore not surprising to learn that in the last few days the Kuomintang's

majority had faded away, like snow upon desert, and its fiery energies have shown distinct signs of relaxation. . . .

While this account might have been exaggerated, it nevertheless carried a good deal of truth. The Nationalist Parliamentary Party split into five factions. Some pretended to be neutral and some simply defected to Yuan's camp. Those who maintained their ground under the Nationalist banner also divided into two factions, the radicals and the moderates. The radicals, seeing no chance of either attaining justice or establishing democracy, left Peking for the south, to support the imminent uprising against Yuan. But the moderates stayed on in the hope of allying themselves with the Progressive Party, to form a restraining force on the ruthless President.[7]

Thus the picture of division after Sung's death was complete, and coincided with the *North China Herald's* observation on 29 March 1913, that 'Alive, we have been told by the Chinese papers, Mr. Sung worked for the union of China. Dead, he appears most likely to promote disunion.'[8] But no one, except perhaps Yuan Shih-k'ai, had foreseen the ease with which the government could liquidate resistance and restore effective order and tranquillity. Within a few weeks, the militant wing of the Nationalist Party was crushed by Yuan's forces, and its leaders fled to Japan. In another few weeks, the Nationalist Party was dissolved by the President, and the Parliament closed down, marking the end of an era during which democracy was believed to be the only hope for China, and the beginning of another, which saw China embark on a long and tortuous course, groping for an answer to her ills.[9]

As for Shanghai's railway station where Sung lost his life, it was regarded in later years as a danger point for all important Chinese figures, provincial military governors and warlords alike. Feng Yu-hsiang, a well-known warlord, was seen on the station in 1927. An eye-witness described it vividly: 'He was entirely surrounded by a "rugger scrum" of bodyguards who clung to him like bees so that only the crown of his straw hat was visible as they slowly moved down the platform'.[10] There could be little doubt that he had Sung's fate in mind.

Following the burial of Sung Chiao-jen on the outskirts of Shanghai, and as his fleeing friends regrouped themselves outside the reach of their foes to reflect on their recent experience, a human endeavour that is now remembered as the 1911 Chinese revolution came to an end, and with it this narrative of one of the heroes also draws to a close. How should Sung Chiao-jen's role in this period be viewed? What place does the 1911 revolution occupy in the modernisation of China? Did it constitute part of a great change predicted by a nineteenth-century Chinese who foresaw that 'among the mountain people there will rise a big voice to which Heaven and Earth will respond with bells and drums, and the Gods will aid with waves and storm'?[11] Or was it merely as a scathing contemporary observer of the 1911 upheaval put it: 'The dregs rose and became scum, and lashed themselves into foam, but when all was over they sank once more to the bottom'?[12]

Sung Chiao-jen began his revolutionary career at the age of twenty-two when he participated in 1904 in the founding of the China Resurgence Society in Hunan and the Science Study Group in Hupeh. He left little writing in this period for us to have a glimpse of his inner thought. It was possible that, like many other young revolutionaries of this time, his initial action mainly stemmed from nationalism and anti-Manchu sentiment, though he might also have had a vague notion of democracy. However, his sympathy for the downtrodden and the outlaws of Manchuria, and his belief in intuitive thought and basic human goodness as taught in the philosophy of Wang Yang-ming, reveal a democratic strain in him. It is not surprising that, when he was exposed more fully to Western political thought in the intervening years between his first revolutionary action in the Changsha revolt of 1904 and his decision to assume a front role in the revolutionary movement in 1910 with the formation of the Central China Office, he was strongly attracted to the idea of democracy, and formed the conviction that it was the best political system for China. Thus for the rest of his life he fought determinedly for the cause of democracy. Within the revolutionary party he stood for collective leadership, in contrast to Sun Yat-sen's insistence on personal leadership. In government he opposed the presidential form and advocated parliamentary supremacy and a responsible cabinet system. He preferred government by institutions, and wished to see institutional growth in China supplant the deeply rooted practices of government by personalities or through a network of personal ties. There might be many who had expressed similar views, but Sung seems to be the first one to make a serious attempt to realise them. In view of the long tradition behind China's established practices, perhaps it is not surprising that he failed in his attempt.

Apart from the overthrow of the Manchu dynasty, the 1911 Chinese revolution had few tangible achievements. It failed to establish a satisfactory and enduring political system, and China was not regenerated. It had failed to clean up the remnants of reactionary forces, which remained to plague China for many years to come. Because of its failure and the chaos that followed it, posterity tends to regard the 1911 revolution with mixed feelings. While historians recognise it to be an important event, they lament that it was not more thorough. Historical judgment was further clouded by the opinion of some surviving revolutionaries of 1911, who blamed their deceased colleagues for the failure. Thus Sung Chiao-jen became the whipping boy of some of his surviving colleagues and some historians. Many charges have been brought against him, among the most serious being that he was a separatist who undermined the unity of the revolutionary movement, and that he was an opportunistic politician who abandoned the revolutionary party to seek his own political life.

Only in a sense was Sung Chiao-jen a separatist. He brought into existence an organisation, and refused to put it under Sun Yat-sen's command. Otherwise one could not see a more devoted revolutionary. Having taken the revolutionary path, he never regretted his choice or wavered from his purpose. Despite his dissatisfaction and unhappiness with the Chinese League under Sun Yat-sen's leadership, he remained in the League. It was not until 1910, after his efforts to seek Sun Yat-sen's co-operation in an attempt to revive the League's headquarters in Tokyo, that he began to regard Sun as retrogressive, and took steps to organise his Central China Office.[13] Even then he and his colleagues took great pains to preserve their tie with the League. This is evident in the title of their organisation. Unlike other dissidents, who chose totally different names for their organisations, such as the Mutual Advancement Society, they called theirs the Central China Office of the Chinese League. As later events reveal, the Chinese League was able to regroup to become an important political force in the 1911 revolution and in the new republic, largely because of the existence of the Central China Office, not in spite of it.

Sung's reorganisation of the Chinese League into the Nationalist Party has also been much criticised, but few critics would attempt to suggest an alternative. As Chang Chi, Sung's associate in the formation of the Nationalist Party and a prominent revolutionary figure for many years after Sung's death, explained some years later:

> The role of Mr Sung in reorganising the Nationalist Party is now misunderstood by many people. Some say he should not have reorganised the Chinese League into the Nationalist Party. This view is not correct. Since a provisional constitution had been promulgated, there had to be a Parliament, and since there was to be a Parliament, there had to be large political parties to carry out its functions. Since the Chinese League did not wish to see its own clean record spoiled by disagreeable political party practices,

it had to make a clean end. That was the opinion of a section of the Chinese League's leading colleagues, and not completely the private wish of Mr Sung. Some say he wanted to be the Prime Minister, but that is the opinion of the ungenerous.[14]

Following Sung's death, the Nationalist Party was knocked out of action by Yuan Shih-k'ai. Yet, during its short existence it was a great organisational success. Its victory in the national election of 1913 is conclusive evidence of its effectiveness as a political party. The fact that Yuan Shih-k'ai and his followers had to resort to criminal methods against Sung Chiao-jen is a further proof of his party's importance. True, the Nationalist Party after Sung's death failed to withstand Yuan's oppression, but was it the fault of Sung Chiao-jen, a dead man? It was already a difficult enough task for any man to hold together a group of intellectuals with new ideas and old habits, to whom regional loyalty was still all-important. Sun Yat-sen's failure to maintain the unity of the Chinese League indicates the extent of this difficulty. It was to Sung's credit that he succeeded where Sun had failed, and at the cost of only two remote political planks, namely the equality of the sexes and the principle of social welfare. Undeniably, Sung resorted to expedient means in the war against the Manchus, and again in forming the Nationalist Party. But he seems to have done so in recognition of the existing realities. On both occasions the revolutionaries were placed in a passive position. They had either to adjust themselves to existing conditions or to face exclusion from the game and admit defeat from the outset. Flexibility at least kept the revolutionary party in the run and provided it with a chance to reassert itself. Otherwise, Sung had an unblemished record. He held fast to his political convictions, and refused to exchange them for either money or official position.

The critics of Sung Chiao-jen and his colleagues come mainly from two camps, the later Nationalists and the Communists. Later Nationalists tend to blame Sung Chiao-jen and his friends, whom they call 'moderates' to distinguish them from themselves, for their failure to follow the so-called 'Plan of Revolution' of the Chinese League, which specified that the revolutionary war was to be carried out in three stages—military dictatorship, provisional government, and, finally, constitutional government.[15] The Communists, in the light of their own experience, believe that the irresolution and half-heartedness of the revolutionaries of 1911 were the main causes of the failure of the revolution. In short, both views emphasise the immediate human factor, and a number of particular individuals or a special class of man is held responsible for the failure of the revolution. The other factors, such as the loosely knit nature of the pre-

Republican revolutionary movement, the circumstances under which the revolution broke out, the revolutionaries' dependence on the co-operation and support of the conservative forces in the anti-Manchu war, the fear of foreign intervention, and the power and appeal of Yuan Shih-k'ai, are not sufficiently taken into account. In fact few would now dispute the assertion that these factors contributed to the rise of Yuan Shih-k'ai, or that the north-south compromise was the key to subsequent developments to the detriment of the revolutionary cause. It would not be an exaggeration to say that the revolutionary party had begun losing its grip on the reins of leadership as early as December 1911, when Wu Ting-fang, a non-revolutionary, was appointed to take charge of negotiations with the north. For behind Wu Ting-fang and his negotiations was the influence of the powerful gentry, represented by men like Chang Ch'ien and Chao Feng-ch'ang, who had wide connections with foreign powers as well as with ex-bureaucrats, reformers, constitutionalists, and local forces in central China.*

The revolutionaries of 1911 possessed an ideal but no effective tools for its realisation. Unlike later revolutionaries who had the advantage of learning from the mistakes of their forerunners, and drawing inspiration from such experiences as the Russian revolution of 1917, the revolutionaries of 1911 had only such remote examples as the American and French revolutions, and the more recent ones of Turkey and Portugal. The revolutionaries of 1911 cannot be accused of not taking advantage of the lessons of history. They learned from the Turkish revolution the importance of winning the support of government troops for revolution; from Portugal the strategy and tactics of 'capital' revolution; and from the Taiping rebellion the importance of maintaining harmony, and the need to avoid conflicts with foreign nations during revolution.

The last two historical observations exercised particularly powerful influence on the actions of the revolutionaries of 1911. Sung Chiao-jen and his colleagues took great pains to observe them, and the result was tolerance and conciliation, to the utmost limit of the revolutionary party, towards diverse and even deviating forces.

In 1911 the Chinese revolutionaries were not aware either of the necessity or of the technique for organising the masses for revolution. Consequently, the overwhelming majority of the Chinese people were not involved in the revolution. Participation was confined to

---

* According to Liu Hou-sheng, *Chang Ch'ien chuan-chi*, pp. 194-5, the peace negotiations between Wu Ting-fang and T'ang Shao-yi were merely a formality. Decisions were made at secret meetings between Huang Hsing, Sun Yat-sen, T'ang Shao-yi, Chang ch'ien, and other leading members of the gentry in Chao Feng-ch'ang's house in Shanghai.

students, soldiers, members of secret societies, members of local
gentry, and some government officials. Their backgrounds were
diverse, and their objectives differed. The sincere revolutionaries,
who came mostly from the younger generation of students and
themselves an incoherent force, were vastly outnumbered by the
well-established and widely influential local gentry in the anti-
Manchu war. The masses were unconcerned and inarticulate, but
the gentry were ambitious and vociferous. In the name of democracy,
which was one of the professed goals of revolution, the revolutionaries
were bound to take their views into consideration, and even bow
to their wishes. The gentry still possessed real power, and could easily
turn into a hostile force.

The concept of democracy was itself not a suitable ideology for
revolution in China. For, with its emphasis on individuality and
individualism, it was not compatible with a revolution in the Chinese
setting, which demanded a high degree of discipline. Much organisational experience and adjustment in the use of methods and ideological training were needed to produce the type of parties which
featured later revolutionary movements in China.

In the 1911 revolution, few saw the need of acquiring a wider
basis for revolution than in the ranks of students, soldiers, and secret
societies. Even these three elements would have given the movement
a much greater strength than they actually did if their preparations
had been extended to more than just the few cities in central China.
The revolutionaries' initial successes in Wuchang and Shanghai in
1911 argued strongly for the possibilities that might have followed
similar but more extensive and more thorough preparations.
Significantly, the Central China Office's original date for the uprising
was 1913, not 1911. But Sun Yat-sen took no part in such a scheme.
From 1906 to 1911 his movement was entirely externally-based and
externally-powered, and as a result none of his attempted uprisings
in this period managed to hold one square inch of Chinese territory.

This brings our attention to a frequently heard assertion that Sun
Yat-sen had more distant goals in view than his colleagues in the
1911 revolution. It has been argued that, while Sun Yat-sen regarded
the overthrow of the Manchu dynasty as a means to an end, most
other revolutionaries deemed it as their ultimate goal, so that, when
the Manchu Dynasty was toppled, they lost the desire to go further,
thus precipitating an attitude of compromise.

While recognising some truth in this argument, one must also bear
in mind the difficulties in qualitative and quantitative analyses of
the so called 'revolutionaries' which such an assertion entails. Who
were the revolutionaries? If they were only those who had consistently

participated in the revolutionary movement before 1911, clearly there was one faction which was suspicious of socialistic doctrines, and preferred to dissociate themselves from them. But there were, besides Sun Yat-sen and his southern colleagues, others who, though adopting a cautious attitude, were deeply interested in the question of socialism. Sung Chiao-jen, for example, had shown keen interest in socialist ideas and movements in Europe and had written articles on the subject. It is not obvious that the anti-socialist faction overhwelmed the socialists in number and strength. The reappearance of the principle of social welfare in the platform of the reorganised Chinese League in January and again in March 1912 was surely an indication of the influence of the more socialist-minded group.

If some revolutionaries' neglect of socialist principles was held to have contributed to the failure of the 1911 revolution, in the sense that, as a result, they failed to broaden the basis of their revolution by involving the peasants in their task, then Sun Yat-sen probably should shoulder a large share of the blame. In this period, he made no real attempt to build a widely based revolutionary movement in China itself. It was left to the initiative of the so-called 'separatists' to organise movements at or near the grass-roots level. It was no mere coincidence that the latter succeeded, where Sun repeatedly failed, in initiating uprisings in China.

The spontaneous nature of the 1911 uprisings and the limited influence and control of the revolutionaries over its development had decisively restricted the scope of the revolutionary camp. What happened in Hupeh, Hunan, and Kiangsu were standard examples of the way various provinces gained independence. The uprisings were initiated by either the revolutionaries or the gentry or both, and later dominated by anti-Manchu but non-revolutionary elements. The cases of Hupeh, Hunan, and Kiangsu were manifestations of the strength of non-revolutionary forces which the revolutionaries of 1911 had to contend with. They might be led, or even listen to reasoned argument, but they would not be controlled. To coerce these forces before the fall of the Manchus was obviously inadvisable, apart from the consideration that the revolutionaries might not be successful in such attempts. The deaths of two revolutionary leaders at the hands of the conservative gentry of Hunan, the home province of such revolutionaries as Sung Chiao-jen and Huang Hsing, exemplified the existing power struggle between the two camps, and the uncertain and precarious position of the revolutionaries.*

---

* The two murdered revolutionaries were Chiao Ta-feng and Ch'en Tso-hsin, who were the first Governor and Deputy-Governor of Hunan's revolutionary government.

Bearing in mind the course of the 1911 revolution, which began with the fusion of the already incoherent revolutionary factions with diverse non-revolutionary and conservative elements, and ended in a compromise which meant domination by the still more reactionary forces of the north, nothing could be more misleading than to ascribe the term 'moderate' to Sung Chiao-jen, who, in face of overwhelming odds, made a gallant attempt to correct an obviously dangerous trend. The following was a contemporary image of Sung Chiao-jen:

> Sung's voice was undoubtedly the most effective and probably the most sincere, of all those raised in the struggle of the provinces for local autonomy and against the concentration of power in the hands of the President. Less pliable than Sun Yat-sen, and an earnest believer in the efficacy of constitutional republicanism, Sung presented a serious obstacle to the smooth 'making' of the Presidential election, and to the reinforcement of authority at Peking. By his death a grim warning has been given to those of the Nationalist Party who openly oppose centralization. . . .[16]

Sung Chiao-jen was anything but a moderate. His determination to curtail Yuan's power and to recapture the lost political influence of the revolutionary party proved that he was not. Undeniably he failed to realise his objectives, and the causes of his failure seem to lie as much in his misjudgment of the characters of his political foes as in his over-reliance on constitutional means. But, as already pointed out, the alternative courses of action, including armed struggle, would in 1913 have been equally ineffective. Capitulation, indifference, and passivity would probably have enabled Sung to live a longer life, but then he would have ceased to be an active revolutionary.

The 1911 revolution provided China with its first opportunity of adopting democracy, but the failure of this experiment drove many to follow an opposite course of action. After Sung's death, lip service to the cause of democracy continued to be heard, but many began to doubt its validity under Chinese conditions. Thus in 1914 Sun Yat-sen, who was democratic in words but never in action, demanded from his followers personal loyalty to his leadership.[17] The following, translated from Chinese, and alleged to be the words of Chiang Kai-shek, who dominated Chinese politics for over two decades prior to 1949, reveals China's aversion to democracy.

> In the first year of the Republic, why were political parties such as the Republican and the Progressive able to appear? It was because we did not lay down the rule of party dictatorship, thus enabling

all anti-revolutionary parties to appear; and when they appeared, the revolutionary party was destroyed by them. Why was the revolutionary party defeated in 1912? How did Yuan Shih-k'ai manage to make himself emperor? All of us must know the reason. It was because at that time there were many parties and we did not adopt the policy of party dictatorship.[18]

In China's intellectual circles, the call for dictatorship was also heard. The following, published in 1934 in a popular journal, the *Eastern Miscellany*, was written by Ch'ien Tuan-sheng, a prominent Chinese political scientist and a Harvard graduate. It read:

In my view what China needs is an able and idealistic dictator. China wants to become a strong nation in the shortest possible time. The goal of industrializing China definitely cannot be achieved within ten or twenty years, . . . and to attain this goal the government must possess power. In order to give the government his power, apart from a popular dictatorship, there is no other effective alternative. . . .

There are among us some people, including myself, who have undergone long periods of liberal education. These people naturally find undemocratic practices extremely distasteful. But if we want to make China into a strong modern nation, I fear there is no alternative except to throw aside our democratic conviction.[19]

Chinese aversion to democracy after 1911 is unmistakable, and there can be little doubt that the revolutionaries' frustration in the 1911 revolution contributed much to its beginning. Perhaps it is particularly in this latter respect that for the supporters of Western-style democracy Sung Chiao-jen's life and death assumes an ominous historical significance.

REFERENCES

INTRODUCTION

1 Ch'en Hsü-lu, 'Lun Sung Chiao-jen', *Hsin-hai ko-ming wu-shih chou-nien chi-nien lun-wen-chi* (*Hsin-hai lun-wen-chi*), ed. Hupeh sheng che-hsüeh she-hui k'o-hsüeh hsüeh-hui lien-ho-hui, Vol. I, pp. 354-74.

2 G. E. Morrison, Diary, 31 March 1912, Morrison Papers, item 95.

3 *The Times*, 24 March 1913, reported that 'His death is universally lamented'. For public opinion in China after Sung's death see 'Sung hsien-sheng pei-hai hou chih yü-lun', in Yeh Ch'u-ts'ang *et al.* (eds.), *Sung Yü-fu*, reprint, Taipei, 1963.

4 Sun Yat-sen, 'Chih Teng Tse-ju lun t'ung-i shih-ch'üan yü t'ung-i ch'ou-k'an shu (1914)', in Chang Ch'i-yun (ed.), *Kuo-fu ch'üan-shu*, Taipei, 3rd ed., 1963, pp. 586-7; Tsou Lu, *Chung-kuo Kuo-min-tang shih-kao* (*Tang-shih-kao*), Vol. I, pp. 105-6, 120, 136. Also 'Ch'en Ch'i-mei chih Huang Hsing shu', ibid., pp. 273-81, and 'Hu Han-min tzu-chuan' ('Tzu-chuan'), in Chung-kuo kuo-

min-tang chung-yang wei-yüan-hui tang-shih shih-liao p'ien-tsuan wei-yüan-hui (ed.), *Ko-ming wen-hsien*, (*KMWH*), 2nd ed., 1958, Vol. II, p. 436.

5 Feng Tzu-yu, *She-hui chu-i yü Chung-kuo*, p. 6.

6 Tai Chi-t'ao, *Sun Wen chu-i chih che-hsüeh ti chi-ch'u*, pp. 13-14.

7 'Chung-kuo kuo-min-tang ti-i-chieh chung-yang chih-chien wei-yüan ti-shih-tz'u ch'üan-t'i hui-i chueh-i', in Chü Cheng (ed.), *Ch'ing-tang shih-lu*, pp. 50-2. This resolution was passed by the Nationalist leaders in Peking on 8 December 1925. Tai Chi-t'ao's book containing his criticism of Sung Chiao-jen was completed in June 1925 and published in Shanghai in 1926.

8 Tu-hsiu, 'Hsin-hai ko-ming yü Kuo-min-tang', *Hsiang-tao chou-pao*, No. 86, Oct. 1924, pp. 703-5; Feng Tzu-yu, *Ko-ming i-shih* (*KMIS*), Vol. II, Shanghai, 1946, p. 94, contains a similar criticism.

9 'Hsin-hai ko-ming wu-shih chou-nien hsüeh-shu t'ao-lun-hui t'ao-lun ti i-hsieh wen-t'i', *Hsin-hai lun-wen-chi*, Vol. II, pp. 707-10.

2 FORMATIVE YEARS

1 Sung Chiao-jen, *Wo-chih-li-shih (Diary)*, 15 March 1906.

2 Lo Jun-chang, 'Sung-mu wan-t'ai fu-jen ch'i-chih shou-hsü', *Min-li-pao*, 21 April 1913, p. 11.

3 Ibid.

4 Chü Fang-mei, 'Sung Chiao-jen lei', *Min-li-pao*, 28 April 1913, p. 13.

5 Feng Wei-ying, 'Chuan', in Sung, *Diary*, p. 33.

6 These descriptions of the town and district of T'ao-yüan are drawn from 'Hsi-lu shih-shen Feng Kao-yü, Wu Ching-hung chi Sung t'ung-tsu Sung Chiao-yü Chiao-k'uan teng chih T'an-tu Yen-k'ai shu', *Min-li-pao*, 15 April 1913, and Chien Po-tsan, 'Ch'ang-te T'ao-yüan lun-hsien-chi', collected in his *Chung-Kuo shih lun-chi*, Vol. I, p. 354.

7 Feng, 'Chuan', p. 33.

8 Chü, 'Sung Chiao-jen lei', p. 13.

9 'Cities of Old Cathay-Chang-sha', *North China Herald (NCH)*, 24 Aug. 1912.

10 Teng and Fairbank, *China's Response to the West*, p. 10; Hou Wai-lu, *Chung-Kuo tsao-ch'i ch'i-meng ssu-hsiang shih (1600-1840)*, pp. 817-19; Hummel (ed.), *Eminent Chinese of the Ch'ing Period*, pp. 817-19.

11 Chang T'ai-yen, 'Shu Tseng ke Ch'uan-shan i-shu hou', *T'ai-yen wen-lu hsu-pien*, Ch. 2, Pt 1, p. 10.

12 Sung Chiao-jen, 'Hsüeh-sheng tsu-chih i-yu tsui hu', *Hsing-shih*, No. 1, pp. 128-9.

13 Sung Chiao-jen, 'Ch'ing t'ai-hou chih hsien-cheng t'an', ibid., pp. 125-6.

14 Ti Chu-ch'ing, 'Jen-Kung hsien-sheng shih-lüeh', in Ting Wen-chiang (comp.), *Liang Jen-kung hsien-sheng nien-p'u ch'ang-p'ien ch'u-kao*, Vol. I, p. 44.

15 Liang Ch'i-ch'ao, *Intellectual Trends in the Ch'ing Period*, p. 101; *Ch'ing-tai hsüeh-shu k'ai-lun*, p. 140.

16 Chiang Piao, 'Hsiang-hsüeh-pao hsü', *Hsiang-hsüeh-pao*, No. 1, 22 April 1897, *Wu-hsü pien-fa (WHPF)*, Vol. IV, pp. 530-1.

17 Ch'en Pao-chen, 'Hunan wu-yen ch'ih ko-chou-hsien ting-kou Hsiang-hsüeh-hsin-pao cha', *Hsiang-hsüeh-pao*, No. 5, 31 May 1897, *WHPF*, Vol. IV, p. 553.

18 Chang Chih-tung, 'Liang-hu tu-yüan Chang tzu-hui hsiang-hsüeh-yüan t'ung-ch'ih Hupeh ko tao fu chou hsien kou-yüeh Hsiang-hsüeh-pao kung-tu', *Hsiang-hsüeh-pao*, No. 15, 7 Sept. 1897, *WHPF*, Vol. IV, pp. 554-5; 'Cha shan-hou-chü t'ing-fa Hsiang-hsüeh-pao', 6 May 1898, ibid., p. 555.

19 Liang Ch'i-ch'ao, *Wu-hsü cheng-pien-chi*, pp. 137-8; *WHPF*, Vol. I, pp. 299-304.

20 'Liang Ch'i-ch'ao shang Ch'en Pao-chen shu lun Hunan ying-pan chih-shih', included in 'Liang Ch'i-ch'ao shu-tu', *WHPF*, Vol. II, pp. 551-8.

21 'Ch'ang-te Ming-ta hsüeh-hui chang-ch'eng', *Hsiang-hsüeh-pao*, No. 30, 13 March 1898, *WHPF*, Vol. IV, pp. 468-70.

22 Chü, 'Sung Chiao-jen lei', p. 13. See also Chü Yü, 'Hsü', in Sung, *Diary*, p. 23.

23 Lo Chi, 'Hsü', in Sung, *Diary*, p. 17.

24 Feng, 'Chuan', p. 33.

25 Lo, 'Sung-mu shou-hsü', p. 11.

3 REBELS IN THE MAKING

1 Chang Huang-ch'i, 'Chi Tzu-li hui', *Hsin-hai ko-ming*, (*HHKM*), Vol. I, p. 253; Smythe, E. Joan, 'The Tzu-li-hui: Some Chinese and Their Rebellions', *Papers on China*, Vol. XII, pp. 51-68; Feng Tzu-yu, *Ko-ming i-shih* (*KMIS*), Vol. II, pp. 76-7.

2 *Ta-ch'ing li-ch'ao shih-lu: ta-ch'ing te-tsung-ch'ao Ch'ing-huang-ti shih-lu*, Ch. 486, pp. 2a-2b.

3 Chang Chih-tung, 'Tsou-i 57: ch'ou-ting hsüeh-t'ang chi-mu t'zu-ti hsing-pan che', *Chang Wen-hsiang-kung ch'üan chi*, Ch. 57, p. 5a.

4 'Tsou-i 70: Ch'ing-chiang ko-hsüeh-t'ang pi-yeh-sheng chi kuan-li-yüan che', ibid., Ch. 70, pp. 13b-14a.

5 'Chiang Yü-yen hsien-sheng tzu-chuan', in Wu Hsiang-hsiang (ed.), *Chung-kuo hsien-tai-shih ts'ung-k'an*, Vol. VI, p. 249. See also Feng Tzu-yu, 'T'ien T'ung shih-lüeh' and Hsiung Shih-li, 'Wu K'un chuan', Chang Nan-hsien, *Hupeh ko-ming chih-chih-lu* (*Chih-chih-lu*), pp. 126 and 137 respectively.

6 Paul S. Reinsch, *Intellectual and Political Currents in the Far East*, pp. 216-17.

7 Yang Shou-jen, 'Hsin Hunan', in Chang Nan and Wang Jen-chih (eds.), *Hsin-hai ko-ming ch'ien shih-nien chien shih-lun hsüan-chi* (*SLHC*), Ser. 1, Vol. II, pp. 628-9, 615.

8 Li Shu-ch'eng, 'Hsüeh-sheng chih ching-cheng', *Hupeh hsüeh-sheng chieh*, No. 2, Tokyo, 1903, pp. 1-2.

9 'Min-tsu chu-i chih chiao-yü', *Yu-hsüeh i-p'ien*, No. 10, Tokyo, 1902-3, pp. 1-9. Also *SLHC*, Ser. 1, Vol. I, pp. 404-10.

10 Feng, *KMIS*, Vol. I, pp. 97-9. T'ao ch'eng-chang, 'Che-an chi-lüeh', *HHKM*, Vol. III, p. 15, states that it was primarily an anti-foreign society.

11 Li Chien-nung, *Tsui-chin san-shih-nien Chung-kuo cheng-chih-shih* (*Chin san-shih-nien shih*), p. 88.

12 Feng, *KMIS*, Vol. I, p. 98.

13 Feng Tzu-yu, *Chung-hua min-kuo k'ai-kuo-ch'ien ko-ming-shih* (*KMS*), Vol. I, p. 56.

14 Feng, *KMS*, Vol. I, p. 56.

15 Feng, *KMIS*, Vol. I, p. 113. Sung Chiao-jen, 'Ch'eng Chia-sheng Ko-ming ta-shih-hüeh, *Kuo-shih-kuan kuan-k'an* (*Kuan-k'an*), Vol. I, No. 3, p. 70.

16 For a list of journals publish-ed or sold in Shanghai in this period see Feng, *KMIS*, Vol. I, p. 140. See also Feng, *KMS*, Vol. I, p. 126.

17 Chang Ping-lin, 'Tseng ta-chiang-chün Tsou-chün mu-piao', *T'ai-yen wen-lu hsü-p'ien*, Ch. 5, Pt I, pp. 1-3. For information on the Educa-tional Society, see Wu Tse-chung (ed.), *Chih-hui hsien-sheng i-p'ien tsung-yao hui-i*, which includes Chiang Wei-ch'iao, 'Chung-kuo Chiao-yü-hui chih hui-i', and Yu Te-chi, 'Wu chih-hui hsien-sheng yü Ai-kuo hsüeh-she'.

18 Chu Ho-chung, 'Ou-chou T'ung-meng-hui chi-shih' ('Chi-shih'), *KMWH*, Vol. II, pp. 252, 113. Yang Yü-ju, *Hsin-hai ko-ming hsien-chu-chi* (*Hsien-chu-chi*), p. 10.

19 Li Lien-fang, 'Wu-han ko-ming t'uan-t'i chi-ch'i kung-tso', *Chung-hua min-kuo k'ai-kuo wu-shih-nien Wen-hsien*, Ser. 2, Vol. I, *Wuchang shou-i* ('Wu-han ko-ming', *Wuchang shou-i*), p. 39; Chang, *Chih-chih-lu*, p. 29; Chu, 'Chi-shih', *KMWH*, Vol. II, p. 113.

20 Li, 'Wu-han ko-ming', *Wu-chang shou-i*, pp. 39-40.

21 Feng, *KMIS*, Vol. I, pp. 102-4

22 *Su-pao*, 15, 30 May 1903.

23 Chu, 'Chi-shih', *KMWH*, Vol. II, p. 113.

24 Ibid., 21 May 1903.

25 Feng, *KMIS*, Vol. I, pp. 109-12.

26 For an account of Huang Hsing's career see Hsüeh Chün-tu, *Huang Hsing and the Chinese Revolution*.

27 Liu K'uei-i, *Huang Hsing chuan-chi*, p. 2.

28 Huang I-ou, 'Huang Hsing yü Ming-te hsüeh-t'ang', in

Chung-kuo jen-min cheng-chih hsieh-shang hui-i ch'üan-kuo wei-yüan-hui wen-shih tzu-liao yen-chiu wei-yüan-hui (ed.), *Hsin-hai ko-ming hui-i-lu* (*Hsin-hai hui-i-lu*), Vol. II, pp. 132-3.

29 Ibid., p. 134; Huang I-ou, 'Hui-i hsien-chün Huang K'e-ch'iang hsien sheng' (Hui-i'), *Hsin-hai hui-i-lu*, Vol. I, p. 609; Chou Chen-lin, 'Kuan-yü Huang Hsing, Hua-hsing-hui ho Hsin-hai ko-ming hou ti Sun-Huang kuan-hsi' ('Huang Hsing'), *Hsin-hai hui-i-lu*, Vol. I, p. 330. There are discrepancies concerning the number of people at this meeting. The above accounts give the number as more than 20; Liu, *Huang Hsing*, p. 3, gives 29 names besides Huang Hsing and the author himself. Chang Shih-chao, 'Yü Huang K'e-ch'iang hsiang-chiao shih-mo', *Hsin-hai hui-i-lu*, asserts that there were only 12 participants and all but 2 were Hunanese.

30 Huang, 'Hui-i', *Hsin-hai hui-i-lu*, Vol. I, p. 609.

31 Ibid. This is the only account of a second meeting of the China Resurgence Society. This could be the cause of the discrepancy in the attendance numbers referred to in note 29.

32 Liu, *Huang Hsing*, p. 3; Huang, 'Hui-i', *Hsin-hai hui-*

i-lu, Vol. I, p. 610. Kung I-shing, 'Kuang-fu-chün chih', *HHKM*, Vol. I, p. 530, mentioned that the Huang-han-hui was established by Li Hsieh-ho and five others but did not explain its relation to the China Resurgence Society.

33 Liu, *Huang Hsing*, pp. 3-4. See also Chang Huang-ch'i, 'Kuang-fu-hui ling-hsiu T'ao Ch'eng-chang ko-ming-shih' ('T'ao . . . ko-ming-shih'), *HHKM*, Vol. I, pp. 522-3.

34 Liu, *Huang Hsing*, p. 4.

35 Chang, *Chih-chih-lu*, p. 62.

36 Ibid. S. H. Cheng, 'The T'ung-meng-hui: Its Organization, Leadership and Finance, 1905-1912' (TMH), p. 88, mentions that some forty students from the Wu-chang Civil High School joined the Science Study Group.

37 Chou, 'Huang Hsing', pp. 331-2. Feng, *KMS*, Vol. I, p. 166, states that no less than 100,000 members of the *Ko-lao-hui*, a powerful secret society in central China, joined the revolutionary movement. As Hsüeh, *Huang Hsing*, p. 21, points out, the figure was probably an exaggeration.

38 Chang, *Chih-chih-lu*, p. 55, and Chang, 'T'ao . . . ko-ming-shih', pp. 522-3.

39 Chang, *Chih-chih-lu*, p. 55.

40 Liu, *Huang Hsing*, p. 4.

41 Huang, 'Hui-i', p. 610. There are some discrepancies on the date of the arrest order. Chou, 'Huang Hsing', p. 334, states that the news of the government's order for his arrest did not reach Huang Hsing until 2 November. Ts'ao Ya-po, *Wuchang ko-ming chen-shih (Chen-shih)*, Vol. I, pp. 1-3, states that it occurred ten days before the scheduled uprising. However, after comparing various sources on this incident, 24 October seems the more reliable date. See also Hsüeh, *Huang Hsing*, Ch. 2, n. 35.

42 Sung, *Diary*, 17 Nov. 1904, indicated that he was not in Wuchang after early September 1904. It should be noted that the dates in Sung's diary for 1904 were according to Chinese lunar calendar reckoning. The dates supplied in these notes are according to solar calendar system.

43 Sung, *Diary*, 31 Oct., 2 Nov. 1904.

44 Sung, *Diary*, 5, 6, 7 Nov. 1904. Note that Sung's name was not among the names of wanted persons listed in the official bulletin, quoted in Tsou Lu, *Chung-kuo kuo-min-tang shih-kao (Tang-shih-kao)*, Vol. III, pp. 676-7.

45 Chang, *Chih-chih-lu*, p. 56.

46 Sung, *Diary*, 17 Nov. 1904.

47 Tsou Lu, *Tang-shih-kao*, Vol. III, pp. 678-83.

48 Sung, *Diary*, 22 Nov. 1904.

49 Ibid., 4, 5 Dec. 1904.

4 THE THEME OF UNITY

1 Kung-Ming (Sung Chiao-jen), 'Hsi-fang ti-erh chih Man-chou wen-t'i', *Erh-shih shih-chi chih Chih-na*, No. 1, May 1905, p. 105; Ch'iang-tsai, 'I-ch'ien chiu-pai-ling-wu nien Lu-kuo chih ko-ming', *Min-pao*, No. 3, 1906, and No. 7, 1906; Sung, *Diary*, 15 Jan., 3 May 1905.

2 Sung, *Diary*, 9 June, 8 Feb. 1905, collated with notes 1 and 13 to this chapter.

3 Sung, *Diary*, 13 Dec. 1904.

4 Ibid., 3 Jan. 1905.

5 Ping Hsin, 'Sung hsien-sheng liu-Jih-shih chih i-shih' under 'Sung Yü-fu hsien-sheng i-shih', p. 15, in Yeh et al. (eds.), *Sung Yü-fu*.

6 Sung, *Diary*, 13 Jan., 24 April, 8 Aug. 1905; *Hsing-shih*, No. 1, pp. 125-6.

7 Sung, *Diary*, 2, 8 Jan. 1905.

8 Ibid., 12 Feb., 19, 22, 26, 27, 28 March 1905.

9 Ibid., 24 June 1905.

10 'Pen-she-chien-chang', *Erh-shih shih-chi chih Chih-na*, No. 1, Tokyo, 1905, back cover.

11 Wei-chung, 'Erh-shih shih-chi chih chih-na ch'u-yen: fa-k'an chih ts'ü-i', *Erh-shih shih-chi chih Chih-na*, No. 1, pp. 1-14.

12 Ch'en Hung-chü, 'Mei-chou t'ung-hsin', *Erh-shih shih-chi chih Chih-na*, No. 1, pp. 117-22.

13 Kung-ming, 'Han-tsu ch'in-lueh-shih', *Erh-shih shih-chi chih Chih-na*, No. 1, pp. 31-42.

14 Sung, *Diary*, 2 Dec. 1906.

15 Wei-chung, *Erh-shih shih-chi chih Chih-na*, No. 1, pp. 1-14.

16 Sung, *Diary*, 28, 31 Jan., 1 Feb. 1905.

17 Ibid., 28 Aug. 1905.

18 Ibid., 20 Aug. 1905.

19 Ibid., 2 Dec. 1906.

20 Ibid., 28 July, 20 Aug. 1905.

21 *Su-pao*, 6 April 1903.

22 'Fei-sheng-chieh', *Chekiang-ch'ao*, No. 3, April 1903, pp. 13-32.

23 'Lun Chung-kuo hsüeh-sheng t'ung-meng-hui chih fa-ch'i', *Su-pao*, 30, 31 May 1903.

24 *Han-sheng*, No. 1, June 1903, p. 4.

25 'Hsing-chung-hui shih-liao', *KMWH*, Vol. III, p. 322; Lo chia-lun, *Kuo-fu nien-p'u*, Vol. I, pp. 63-4.

26 Lo Chia-lun, *Kuo-fu nien-p'u*, Vol. I, pp. 76-8; Chang, *Chih-chih-lu*, p. 18.

27 Feng Tzu-yu, 'Hsing-chung-hui jen-ming shih-chi k'ao', *KMWH*, Vol. III, pp. 331-72.

28 Feng Tzu-yu, 'Hsing-chung-hui tsu-chih-shih', *KMWH*, Vol. III, p. 323; Chu, 'Chi-shih', *KMWH*, Vol. II, p. 256.

29 Feng, *KMIS*, Vol. I, p. 98.

30 Ibid., pp. 61-2.

31 Liu Ch'eng-yü, 'Hsien-tsung-li chiu-te-lu', *Kuo-shih-kuan kuan-k'an*, Vol. I, No. 1, p. 46.

32 Hu I-sheng, 'T'ung-meng-hui ch'eng-li ch'ien erh-san shih chih hui-i' ('Hui-i'), *KMWH*, Vol. II, pp. 248-9.

33 Feng, *KMIS*, Vol. I, p. 134; *KMWH*, Vol. III, pp. 363-6.

34 Hu I-sheng, 'Hui-i', *KMWH*, Vol. II, p. 249; Vol. III, p. 364.

35 I-hsien (Sun Yat-sen), 'Chih-na pao-ch'üan fen-ko ho-lun', *Kiangsu*, No. 6, Nov. 1903, pp. 13-21.

36 Feng, *KMIS*, Vol. III, p. 2, n. 183.

37 Ibid., Vol. I, pp. 132-3.

38 Lo Chia-lun, *Kuo-fu nien-p'u*, Vol. I, p. 85; Chang, *Chih-chih-lu*, p. 18; Chu Ho-chung, 'Hsin-hai ko-ming ch'eng-yü Wu-han chih yüan-yin', *Chien-kuo yüeh-k'an*, Vol. II, No. 4, p. 63.

39 Sung Chiao-jen, 'Ch'eng Chia-sheng ko-ming ta-shih-lüeh', *Kuan-k'an*, Vol. I, No. 3, p. 70.

40 Ibid.

41 Chu, 'Chi-shih', *KMWH*, Vol. II, p. 255.

42 Ho Chih-ts'ai, 'Ou-chou T'ung-meng-hui ch'eng-li shih-mo', in Feng, *KMIS*, Vol. II, p. 138.

43 Feng Tzu-yu, 'Chi Chung-kuo t'ung-meng-hui', *KMWH*, Vol. II, pp. 146-7.

44 Sung, *Diary*, 19 July 1905.

45 Katsuo Yoshihisa, *Tōa senka-ku shishi Kiden*, Vol. II, pp. 374-5.

46 M. B. Jansen, *The Japanese and Sun Yat-sen*, p. 117; T'ien T'ung, 'T'ung-meng-hui ch'eng-li-chi', *KMWH*, Vol. II, p. 142; Chü Cheng, 'Fang-wen Teng Chia-yen hsien-sheng ti-i-chiang', in K'ai-kuo wen-hsien, T'ung-meng-hui, Vol. I, pp. 342-5; Tsou Lu, *Tang-shih-Kao*, Vol. I, pp. 37-8.

47 Sung, *Diary*, 25, 28 July 1905. Some record that Sun Yat-sen met Sung Chiao-jen and Huang Hsing at the same time in Huang Hsing's residence. See Katsuo Yoshi-hisa, pp. 374-5.

48 Sung, *Diary*, 28 July 1905.

49 Ibid., 29 July 1905.

50 Teng Mu-han, 'Chung-kuo T'ung-meng-hui ch'eng-li shih-jih k'ao', *KMWH*, Vol. II, pp. 246-7.

51 Sung, *Diary*, 30 July 1905.

52 Ibid., 13 Aug. 1905. Kuo-t'ing, 'Chi Tung-ching liu-hsüeh-sheng huan-ying Sun chün I-hsien shih', *Min-pao*, No. 1, Dec. 1905, p. 69, states that more than 1,300 people attended the meeting.

53 Sung, *Diary*, 20 Aug. 1905.

54 Ibid., 29, 30 Aug. 1905.

55 Sung Chiao-jen, 'Ch'eng chia-sheng ko-ming ta-shih lüeh', *Kuan-k'an*, Vol. I, No. 3, p. 71.

56 Ibid.

5 EDUCATION AND REVOLUTION

1 Sung, *Diary*, 25 Sept. 1906.

2 K'ang Pao-chung, 'Ai-tz'u', under 'Sung Yü-fu hsien-sheng ai-lei', Pt 1 in Yeh *et al.* (eds.), *Sung Yü-fu*.

3 Sung, *Diary*, 2, 20, 28 Aug., 3 Sept. 1905.

4 Ibid., 6, 19, 20, 21 Sept. 1905; 17, 20, 21, 26, 27 Jan., 7, 20 Feb., 8, 10 March 1906, collated with 'Chang Chi tzu-chuan nien-p'u', entry for 1905 in *Chang P'u-ch'üan hsien-sheng ch'üan-chi: Hui-i-lu* (*Chang Chi Collection*), Vol. I, p. 235.

5 Han-min, 'Min-pao chih liu-ta chu-i', *Min-pao*, Vol. III, No. 3, pp. 1-22; Wei-chung, 'Erh-shih shih-chi chih Chih-na ch'u-yen', *Erh-shih shih-chi chih Chih-na*, No. 1, p. 4.

6 Sung, *Diary*, 2 Dec. 1906.

7 Ibid., 10, 11 Jan. 1907.

8 Huang Hsing and Hu Han-min, 'Chih T'an Te-tung Teng Tse-ju chu t'ung-chih shu', in Lo Chia-lun *et al.* (eds.), *Huang K'e-ch'iang hsien-sheng shu-han mo-chi* (*Huang Hsing mo-chi*), plates 60, 61.

9 Man-hua, 'T'ung-meng-hui shih-tai *Min-pao* shih-mo-chi', *KMWH*, Vol. II, p. 224.

10 'Shin-koku-jin wo ryū-gaku seshimuru koshi ritsu gakkō ni kan suru kitei', in *Hsin-min ts'ung-pao*, No. 23, 1905, pp. 1-7; Tu-li ts'ang-mang-tzu, 'Tung-ching hsüeh-chieh kung-fen shi-mo kao hsiang-jen fu-lao hsing-hsüeh shu', *HHKM*, Vol. II, p. 222.

11 Chung-kuo chih hsin-min, 'Chi Tung-ching liu-hsüeh-chieh kung-fen shih ping shu i chih i-chien', *Hsin-min ts'ung-pao*, No. 23, p. 12.

12 Sung, *Diary*, 4 Sept. 1905.

13 Sanetō Keishiu, *Chūkokujin Nihon ryūgaku-shi* (*Chūkokujin*), pp. 465-6; *Hsin-min ts'ung-pao*, No. 23, p. 23.

14 The dates cited are according to Huang Tsun-san, *San-shih-nien jih-chi*, Vol. I, entry for 5th day of the winter month. According to Sanetō, *Chūko-kujin*, p. 48, the correct date for Huang's entry should be the 4th day, which was 30 November.

15 Ibid., 11 Dec. 1905; 'Kyūsat-suin seisai', *Ni-roku shimbun*, 13 Dec. 1905, quoted in Sanetō, *Chūkokujin*, p. 477.

16 Ch'en t'ien-hua, 'Ch'en Hsing-t'ai chüeh-ming-shu', *Min-pao*, No. 2; Ch'ian-tsai, 'Pa', ibid.

17 Sanetō, *Chūkokujin*, p. 484.

18 'Mombushō-rei dai-jūkyū-gō no kaishaku', *Asahi shimbun*, 16 Dec. 1905; *Hsin-min ts'ung-pao*, No. 23, pp. 26-8.

19 Ch'en Chia-sheng, 'Shinkoku ryūgakusei torishimari kitei ni hantai no riyū', in Nagai Kazumi, 'Iwayuru shinkoku ryūgakusei torishimari kisoku jiken no seikaku', *Shinshū daigaku kiyō*, No. 2, 1952, pp. 19-20.

20 'Ko-hsiao lien-ho-hui kung-pu', No. 3, 5 Dec. 1905, quoted in Sanetō, *Chūkokujin*, pp. 471, 468; K'ang Pao-chung, 'Ai-tz'u', in 'Sung Yü-fu hsien-sheng ai-lei, Pt 1', in Yeh *et al.* (eds.), *Sung Yü-fu*. 'Tsung-hui ti erh-ch'i hsüan-chü chih-yüan', in *Li Chung-t'ang jih-chi*, quoted in Sanetō, *Chūkokujin*, p. 472.

21 Hu, 'Tzu-chuan', *KMWH*, Vol. III, pp. 380-1; Chiang Yung-ching, 'Hu Han-min hsien-sheng nien-p'u kao', in *Chung-kao hsien-tai-shih ts'ung-k'an*, Vol. III, pp. 90-1. It should be noted that Hu, in his 'Tzu-chuan', misplaced the event to 1903.

22 Hu, 'Tzu-chuan', *KMWH*, Vol. III, p. 391; Sanetō, *Chūkokujin*, p. 473.

23 *Hsin-min ts'ung-pao*, No. 23, 1905, pp. 1-44.

24 Hu, 'Tzu-chuan', *KMWH*, Vol. III, p. 391; Sanetō, *Chūkokujin*, pp. 487-9.

25 Ching Mei-chiu, 'Tsui-an', *HHKM*, Vol. II, p. 243.

26 Sanetō, *Chūkokujin*, p. 490; Sung, *Diary*, 13 Jan. 1906.

27 Huang Tsun-san, *San-shih-nien jih-chi*, 2 Dec. 1905.

28 Sung, *Diary*, 4 Jan. 1906.

29 'Jih-hua hsüeh-sheng-hui-tse', in Sanetō, *Chūkokujin*, p. 490.

30 Sung, *Diary*, 24 Jan. 1905, 10 March 1906.

31 Ibid., 28 July 1905.

32 Ibid., 3 Jan., 14 Aug. 1905.

33 Ibid., 12, 16, 28 Jan. 1906.

34 Ibid., 11 May, 17 June 1906. See also *Meiji szu-shih-erh-nien san-yüeh Ta-ch'ing-kuo kung-shih-kuan shao-chieh hsüeh-sheng so-yin-pu chao-t'ao-t'ien ta-hsüeh ch'ing-kuo liu-hsüeh-sheng pu*, No. 240.

35 Sung, *Diary* 12, 27 Jan., 5, 8, 13 Feb., 25 March 1906.

36 Ibid., 7 April, 3, 26 May, 1, 8, 14 June, 9, 18, 20 Aug., 3 Nov. 1906, 9 Jan. 1907.

37 Chieh, 'Erh-shih shih-chi chih Liang-shan-p'o', *Erh-shih shih-chi chih Chih-na*, No. 1, p. 115.

38 Sung, *Diary*, 4, 29 Sept. 1906.

39 Chieh, *Erh-shih shih-chi chih Chih-na*, No. 1, p. 115.

40 Ling Wu, 'Tung-pei hsin-hai ko-ming chien-shu', *Hsin-hai hui-i-lu*, Vol. V, p. 537; Chu Yen-chia, 'Wu Lu-chen yü Chung-kuo ko-ming,' in H. H. Wu (ed.), *Chung-kuo hsien-tai-shih ts'ung-k'an*, Vol. VI, Taipei, 1964, pp. 181-2.

41 All details concerning Sung's Manchurian trip are derived from his diary for the period from September 1906 to April 1907.

42 *Kuo-fu nien-p'u*, Vol. I, p. 174, entries for 1907; Hsiung Shih-li, 'Wu K'un chuan', in Chang, *Chih-chih-lu*, p. 137; Chang Ping-lin, 'T'ai-yen hsien-sheng tzu-ting nien-p'u', *Chin-tai-shih tzu-liao*, No. 1, Peking, 1957 ('T'ai-yen nien-p'u', *CTSTL*), p. 116, entry for 1907.

43 K'ang Pao-chung, 'Ai-tz'u', in Yeh *et al.* (eds.), *Sung Yü-fu*; Wang Yün-sheng, *Liu-shih-nien lai Chung-kuo yü Jih-pen* (*Chung-kuo yü Jih-pen*), Vol. V, p. 116.

44 Wang, *Chung-kuo yü Jih-pen*, Vol. V, pp. 117-19.

45 Ma Wen-i, 'Sung Chiao-jen yü Chien-tao wen-t'i', *Hsin-hai hui-i-lu*, Vol. VI, p. 38; Sung Chiao-jen, *Chien-tao wen-t'i*, p. 98.

46 Sung, *Chien-tao wen-t'i*, pp. 103-5, 111-12.

47 Sung's letter to the Chinese Minister for Japan was reported under the title, 'Ch'ing cheng-fu nai-yü chao ko-ming-tang pan-li wai-chiao', *Chung-hsing jih-pao*, 12 Oct. 1908, p. 2, collated with Ch'ien Tso-ch'i, 'Pa Wu Lu-chen Yen-chi-t'ing pien-wu pao-kao-shu', in Chang, *Chih-chih-lu*, pp. 39, 41; Ma Wen-i, 'Sung Chiao-jen yü Chien-tao wen-t'i', *Hsin-hai hui-i-lu*, Vol. VI, p. 39; Liu Yü-sheng, *Shih-tsai-t'ang tsa-i*, p. 106.

48 C. W. Young, *The International Relations of Manchuria*, pp. 90-2; J. V. A. MacMurray, *Treaties and Agreements with and Concerning China*, Vol. I, pp. 776-98.

49 *Chung-hsing jih-pao*, 12 Oct. 1908, p. 2.

50 T'an Jen-feng, 'Shih-shou p'ai-tz'u hsü-lu', *CTSTL*, No. 3, 1956 ('P'ai-tz'u', *CTSTL*), p. 42; 'T'ai-yen nien-p'u', *CTSTL*, No. 1, 1957, p. 121.

6 INTRA-PARTY DISPUTES

1 'Fu Ch'en Ch'u-nan kao ts'ang-pan *Min-pao* ping chu Ch'ou-k'an han', *Kuo-fu ch'üan-shu*, p. 398.

2 'Chih Hsiang-kang tsung-tu li-shu Man-ch'ing cheng-fu tsui-chuang ping i-ting p'ing-chih chang-ch'eng ch'ing chuan-shang ko-kuo tsan-ch'eng shu (24 July 1900)', *Kuo-fu ch'üan-shu*, p. 358; 'The true solution of the Chinese question (1904)', ibid., pp. 369-71; Han-min, 'Min-pao chih liu-ta chu-i', *Min-pao*, No. 3, pp. 19-21.

3 Jansen, *Sun Yat-sen*, pp. 113-15.

4 Chang Ping-lin, 'Tai-i jan-fou-lun', *Min-pao*, No. 24, p. 10.

5 Chang Ping-lin, 'Szu-huo-lun', ibid, No. 22, p. 11.

6 Sung, *Diary*, 6 June 1906.

7 'T'ai-yen nien-p'u', *CTSTL*, No. 1, 1957, p. 121.

8 Sung, *Diary*, 28 Feb. 1907; Feng Tzu-yu, *KMS*, Vol. I, p. 200.

9 Sung, *Diary*, 28 Feb. 1907.

10 Jansen, *Sun Yat-sen*, p. 122; Sung, *Diary*, 25, 27 Feb. 1907; Wang Tung, 'T'ung-meng-hui ho "Min-pao" p'ien-tuan hui-i', *Hsin-hai hui-i-lu*, Vol. VI, p. 29; *Kuo-fu nien-p'u*, Vol. I, p. 176.

11 *Kuo-fu nien-p'u*, Vol. I, p. 175; Feng, *KMS*, Vol. I, p. 201.

12 Feng Tzu-yu, 'Chi Chung-kuo t'ung-meng-hui', *KMWH*, Vol. II, p. 156.

13 Hu Han-min, 'Nan-yang yü Chung-kuo ko-ming', *Chung-hua min-kuo k'ai-kuo wu-shih-*

nien wen-hsien: Chung-kuo T'ung-meng-hui, Vol. I, p. 461; T'an Jen-feng, 'P'ai-tz'u', *CTSTL*, No. 3, 1956, p. 35.

14 Feng, *KMS*, Vol. I, p. 210.

15 Liu K'uei-i, *Huang Hsing*, p. 16.

16 Feng, 'Chi Chung-kuo t'ung-meng-hui', *KMWH*, Vol. II, p. 156.

17 Liu K'uei-i, *Huang Hsing*, p. 16.

18 Feng, *KMIS*, Vol. II, p. 38; Vol. IV, pp. 188-9; *KMS*, Vol. II, p. 182; Kayanō Chōchi, *Chūka minkoku kakumei hikyū*, pp. 107-8; Hu Han-min, 'Tzu-chuan', *KMWH*, Vol. III, p. 399.

19 'Fang-ch'eng ch'i'-i wang ch'ou-hua chieh-chi hsiang-hsieh chih Miyazaki Torazō han (19 October 1907)', *Kuo-fu ch'üan-shu*, pp. 402-3; Jansen, *Sun Yat-sen*, p. 119, Plate 2.

20 T'an, 'P'ai-tz'u', *CTSTL*, No. 3, 1956, p. 39.

21 Yüan Shu-i, 'Kung-chin-hui yü T'ung-meng-hui ti kuan-hsi', in *Pei-ching-shih li-shih hsüeh-hui ti-i ti-erh chieh nien-hui lun-wen hsüan-chi*, Peking, 1964, pp. 281-95.

22 'Kung-chin-hui shih-mo', in Chang, *Chih-chih-lu*, p. 179; Li Lien-fang, *Hsin-hai Wuchang shou-i-chi*, p. 16b; Hu Tzu-shun, 'Wuchang k'ai-kuo shih-lu', *KMWH*, Vol.

IV, p. 451; Chü Cheng, *Mei-ch'uan p'u-chi*, p. 13a; Teng Wen-hui, 'Kung-chin-hui ti yüan-ch'i chi ch'i jo-kan chih-tu' ('Kung-chin-hui'), *CTSTL*, No. 3, 1956, pp. 10-11.

23 Sung, *Diary*, 5, 7 Jan., 28 Feb. 1907. For Huang's and T'an's attitudes see Li, *Huang K'e-ch'iang nien-p'u*, in H.H., Wu (ed.), *Chung-kuo hsien-tai-shih ts'ung-k'an*, Vol. IV, p. 229, also T'an, 'P'ai-tz'u', *CTSTL*, No. 3, 1956, p. 39.

24 Chang Ping-lin, 'Chiao Ta-feng chuan', in Chang, *Chih-chih-lu*, p. 232.

25 Ts'ai Chi-min and Wu Hsing-han, 'Hsin-hai Wu-han shou-i shih-lu', in *KMWH*, Vol. IV, p. 497.

26 Shen Tieh-min, 'Chi Kuang-fu-hui erh-san-shih', *Hsin-hai hui-i-lu*, Vol. IV, pp. 131-42; Kung I-hsing, 'Kuang-fu-chün chih', *HHKM*, Vol. I, p. 530; 'Chih Ch'en Chiung-ming chi Chung-kuo t'ung-meng-hui t'iao-ho tang-cheng tien (28 January 1912)', *Kuo-fu ch'üan-shu*, p. 456.

27 The account of T'ao Ch'eng-chang's quarrel with Sun Yat-sen is based on 'Yu Ou ti Mei ch'ien-hou chih Wang Tzu-k'uang yü liu Pi t'ung-chih ko-han (22 October 1909)', *Kuo-fu ch'uan-shu*, pp. 416-17; 'Chih Wu Ching-

heng ch'ing yü hsin-shih-chi p'ing lun *Jih-hua hsin-pao* p'o-huai tang-shih miu-lun ko-han, No. 1 (4 December 1909)', ibid., p. 420; Chang Huang-ch'i, 'T'ao Ch'eng-chang Ko-ming-shih', *HHKM*, Vol. I, pp. 525-6; Kung I-hsing, 'Kuang-fu-chün chih', ibid., p. 532; 'Hu Han-min chih Nan-yang t'ung-chih shu' in Li, 'Huang k'e-ch'iang nien p'u', in Wu, *Chung-kuo hsien-tai shih ts'ung-k'an*, Vol. IV, p. 231; T'ao Ch'eng-chang, 'Che-an-chi-lüeh', *HHKM*, Vol. III, pp. 3-111; 'T'ai-yen nien-p'u', *CTSTL*, No. 1, 1957, p. 122.

28 'T'ai-yen nien-p'u', *CTSTL*, No. 1, 1957, pp. 121-2.

29 T'an, 'P'ai-tz'u', *CTSTL*, No. 3, 1956, p. 40.

30 Sun Yat-sen's letter to Wu Chih-hui, 4 Dec. 1909, *Kuo-fu ch'üan-shu*, p. 420.

31 T'an, 'P'ai-tz'u', p. 42.

32 Sun Yat-sen, 'Yu nan-yang chih Wu ching-heng han (20 July 1910)', *Kuo-fu ch'üan-shu*, pp. 427-8.

33 'Yu Jih-pen ti Sing-chia-po hou chih Teng Tze-ju teng han, No. 3 (24 August 1910)', *Kuo-fu ch'üan-shu*, pp. 428-9.

34 T'ien T'ung, 'T'ung-meng-hui ch'eng-li-chi', *KMWH*, Vol. II, p. 142.

35 T'an, 'P'ai-tz'u', p. 42.

36 Ibid.; Yang, *Hsien-chu-chi*, p. 31.

37 Chü Cheng, *Mei-ch'üan, p'u-chi*, p. 15b; 'Tsou Yung-ch'eng hui-i-lu', *CTSTL*, No. 3, 1956, p. 93; Chü Cheng, 'Hsin-hai tsa-chi', *Chü Chüeh-sheng hsien-sheng ch'üan-chi*, Vol. II, p. 474; Yang, *Hsien-chu-chi*, p. 32.

38 *Gaimushō Kiroku* (Japan Foreign Office Records): *Kakkoku naisei zassan Shina no bu—Kakumeitō Kankei (Bōmei-sha wo fukumu)*, Mon 1 Rui 6 Kō 1 Gō 4-2-1, Vol. 4, pp. 450156-450157 (Confidential Report No. 66, 10 Jan. 1911) records that Sung Chiao-jen left Yokohama for Shanghai on 31 December 1910.

39 Ibid.; also Sao-hsin, 'Pu-k'an hui-shou', under Sung hsien-sheng i-shih, in Yeh *et al.* (eds.), *Sung Yü-fu*.

40 Confidential Report No. 985, 21 March 1911, in Gaimushō Kiroku, p. 450184; also No. 1167, 13 April 1911, and No. 534, 16 Feb. 1911, ibid., pp. 450203, 450166 respectively.

7 PRELUDE TO A STORM

1 Ch'ou Ngao, 'Hsin-hai ko-ming ch'ien-hou tsa-i', *Hsin-hai hui-i-lu*, Vol. I, p. 442; Chang Ping-lin, 'Chi Cheng-wen-she-yüan-ta-hui p'o-huai-chuang', *T'ai-yen wen-lu*

ch'u-p'ien pei-lu, Vol. II, pp. 65b-71a. Cf. Ting, *Liang Jen-kung*, Vol. I, pp. 250-1.

2 Tan Mou-hsin, 'T'ung-meng-hui-yüan yü Pao-huang-tang fen-tzu tsai Jih-pen ti chi-ch'ang jan-tou', *Hsin-hai hui-i-lu*, Vol. VI, pp. 35-6.

3 *Kuo-fu nien-p'u*, pp. 174-206.

4 K'ang Yu-wei, 'K'ang Nan-hai yü Jen-ti shu', 15 Dec. 1908 or 6 Jan. 1909, in Ting, *Liang Jen Kung*, Vol. I, pp. 294-5; *The Chinese Times*, 18 Sept. 1909, p. 4.

5 Cameron, *The Reform Movement in China, 1898-1912*, pp. 122-4, 126.

6 Ibid., p. 128; *NCH*, 8 April 1911.

7 Huang Hsing, 'Chih Hsien-lo t'ung-chih shu', *Huang Hsing Mo-chi*, pp. 13-14.

8 *Tsou Lu, Kuang-chou san-yüeh erh-shih-chiu ko-ming shih* (*Kuang-chou ko-ming-shih*), pp. 30, 4.

9 Ibid., p. 19; T'an Jen-feng, 'P'ai-tz'u', *CTSTL*, No. 3, 1956, p. 44.

10 Ibid.

11 Ibid., p. 48; Hsü T'ien-fu, 'Sung hsien-sheng chuan-lüeh', in Yeh Ch'u-ts'ang (ed.), *Ko-ming shih-wen-hsüan*, p. 170; 'Sung Yü-fu hsien-sheng i-shih', in Yeh *et al.* (eds.), *Sung Yü-fu*.

12 Tsou Lu, *Kuang-chou ko-ming-shih*, pp. 57-69

13 Ibid., p. 38.

14 Ibid., pp. 38-9, 63, 43.

15 'Sung Chiao-jen t'an Hsin-hai ko-ming', *Min-li-pao*, 17 Oct. 1912, pp. 6-7.

16 Tan Jen-feng, 'P'ai-tz'u', p. 46; Huang Hsing, 'Chih hai-wai t'ung-chih shu', *Huang Hsing Mo-chi*, Pt 1, plate 51.

17 *Huang Hsing Mo-chi*, Pt 1, plate 68; Sun Yat-sen, 'Huang-hua-kang lieh-shih lüeh hsü' (December 1921), *Kuo-fu ch'uan-shu*, p. 1052; Hu Han-min, 'Tzu-chuan', *KMWH*, Vol. III, p. 411.

18 Hu Han-min, 'Tzu-chuan', *KMWH*, Vol. III, p. 411.

19 'Chih Feng Tzu-yu shu', *Huang Hsing mo-chi*, Pt 1, plate 80; *CTSTL*, No. 3, 1956, p. 48; Hu Han-min, 'Tzu-chuan', *KMWH*, Vol. III, pp. 40-1.

20 Sao hsin, 'Pu-k'an hui-shou' in Yeh *et al.* (eds), *Sung Yü-fu*.

21 *KMWH*, Vol. II, pp. 238-40.

22 Lo, *Kuo-fu nien-p'u*, Vol. I, p. 217.

23 Chü Cheng, *Mei-ch'uan p'u-chieh*, pp. 15b-16a.

24 Tan Jen-feng, 'P'ai-tz'u', p. 43.

25 Ibid.

26 Ibid., pp. 42-3.

27 Sao-hsin, 'Pu-k'an hui-shou'; Lo Chia-lun, 'Hsü', in Sung Chiao-jen, *Erh-pai-nien lai chih O-fan*, pp. 1-2.

28 T'an Jen-feng, 'P'ai-tz'u', p. 44; S. H. Cheng, TMH, p. 116.

29 Tsou Yung-ch'eng, 'Hui-i-lu', *CTSTL*, No. 3, 1956, p. 97.

30 Sao-hsin, 'Pu-k'an hui-shou'.

31 Yang, *Hsien-chu-chi*, pp. 35-6, 40; Li Lien-fang, *Hsin-hai Wuchang shou-i-chi*, p. 71b.

32 T'an Jen-feng, 'P'ai-tz'u', p. 48; Tseng Po-hsing, 'Huang-hua-kang yü Chung-pu T'ung-meng-hui', *Wuchang shou-i*, p. 19; 'Ch'eng-li ta-hui ch'ien-ming-tan', *Wuchang shou-i*, plate 1.

33 'Chung-kuo t'ung-meng-hui chung-pu tsung-hui hsüan-yen', *Wuchang shou-i*, pp. 9-10, plates 12-14.

34 'Tsai-mei chih Jih-pen Munakata kun k'ang-i Jih-pen tui pen-tang t'ai-tu p'an ch'i-tao Jih-pen yü-lun chi cheng-fu t'ung ch'ing wo-kuo ko-ming han', *Kuo-fu Ch'üan-shu*, pp. 435-6.

35 'Chung-kuo t'ung-meng-hui chung-pu tsung-hui chang-ch'eng', article 13 in *Wuchang shou-i*, pp. 5-7, plates 3-7.

36 'Chung-kuo t'ung-meng-hui chung-pu tsung-hui tsung-wu-hui chih-yüan lu', *Wuchang shou-i*, plate 15.

37 Ch'en Hsü-lu, 'Lun Sung Chiao-jen', *Hsin-hai lun-wen-chi*, Vol. I, p. 358.

38 'Tsung-wu-hui chang-ch'eng', articles 2, 4; 'Chung-kuo t'ung-meng-hui chung-pu tsung-hui hsüan-yen' and 'Chung-kuo t'ung-meng-hui chung-pu tsung-hui chang-ch'eng', articles 17, 18, *Wuchang shou-i*, pp. 9, 6.

39 Ch'eng Ch'ien, 'Hsin-hai ko-ming ch'ien-hou hui-i p'ien-tuan', *Hsin-hai hui-i-lu*, Vol. I, p. 76.

40 Tseng Po-hsing, 'Huang-hua-kang yü Chung-pu Tung-meng-hui', p. 20.

41 'Ch'eng-li ta-hui ch'ien-ming tan' and 'Chung-kuo t'ung-meng-hui chung-pu tsung-hui chang-ch'eng', article 1 in *Wuchang shou-i*, plates 1-2, 3.

42 Chang Hsiang-wen, 'Sung Chiao-jen chuan', *Nan-yüan ts'ung-kao*, Vol. VIII, p. 20a; Sung Chiao-jen, 'Hupeh hsin-shih ti-ti shuo', *Min-li-pao*, 15 Oct. 1911, p. 1.

43 Hsü T'ien-fu, 'Sung hsien-sheng chuan-lüeh', p. 171; Wu Yü-chang, 'Wuchang ch'i-i ch'ien-hou tao erh-tz'u ko-ming', *Hsin-hai hui-i-lu*, Vol. I, p. 95.

44 'Chung-kuo t'ung-meng-hui chung-pu tsung-hui chung-yao chüeh-i', *Wuchang shou-i*, plates 16-19.

45 Ibid.

46 Lin Yu-tang, *Public Opinion in China*, Chicago, 1936, p. 113; K'o Kung-chen, *Chung-kuo pao-hsüeh-shih*, p. 158.

47 Sung Chiao-jen, 'Lun ch'uan-jen cheng-lu shih', *Min-li-pao*, 14 Sept. 1911.

48 Yü-fu (Sung Chiao-jen), 'P'u-kuo kai-ko chih ta-ch'eng-kung', *Min-li-pao*, 28 Sept. 1911, p. 1.

8 THE REVOLUTION OF 1911

1 Chü Cheng, *Hsin-hai cha-chi Mei-ch'uan jih-chi ho-k'an (Ho-k'an)*, p. 1.

2 Ibid.

3 T'an Jen-feng, 'P'ai-tz'u', *CTSTL*, Vol. 3, 1956, p. 49.

4 'Chung-kuo t'ung-meng-hui chung-pu tsung-hui chung-yao chüeh-i', *Wuchang shou-i*, plate 18.

5 'Sun Wen hsüeh-shuo', *Kuo-fu ch'üan-shu*, p. 37.

6 Chang, *Chih-chih-lu*, pp. 258-59; Li Lien-fang, *Hsin-hai Wuchang shou-i-chi*, pp. 84b-85a; Wu Hsiang-hsiang, *Sung Chiao-jen*, p. 102; Li Shih-yüeh, *Liang-hu ko-ming yün-tung*, pp. 71-4; J. Ch'en, *Yuan Shih-k'ai 1859-1916*.

7 *NCH*, Nov. 1904, quoted in Powell, *The Rise of Chinese Military Power*, pp. 230-1.

8 Chang Nan-hsien, 'Jih-chih-hui shih-mo', *Chih-chih-lu*, p. 81.

9 Li Lien-fang, *Hsin-hai Wuchang shou-i-chi*, p. 7b; Chang Nan-hsien, 'Wei wu-shih-liu nien-ch'ien ti i-pi li-shih-chang ta-k'e-wen', *Hsin-hai hui-i-lu*, Vol. VI, pp. 42-5;

Chang Nan-hsien, *Chih-chih-lu*, p. 83; Sung Chiao-jen, *Diary*, 3 June 1905.

10 Li Lien-fang, p. 9a; Feng, *KMIS*, Vol. II, p. 65.

11 Chang Nan-hsien, *Chih-chih-lu*, pp. 142, 145, 148.

12 Liang Ch'i-ch'ao, 'Hsiang-luan kan-yen', *Yin-ping-shih ho-chi*, Vol. IX, pp. 58-67; M. Hewlett, *Forty Years in China*, pp. 59-71.

13 'Chen-wu hsüeh-she shih-mo', Chang Nan-hsien, *Chih-chih-lu*, pp. 152-4, 158-9. On the origin of the Literary Society cf. 'Wuhan ko-ming t'uan-t'i Wen-hsüeh-she chih li-shih', *Min-li-pao*, 7, 8 Oct. 1912; Yang Yü-ju, *Hsin-hai ko-ming hsien-chu-chi*, p. 29; Chang Yü-k'un, 'Wen-hsüeh-she Wuchang shou-i chi-shih', *Wuchang shou-i*, pp. 109-12; Hu Tze-shun, 'Wu-chang k'ai-kuo shih-lu', *KMWH*, Vol. IV, p. 18; Chang Kuo-kan, *Hsin-hai ko-ming shih-liao*, p. 32.

14 Li Lien-fang, *Hsin-hai Wuchang shou-i-chi*, pp. 14a-18a; 'Wuhan ko-ming t'uan-t'i Wen-hsüeh-she chih li-shih', *Min-li-pao*, 7, 8 Oct. 1912.

15 'Chiang I-wu shih-lüeh', Chang Nan-hsien, *Chih-chih-lu*, pp. 166; 63; Hu Tze-shun, 'Wu-ch'ang k'ai-kuo shih-lu', *KMWH*, Vol. IV, p. 461; Li Lien-fang, pp. 14a-14b.

16 Yeh Shu, 'K'ai-kuo yüan-hsun Chiang shang-chiang I-wu shih-lüeh', in Yung Ch'ien, 'Wuchang Liang-jih-chi', *HHKM*, Vol. V, p. 73.

17 Membership register of the T'ung-meng-hui for 1905-1906, in *KMWH*, Vol. II, p. 179; Chang Yü-k'un, 'Liu Yao-cheng chuan', Chang Nan-hsien, *Chih-chih-lu*, pp. 262-3.

18 Chang Nan-hsien, pp. 179, 190.

19 Hu Tze-shun, 'Wu-ch'ang k'ai-kuo shih-lu', p. 435.

20 Chang Nan-hsien, pp. 179-90; Li Lien-fang, *Hsin-hai Wuchang shou-i-chi*, p. 17a; Feng, *KMIS*, Vol. I, p. 249.

21 T'an Jen-feng, 'P'ai-tz'u', p. 44.

22 Ts'ai Chi-ou, *O-chou hsüeh-shih*, p. 56.

23 Li Lien-fang, *Hsin-hai Wuchang shou-i-chi*, p. 71a.

24 Yang Yü-ju, *Hsin-hai ko-ming hsien-chu-chi*, p. 39.

25 Ibid., pp. 40-1, notes 1 and 2 collated with Li Lien-fang, p. 71b; Jung Meng-yüan (ed.), *Chung-kuo chin-tai-shih tzu-liao hsüan-chi*, p. 636; *Wuchang shou-i*, p. 114; Chang

Nan-hsien, *Chih-chih-lu*, pp. 238, 69; Tsou Yung-ch'eng, 'Hui-i-lu', *CTSTL*, Vol. 3, 1956, p. 99; T'an Jen-feng, 'P'ai-tz'u', p. 50; Chü Cheng, *Ho-k'an*, p. 38.

26 Chü Cheng, *Ho-k'an*, p. 38; T'an Jen-feng, p. 50; 'Ts'en Wei-sheng tzu-shu: Sung hsien-sheng chih ai-wo', *Min-li-pao*, 17 April 1911; Ts'ai Chi-ou, *O-chou hsüeh-shih*, pp. 63-4; Yang Yü-ju, *Hsin-hai ko-ming hsien-chu-chi*, p. 53.

27 *Wuchang shou-i*, plate 18; T'an Jen-feng, p. 50.

28 Chang Nan-hsien, *Chih-chih-lu*, p. 249.

29 T'an Jen-feng, p. 50; *Wuchang shou-i*, plate 18.

30 T'an Jen-feng, p. 51.

31 Yang Yü-ju, p. 48; Li Lien-fang, p. 74a; Chang Nan-hsien, *Chih-chih-lu*, p. 247.

32 Hu Tzu-shun, *Wuchang k'ai-kuo shih-lu*, p. 465; Wu Hsing-han, 'Wuchang ch'i-i san-jih-chi', *HHKM*, Vol. V, p. 78; Teng Yü-lin, 'Hsin-hai Wuchang ch'i-i ching-kuo', *HHKM*, pp. 100-1; Yang Yü-ju, p. 53; Chang Nan-hsien, *Chih-chih-lu*, pp. 247-9; Li Lien-fang, p. 81b, 74b-75a; Li Shih-yüeh, *Liang-hu ko-ming yün-tung*, p. 69, n. 1.

33 Chang Nan-hsien, *Chih-chih-lu*, p. 251; Ts'ai Chi-ou, *O-chou hsüeh-shih*, p. 74.

34 Li Lien-fang, pp. 84, 73b, 76a, 71b; Chang Nan-

hsien, *Chih-chih-lu*, p. 263; Chang Kuo-kan, *Hsin-hai ko-ming shih-liao*, p. 60; *Wuchang shou-i*, pp. 111-18.

35 Chang Nan-hsien, *Chih-chih-lu*, p. 250. Cf. Teng Yü-lin, p. 102.

36 Li Shih-yüeh, pp. 71-2; Jerome Ch'en, 'A Footnote on the Chinese Army in 1911-12', *T'oung-pao*, Vol. 48, Leiden, 1960, pp. 441-3.

37 'Chu Han Ying, O, Te, Jih ling-shih pu-kao-wen', *Wuchang shou-i*, p. 379.

38 *Wuchang shou-i*, plates 434-46.

39 'Sung Chiao-jen chih Yang P'u-sheng Han', 2 Nov. 1911, *Wuchang shou-i*, plates 437-8.

40 Sao-hsin, 'Pu-k'an hui-shou', in Yeh *et al.* (eds.), *Sung Yü-fu*.

41 Sung Chiao-jen, 'Hupeh hsin-shih ti-li-shuo', *Min-li-pao*, 15 Oct. 1911.

42 Sao-hsin, 'Pu-k'an hui-shou'; Fan Kuang-ch'i, 'Chi Sung-hsien-sheng i-shih', in Yeh Ch'u-ts'ang (ed.), *Ko-ming shih-wen hsüan*, p. 163.

43 Ibid.; Tsou Lu, *Tang-shih-kao*, Vol. III, p. 975.

44 Yang Yü-ju, pp. 157-9; Li Lien-fang, pp. 147b-148a; Ts'ao Ya-po, *Chen-shih*, Vol. II, pp. 210-13.

45 Yang Yü-ju, p. 159.

46 Ts'ai Chi-ou, pp. 140-1.

47 Chü Cheng, *Ho-k'an*, pp. 60-1; *Chü Cheng Collection*, Vol. II, pp. 512-13.

48 Ibid., pp. 518-19.

49 *Kita Ikki chosaku shū*, Vol. II, p. 44.

50 Cf. Wu Hsiang-hsiang, *Sung Chiao-jen*, p. 106.

51 Hsieh Shih-ch'ing, 'Shu-kung sui-pi', *Hsin-hai ko-ming tsu-liao*, p. 492.

52 Fan Kuang-ch'i, 'Chi Sung hsien-sheng i-shih', *Ko-ming shih-wen-hsüan*, pp. 163-4.

53 Chang Kuo-kan, *Hsin-hai ko-ming shih-liao*, p. 227.

54 *Kita Ikki chosaku shū*, Vol. II, p. 46.

55 Ibid., collated with *Tokyo Nichinichi Shimbun* (E), 21 Nov. 1911 (Meiji 44th year).

56 Hsü Shen *et al.*, 'Ti chiu-cheng mo-lin ch'i-i ho chiang-che lien-chun kuang-fu Nanking ch'in-li-chi', *Hsin-hai hui-i-lu*, Vol. IV, p. 238.

57 Ibid., p. 240; Ma Yai-min, 'Nan-ching kuang-fu chien-wen so-i', *Hsin-hai hui-i-lu*, Vol. IV, pp. 257, 259.

58 Lin Shu-ching, 'Chiang-tso yung-ping-chi', *Ko-sheng kuang-fu (KSKF)* (*Chung-hua min-kuo k'ai-kuo wu-shih nien wen-hsien, series 2*), Vol. II, p. 48.

59 *Ko-ming shih-wen-hsüan*, p. 164.

60 Ibid.; *KSKF*, Vol. II, p. 80; Chang Kuo-kan, p. 236. Cf. Ch'en Tze-feng, 'Po Wen-

wei t'an P'u-k'ou yü Nanking
chih-i', *KSKF*, Vol. II, p. 84.

61 Chang Kuo-kan, pp. 235-6.

62 Lin Shu-ch'ing, 'Chiang-tso
yung-ping-chi', *KSKF*, Vol.
II, p. 80.

9 THE NANKING PROVISIONAL GOVERNMENT

1 T'an Jen-feng, 'Ai-tz'u' and
'Sung Yü-fu hsien-sheng i-
shih', in Yeh *et al.* (eds.),
Sung Yü-fu.

2 K'ang Pao-chung, 'Ai-tz'u',
ibid.

3 Tson Lu, *Kuang-chou ko-ming-
shih*, pp. 30, 4; T'an Jen-feng,
'P'ai-tz'u', *CTSTL*, No. 3,
1956, p. 44; Hsü T'ien-fu,
'Sung hsien-sheng chuan-
lüeh', in Yeh Ch'u-ts'ang
(ed.), *Ko-ming shih-wen-
hsüan*, p. 170; 'Sung Yü-fu
hsien-sheng i-shih', in Yeh *et
al.* (eds.), *Sung Yü-fu.*

4 Jerome Ch'en, *Yüan Shih-k'ai,
1859-1916'*, p. 118.

5 Sao-hsin, 'Pu-k'an hui-shou'
and 'Sung Yü-fu hsien-sheng
i-shih', in Yeh *et al.* (eds.),
Sung Yü-fu.

6 Yü-fu, 'P'u-kuo kai-ko chih
ta ch'eng-kung', *Min-li-pao*,
28 Sept. 1911, p. 1.

7 Portugal's republican revolution took place on 4 Oct.
1910; see C. E. Nowell, *A
History of Portugal*, pp. 213,
224.

8 Yü-fu, 'P'u-kuo kai-ko chih
ta ch'eng-kung'; Yü-fu,
'Chiao-chan-shih chih chung-
li lun', *Min-li-pao*, 28 Sept.,
14 Oct. 1911, p. 1.

9 Li Lien-fang, *Hsin-hai Wuchang shou-i-chi*, p. 119b. For
a full text of this constitution
see *Min-li-pao*, 2 Dec. 1911.

10 'O-chün tutu Li Yüan-hung
chih ko-sheng cheng-hsun
tui tsu-chih cheng-fu i-chien
tien' 7 Nov. 1911, *KMWH*,
Vol. I, p. 1.

11 'O-chün tutu Li Yüan-hung
fu Ch'en Ch'i-mei ch'ing-p'ai
tai-piao fu O tsu-chih lin-
shih cheng-fu tien', n.d.,
KMWH, Vol. I, pp. 3-4. See
also Ch'en Ch'i-mei's telegram of 13 Nov. 1911; cf.
Ts'ai Chi-ou, *O-chou hsüeh-
shih*, pp. 160-1; Ts'ao Ya-po,
Chen-shih, Vol. II, p. 262.

12 'Kiangsu tutu Ch'eng Te-
ch'üan Chekiang tutu T'ang
Shou-ch'ien lien-ming chih
Fu-chün tutu Ch'en Ch'i-
mei t'i-i tsai Shanghai tsu-
chih lin-shih i-shih chi-kuan
tien', *KMWH*, Vol. I, pp. 1-2.

13 'Chen-chiang tutu Lin Shu-
ch'ing chih Shanghai chün-
cheng-fu chu-chang tsai Fu
k'ai-hui tien', 12 Nov. 1911,
KMWH, Vol. I, p. 2.

14 'Fu-chün tutu Ch'en Ch'i-
mei chih ko-sheng ch'ing
p'ai tai-piao fu Fu i-chien lin-
shih cheng-fu tien', 13 Nov.
1911', *KMWH*, Vol. I, p. 3.

15 Ku Chung-hsiu, *Chung-hua min-kuo k'ai-kuo-shih*, reprint, Taipei, 1962, p. 34; Liu Hsing-nan, 'Hsin-hai ko-sheng tai-piao hui-i jih-chih', *Hsin-hai hui-i-lu*, Vol. VI, p. 241.

16 'O-chün tutu Li Yüan-hung fu ch'en Ch'i-mei ch'ing-p'ai tai-piao fu O tsu-chih lin-shih cheng-fu tien', n.d., *KMWH*, Vol. I, pp. 3-4.

17 The *Tokyo Nichinichi shimbun*, 21 Nov. 1911 (Meiji 44th year), E, reported that Sung Chiao-jen left Wuchang for Nanking on 13 November 1911 at 4 p.m.

18 Ku Chung-hsiu, *K'ai-kuo-shih*, p. 34; Liu Hsing-nan, 'Hsin-hai ko-sheng tai-piao hui-i jih-chih', *Hsin-hai hui-i-lu*, Vol. VI, p. 241; Chang Nan-hsien, *Chih-chih-lu*, p. 390. Instead of Fukien, Ku Chung-hsiu named Chekiang as one of the three provinces of the representatives of which initiated the establishment of this organisation.

19 Lin Shu-ch'ing, 'Chiang-tso yung-ping chi', *Ko-sheng kuang-fu*, Vol. II, p. 48.

20 Ku-hung, 'Sung hsien-sheng i-shih (1)', 'Sung Yü-fu hsien-sheng i-shih', in Yeh *et al.* (eds.), *Sung Yü-fu*.

21 'Chekiang teng-sheng tai-piao chih Li Yüan-hung, Huang Hsing ch'eng-jen O-chün wei min-kuo chung-yang chün-cheng-fu ping

ch'ing wei-jen Wu T'ing-fang, Wen Tsung-yao chu-fu pan-li chiao-hsieh tien', n.d., *KMWH*, Vol. I, pp. 4-5, collated with Tsou Lu, *Tang-shih-kao*, Vol. III, Pt 2, p. 1009.

22 P'ing-i, 'Lin-shih cheng-fu ch'eng-li chi', *HHKM*, Vol. VIII, pp. 3-4, collated with Liu Hsing-nan, 'Hsin-hai ko-sheng tai-piao hui-i jih chih', p. 241; Tsou Lu, *Tang-shih-kao*, Vol. III, Pt 2, p. 1010; 'Chih Shanghai Chü T'ao erh-wei-yüan tien (23 Nov. 1911)', *Li fu-tsung-t'ung cheng-shu*, reprint, Taipei, 1962, Vol. I, pp. 12a-12b; Chang Hsiao-jo, *Nan-t'ung Chang Chi-chih hsien-sheng chuan-chi*, pp. 167-8.

23 *Kita Ikki chosaku shū*, Vol. II, p. 46; Ku-hung, 'Sung hsien-sheng i-shih (1)', in Yeh *et al.* (eds.), *Sung Yü-fu*.

24 Sao-hsin, 'Pu-k'an hui-shou'.

25 Ibid.; *Min-li-pao*, 11 Dec. 1911, p. 1.

26 'Chün-chi-tz'u tien-pao-tang: Hsüan-t'ung san-nien shih-yüeh shih-i-jih (1 Dec. 1911) liu-fu tai-piao Sung Chiao-jen teng chih ko-sheng tzu-i-chü tien', *HHKM* Vol. V, p. 396.

27 'Hsüan-t'ung san-nien shih-yüeh shih-szu-jih liu Fu tai-piao chi T'ang Shou-ch'ien teng chih tzu-i-chü tien', ibid., p. 396, collated with *Chü Chüeh-sheng hsien-sheng*

ch'üan-chi, Vol. II, 528, 525, and Liu Hsing-nan, p. 248.

28 Ku Chung-hsiu, *Chung-hua min-kuo k'ai-kuo-shih*, p. 40; 'Ko-sheng tai-piao-hui chih Shanghai ko-sheng tai-piao lien-ho-hui kao lin-shih cheng-fu she yü Nanking tien (4 Dec. 1911)', *KMWH*, Vol. I, p. 7; P'ing-i, 'Lin-shih cheng-fu ch'eng-li chi', p. 5.

29 Ku Chung-hsiu, p. 48; Liu Hsing-nan, p. 247.

30 Li Yüan-hung, 'Chih ko-sheng tutu (8 Dec. 1911)', *Li fu-tsung-t'ung cheng-shu*, Vol. I, pp. 21b-22a.

31 Liu Hsing-nan, p. 248.

32 Ibid.

33 Ibid., p. 250

34 Ku Chung-hsiu, p. 35.

35 Ibid., p. 48.

36 Li, *Chin san-shih-nien shih*, pp. 203-4.

37 Hsüeh Chün-tu, *Huang Hsing*, p. 122.

38 Ku Chung-hsiu, p. 48; Wang Yu-lan, 'Hsin-hai chien-kuo hui-i-lu' in *Chuan-chi wen-hsüeh*, Vol. 7, No. 5, p. 39.

39 Ku-hung, 'Sung hsien-sheng i-shih (I)'.

40 Ku Chung-hsiu, pp. 48-9.

41 Li Chien-nung, *The Political History of China, 1840-1928*, p. 256.

42 Ku Chung-hsiu, p. 49.

43 Ibid.

44 Ibid.

45 'Fu Nanking ko-sheng tai-piao (20 Dec. 1911)' and 'Chih Nanking ko-sheng tai-piao (21 Dec. 1911)', *Li fu-tsung-t'ung cheng-shu*, Vol. III, pp. 1b, 5b-6a.

46 Wu, *Sung Chiao-jen*, pp. 110-111.

47 Sao-hsin, 'Pu-k'an hui shou', p. 8; *Min-kuo-pao*, No. 2, pp. 1-2.

48 *Sao-hsin*, p. 8.

49 'Sun Wen hsüeh-shuo', *Kuo-fu ch'üan-shu*, p. 38.

50 'Tsung-li Sun Chung-shan hsien-sheng tzu pali chih min-kuo chün-cheng-fu p'an su-ting tsung-t'ung tien (12 Nov. 1911)', ibid., p. 445.

51 'Ch'eng Te-ch'üan chih ko-sheng kung-ch'ing tsung-li fan-kuo tsu-chih lin-shih cheng-fu tien (14 Nov. 1911)', *KMWH*, Vol. I, p. 4.

52 'Changsha T'an tutu fu-tien (24 Nov. 1911)', *Li fu-tsung-t'ung cheng-shu*, Vol. I, p. 12.

53 T'an Jen-feng, 'P'ai-tz'u', *CTSTL*, No. 3, 1956, p. 59, reflects this view.

54 *Kita Ikki chosaku shū*, Vol. II, p. 59, credited Chang Chi for bringing about the reconciliation between Sung and Sun Yat-sen.

55 *Chü Cheng Collection*, Vol. II, p. 529.

56 For details see *Chü Cheng Collection*, Vol. II, p. 530; 'Tsou Yung-ch'eng hui-i-lu', *CTSTL*, No. 3, 1956, p. 117; T'an Jen-feng, 'P'ai-tz'u', ibid., p. 59.

57 *Min-li-pao*, 11 Dec. 1911, p. 1, collated with Sao-hsin, 'Pu-k'an hui-shou'.

58 'Kung-ho lin-shih cheng-fu ta kang chih ch'üeh-tien', *Min-li-pao*, 23 Dec., 1911, p. 1; 24 Dec. 1911, p. 1.

59 Hsü Hsüeh-er, 'Sung Hsien-sheng Chiao-jen chuan-lüeh', in Yeh *et al.* (eds.), *Sung Yü-fu*, gave the date of this meeting as 27 December 1911.

60 Hu Han-min, 'Tzu-chuan', *KMWH*, Vol. III, p. 428. According to Hu, those at the meeting were Sun Yat-sen, Sung Chiao-jen, Huang Hsing, Hu Han-min, Wang Ching-wei, Ch'en Ch'i-mei, Chang Ching-chiang, Ma Chün-wu, and Chü Cheng.

61 Chang Hsiang-wen, 'Sung Chiao-jen chuan', *Nan-yüan ts'ung-kao*, Vol. VIII, p. 20b agrees with Hsü Hsüeh-er's account.

62 Chü Cheng, *Ho-k'an*, p. 86; cf. Ku Chung-hsiu, *Chung-hua min-kuo kai-kuo-shih*.

63 Ku Chung-hsiu, p. 52.

64 Li Chien-nung, *Chin san-shih-nien shih*, p. 205.

65 Ibid., pp. 205-6; Ku Chung-hsiu, pp. 52-3.

66 Kun Chung-hsiu, p. 53.

67 Ibid.; Li Chien-nung, *Chin san-shih-nien shih*, pp. 206-7.

68 Ku Chung-hsiu, p. 53.

69 Li Chien-nung, *Chin san-shih-nien shih*, p. 207.

70 *Chü Cheng Collection*, Vol. II, p. 531.

71 Ts'ai Yüan-p'ei, 'Ta-k'e-wen' *Min-li-pao*, 27 July 1912, p. 2; Hu Han-min, 'Tzu-chuan', *KMWH*, Vol. III, p. 430.

72 *Chü Cheng Collection*, Vol. II, pp. 538-9.

73 Sao-hsin, 'Pu-k'an hui-shou', p. 8. For legislations during the Nanking provisional government period see *Nanking lin-shih cheng-fu kung-pao*, *Hsin-hai ko-ming tzu-liao*, No. 1, 1961.

74 *Chü Cheng Collection*, Vol. II, pp. 548-9. However, according to Yang Yu-chiung, *Chung-kuo chin-tai fa-chih-shih*, p. 44, Sung Chiao-jen was the chief drafter. See also Hsü Shih-shen (ed.), *Kuo-fu tang-hsüan lin-shih ta-tsung-t'ung shih-lu*, Taipei, 1967, Vol. I, p. 175.

75 C. P. FitzGerald, *Revolution in China*, p. 2.

10 THE TRANSFER TO PEKING

1 J. O. P. Bland, *China, Japan and Korea*, pp. 33-4; *Recent Events and Present Policies in China*, p. 142.

2 Li Chien-nung, *The Political History of China 1840-1928*, p. 257. For the Chinese League's Plan of Revolution, see 'Chung-kuo T'ung-meng-hui chün-cheng-fu hsüan-yen (1907)', *Kuo-fu ch'üan-shu*, pp. 393-4.

3 Chang Hsiao-jo, *Nan-t'ung Chang Chi-chih hsien-sheng chuan-chi*, p. 176; *Li fu-tsung-t'ung cheng-shu*, pp. 83, 90; *Shen-pao*'s report on a meeting of the Ts'an-i-yüan on 27 February 1912, published on 1 March 1912. See also Ch'en Chin-t'ao, 'Chiao-tai pu-wu ping li-ch'en k'un-nan ch'ing-hsing', *T'ien-to-pao*, 11 April, 1912, and Hu Han-min, 'Tzu-chuan', *KMWH*, Vol. III, p. 433.

4 *Chang Chi Collection*, p. 30; *Chü Cheng Collection*, Vol. II, pp. 531-2; *CTSTL*, No. 1, 1957, p. 126.

5 News of negotiation for peace began as early as October 28, 1911. See Jerome Ch'en, *Yuan Shih-k'ai*, p. 118. Sun Yat-sen expressed his support for making Yüan Shih-k'ai President in a telegram of 12 November 1911. See 'Tsung-li Sun Chung-shan hsien-sheng tzu pali chih min-kuo chün-cheng-fu p'an su-ting

tsung-t'ung tien (12 Nov. 1911)', *Kuo-fu ch'üan-shu*, p. 445.

6 John N. Jordan, 'Some Chinese I Have Known', *Nineteenth Century China*, December 1920, in *Collected Papers: Hankow Collection*, Hong Kong University Library, Vol. 41, p. 956. The two ministers were Sir John N. Jordan of Britain and W. W. Rockhill of the U.S.A. Cf. Jerome Ch'en, *Yuan Shih-k'ai*, pp. 98-9, which stated that the Manchu Regent, Prince Ch'ün, was in favour of having Yüan executed at once but was stopped by Chang Chih-tung.

7 As late as 16 January 1912, Yüan Shih-k'ai said that 'If he were to accept the presidency he would stultify himself before the people'. See Morrison Papers, item 147.

8 Sao-hsin, 'Pu-k'an hui-shou', pp. 6-7.

9 Ibid.

10 John Gilbert Reid, *The Manchu Abdication and the Powers*, pp. 312-13.

11 Ibid.

12 Jordan, 'Some Chinese I Have Known', p. 957.

13 Morrison, 'Memorandum on Ts'ai T'ing-kan's mission to Wuchang' 16 Nov. 1911, and 'Conversation with Ts'ai T'ing-kan' 15 Jan. 1912,

Morrison Papers, items 147, 172; J. G. Reid's letter, 'Justice to the Manchus', to *NCH*, 24 Aug. 1912, p. 553 in reply to a charge (*NCH*, 24 Aug. 1912, p. 517) that he put pressure on the distracted Manchus to abdicate.

14 Jerome Ch'en, *Yuan Shih-k'ai*, p. 118.

15 *Tokyo Nichinichi shimbun*, No. 12, 566, 21 Nov. 1911, p. 2; Li Chien-nung, *Chin san-shih-nien shih*, p. 124; Li Yüan-hung, 'Chih Pei-chün ko chiang-ling', 10 Nov. 1911, *Li fu-tsung-t'ung cheng-shu*, Vol. I, pp. 6a-6b.

16 *Tokyo Nichinichi shimbun*, 21 Nov. 1911, p. 2. See also 'Chung-hua min-kuo nan-chün ta tu-t'ung Huang Hsing yü-kao' enclosed in Japan's consular report (Jih-pen chu Hankow tsung-ling-shih-kuan ch'ing-pao) of 10 November 1911, *Hsin-hai ko-ming tzu-liao*, pp. 565-6.

17 Liu Hou-sheng, *Chang Ch'ien chuan-chi*, pp. 194-5.

18 Sung Chiao-jen, 'Sung ts'an-mou chih Li ssu-ling han', *Min-li-pao*, 21 Nov. 1911, p. 5.

19 Chou Hao, 'Yüan Shih-k'ai yü lin-shih tsung-t'ung', *Min-li-pao*, 24 Jan. 1912, p. 1. See also *T'ien-to-pao*, 16 Jan. 1912, p. 3; 2 April 1912, p. 3.

20 Li Chien-nung, *Chin-san-shih-nien shih*, p. 206.

21 Hu Han-min, 'Tzu-chuan', *KMWH*, Vol. III, p. 431; Shang Ping-ho, *Hsin-jen ch'un-ch'iu*, Vol. XXVII, p. 17b.

22 Ku Chung-hsiu, *Chung-hua min-kuo k'ai-kuo-shih*, p. 80; *Chü Cheng Collection*, Vol. II, pp. 544-5. This event took place on 14 February 1912.

23 Ibid., also Hu Han-min, p. 431 and Shang Ping-ho, p. 17b.

24 Li Yüan-hung, *Li fu-tsung-t'ung cheng-shu*, Vol. VII, pp. 18-23; 'Conversation with Ts'ai T'ing-kan', 15 Jan. 1912, Morrison Papers, item 147; Li Chien-nung, *Chin san-shih-nein shih*, p. 238.

25 Morrison, 'Memorandum on "Conversation with tsai [Ts'ai] T'ing-kan" ', 15 Jan. 1912, Morrison Papers, item 147.

26 'Chuan-shih i-hsien chih ch'üeh-ch'ing', *Min-li-pao*, 10 March 1912, p. 7; Ku Chung-hsiu, p. 81.

27 G. E. Morrison's letter to Fraser, 20 March 1912, Morrison Papers, item 172.

28 *Chü Cheng Collection*, Vol. II, pp. 546-7.

29 Ibid., p. 574.

30 Hsüeh Chün-tu, *Huang Hsing*, pp. 137-8; T'eng Jen-feng, 'P'ai-tz'u', *CTSTL*, No. 3, 1956, p. 62.

31 Hu Han-min, 'Tzu-chuan', *KMWH*, Vol. III, p. 428.

32 *Min-li-pao*, 16 March 1912, p. 3.

33 'Kuo-wu-yüan t'ung-kuo chi-shih', *Min-li-pao*, 31 March 1912, p. 6.

11 Cabinet versus President

1 'Chung-hua min-kuo lin-shih yüeh-fa', in Ku Chung-hsiu, *Chung-hua min-kuo k'ai-kuo-shih*, pp. 84-92, article 4.

2 'Hsüan-t'ung san-nien shih-erh yüeh erh-shih-wu jih Chang Chia-shen chih Jen-kung hsien-sheng shu', 25 Dec. 1911, Ting, *Liang Jen-kung*, Vol. I, pp. 372-3; 'Min-kuo yüan-nien erh-yüeh erh-shih-san jih chih Yüan Hsiang-ch'eng shu', ibid., Vol. II, pp. 380-3.

3 The forerunner of this party was the Preparatory Public Association for Constitutional Government (*Yü-pei li-hsien kung-hui*), headed by Chang Ch'ien and T'ang Shou-ch'ien. See Hsieh Pin, *Min-kuo cheng-tang-shih*, pp. 3-4.

4 'Chang chia-shen chih Jen-kung hsien-sheng shu', 25 Dec. 1911, in Ting, *Liang Jen-kung*, Vol. I, pp. 372-3; 'Min-kuo yüan-nien erh-yüeh erh-shih-san jih chih Yüan Hsiang-ch'eng shu', ibid., Vol. II, pp. 380-3.

5 Liu K'uei-i, 'Ch'u-hsiao ts'ung-ch'ien tang-hui chih-i', cited in Wu Hsiang-hsiang, *Sung Chiao-jen*, p. 157.

6 *Min-li-pao*, 14 Dec. 1911.

7 Hu Han-min, 'Tzu-chuan', *KMWH*, Vol. III, p. 434.

8 'T'ung-meng-hui pen-pu kai-ting tsan-hsing chang-ch'eng ping i-chien-shu', *T'ien-to-pao*, 2 Jan. 1912. It may also be found in *Kuo-fu ch'üan-shu*, pp. 395-6, under the title, 'Chung-kuo T'ung-meng-hui wei t'uan-chieh t'ung-chih hsüan-yen', and erroneously dated as September 1911.

9 Ibid. Shelley Hsien Cheng, *TMH*, p. 130, gave the date of this meeting as 21 January 1912 and the number of members present as over 1,000.

10 Hu Han-min, 'Tzu-chuan', *KMWH*, Vol. III, p. 435.

11 Ibid., pp. 435-6.

12 Ibid. See also *T'ien-to-pao*, 23 Jan. 1912, p. 1.

13 'Chung-kuo T'ung-meng-hui tsung-chang ch'oa-an', article 3, *Min-li-pao*, 6 March, p. 2. This constitution was adopted later without change. See Tsou Lu, *Tang-shih-kao*, Vol. I, pp. 85-9.

14 *Min-li-pao*, 9 March 1912, p. 3. Cf. Chü Cheng, *Ho-k'an*, p. 117, according to

whom Chang Chi and Wang Ching-wei were elected to take charge of General Affairs, Ma Ho [Ma Chün-wu] and T'ien T'ung to the Secretariat, and Chü Cheng to take charge of Finance.

15 'Chung-kuo T'ung-meng-hui ch'ao-an', article 20c (translation follows Shelley Hsien Cheng, *TMH*, p. 132).

16 Yang Yu-chiung, *Chung-kuo cheng-tang-shih*, p. 50.

17 Wu Hsiang-hsiang, *Sung Chiao-jen*, p. 161. Ch'ou Ngao, 'Hsin-hai ko-ming ch'ien-hou tsa-i', *Hsin-hai hui-i-lu*, Vol. I, p. 449, maintains that, after the abolition of the Nanking provisional government, Wang Ching-wei left politics, and Hu Han-min returned to Kwangtung to become its Governor; Sung in fact also assumed responsibility for the General Affairs Department.

18 Yang Yu-chiung, pp. 51-3, 56.

19 Chang Chia-shen's letter to Liang in Ting, *Liang Jen-kung*, Vol. I, pp. 372-3.

20 Liang Ch'i-ch'ao's letter to Yüan Shih-k'ai, ibid., Vol. II, pp. 380-3.

21 Ku Chung-hsiu, *Chung-hua min-kuo k'ai-kuo-shih*, pp. 101-2.

22 Jerome Ch'en, *Yuan Shih-k'ai*, p. 141.

23 'Sung Chiao-jen fu Sun Wu shu', *Min-li-pao*, 4 July 1912, p. 2.

24 'T'ai-yen nien-p'u', *CTSTL*, No. 1, 1957, p. 126; Ku Chung-hsiu, p. 101.

25 The Provisional Constitution of the Republic of China, Pt V, articles 44, 45.

26 'Sung chiao-jen fu Sun Wu shu', *Min-li-pao*, 4 July 1912, p. 2; Ku Chung-hsiu, p. 101.

27 Ts'en Hsüeh-lü, *San-shui Liang Yen-sun hsien-sheng nien-p'u*, Vol. I, pp. 115-16, 121.

28 'Sung chiao-jen fu Sun Wu shu', *Min-li-pao*, 4 July 1912, p. 2.

29 For details of Sung's plan see 'Kuo-wu-yüan hui-i nung-lin Sung tsung-chang t'i-i kuan-yü kuan-chih hsing-cheng ts'ai-ping li-ts'ai chih pan-fa', *Min-li-pao*, 2 June 1912, p. 3.

30 Huang Yüan-yung, 'Tsui-chin chih pi-mi cheng-wen (9 June 1912)' and 'Cheng-chieh nei-hsing-chi (30 May 1912)' in *Yüan-sheng i-chu*, Vol. I, pp. 147-8, 135-6, 154-5; Ku Chung-hsiu, pp. 101-2.

31 'Sung chiao-jen fu Sun Wu shu', *Min-li-pao*, 4 July 1912, p. 2.

32 Li Chien-nung, *Chung-kuo chin-pai-nien cheng-chih-shih*, Vol. II, pp. 374-6; for the communique of the Chinese League's Peking headquarters to its regional offices on

23 June 1912 see *Min-li-pao*, 24 June 1912, and the Telegraph column, ibid., 22 June 1912, p. 3.

33 'Tai-chieh-k'uan po-che hsiang-chi (12 May 1912)', *Yüan-sheng i-chu*, Vol. I, p. 131.

34 Ibid., Vol. I, pp. 132-3, 135-6.

35 Ibid., p. 135.

36 *Min-li-pao*, 18 March 1912, p. 7; Ku Chung-hsiu, p. 63.

37 Ku Chung-hsiu, pp. 100-1.

38 *Min-li-pao*, 2, 14 May 1912, under 'special telegraphic news' and 'ordinary news' columns respectively.

39 Ts'en Hsüeh-lü, *San-shui Liang Yen-sun hsien-sheng nien-p'u*, Vol. I, p. 122; Jerome Ch'en, *Yuan Shih-k'ai*, pp. 149-50; *Min-li-pao*, 19 June 1912, p. 6.

40 Ts'ai Yüan-p'ei, 'Ta-k'e-wen', *Min-li-pao*, 27 July 1912, p. 2; 'Sung Chiao-jen fu Sun Wu shu', ibid., 4 July 1912, p. 2; J. Ch'en, *Yuan Shih-k'ai*, p. 150.

41 'Ta-hsiao ling-hsing tsa-chi (19 June 1912)', *Yüan-sheng i-chu*, Vol. I, pp. 155-6.

42 'Sung Chiao-jen chih Pei-ching ko-pao shu', *Min-li-pao*, 12 July 1912, p. 2.

43 Yüan Shih-k'ai's reply to the deputation of the Chinese League, *Min-li-pao*, 23 June 1912.

44 *Yüan-sheng i-chu*, Vol. I, p. 155.

45 *Min-li-pao*, 24 June 1912, p. 3.

46 'Sung Chiao-jen fu Sun Wu shu', *Min-li-pao*, 4 July 1912.

47 Li Chien-nung, *Chung-kuo chin-pai-nien cheng-chih-shih*, Vol. II, pp. 375-6.

48 *Min-li-pao*, 24 June 1912, p. 3; 1 July 1912, p. 6.

49 'Sung chiao-jen chih Pei-ching ko-pao shu', *Min-li-pao*, 12 July 1912, p. 2.

50 *Min-li-pao*, 24 June 1912, p. 3.

51 Yüan shih-k'ai's reply to the deputation of the Chinese League, *Min-li-pao*, 23 June 1912.

52 'Chung-yang pien-chü-chi', *T'ien-to-pao*, 5 July 1912, p. 3; *Min-li-pao*, 3 July 1912, published the Chinese League's decisions at this meeting as conveyed in the League's communique to its regional branches. See also 'Chiao-chuang ta-pan chih nei-ko (22 July 1912)', *Yüan-sheng i-chu*, Vol. I, pp. 185-7.

53 Chü Cheng, *Ho-k'an*, p. 121.

54 'Sung Chiao-jen fu Sun Wu shu', *Min-li-pao*, 4 July 1912.

55 'Sung Chiao-jen tz'u nung-lin tsung-chang tien (1 April 1912)', *Min-li-pao*, 4 April 1912, p. 6.

56 'Sung Chiao-jen wei nung-lin tsung-chang shih yü yüan-nien wu-yüeh shih-san-jih

tsai Tsan-i-yüan hsüan-pu chih cheng-chien', *Tung-fang tsa-chih*, Vol. 9, No. 1, 1 July 1912, p. 41. See also Sao-hsin, 'Pu-k'an hui-shou', in Yeh *et al.* (eds.), *Sung Yü-fu*.

57 *Cheng-fu kung-pao*, No. 66, 5 July 1912; No. 75, 15 July 1912; No. 85, 24 July 1912, cited in Wu Hsiang-hsiang, *Sung Chiao-jen*, p. 177, notes 44-7.

12 Struggle for Democracy

1 'Chang Chen-wu an chih yen-chiu (31 August 1912)', *Yüan-sheng i-chu*, Vol. I, p. 226.

2 Hsing-yen [Chang Shih-chao], 'Hui-tang chao-tang shuo' and 'Hui-tang chao-tang chih i-chien erh', *Min-li-pao*, 29 July 1912, p. 3, and 7 August 1912 respectively.

3 'Chien Chi-po, *Hsien-tai Chung-kuo wen-hsüeh-shih*, p. 395; Chang Shih-chao, 'Chieh-hua-lun', *Min-li-pao*, 12 July 1912, p. 2.

4 'Wu-tang ta-ho-ping hsiang-chih', *Min-li-pao*, 18 Aug. 1912, p. 6.

5 See Chang Ch'ien's letter to Huang Hsing in January 1912, in Chang Hsiao-jo, *Nan-t'ung Chang Chi-chih hsien-sheng chuan-chi*, p. 172, and Huang Hsing's reply to Yüan Tsu-ch'eng on 10 March 1912, *Min-li-pao*, 14 March 1912, p. 7.

6 'T'ung-meng-hui ch'üan-t'i chih-yüan hui-i', *Min-li-pao*, 17 July 1912, p. 3; 'T'ung-

meng-hui ta-hui chi-shih', ibid., 21 July 1912, p. 6.

7 Ibid. See also *Min-li-pao*, 23 July 1912, p. 3.

8 For Yüan Shih-k'ai's use of force in this connection see 'Lu tsung-li yen-shuo ho chih cheng-chieh (30 July 1912)', *Yüan-sheng i-chu*, Vol. I, pp. 190-3, and 'San-jih kuan-t'ien-chi (1 August 1912)', ibid., pp. 194-200.

9 'Wu-tang ta-ho-ping hsiang-chih', *Min-li-pao*, 18 Aug. 1912, p. 6.

10 Ibid.; 'T'ung-meng-hui kai-tsu chih hsien-sheng', *Min-li-pao*, 4 July 1912, p. 2; 'Kuo-min-tang hsüan-yen', ibid., 18 Aug. 1912, p. 2.

11 *Min-li-pao*, 18 Aug. 1912, p. 7. This body was later enlarged to nine men. See 'Kuo-min-tang kuei-yüeh', Tsou Lu, *Tang-shih-kao*, Vol. I, pp. 112-18, article 18.

12 Telegraph news column, *Min-li-pao*, 12 Aug. 1912, p. 3. See also 'Wu-tang ta-ho-ping hsiang-chih', *Min-li-pao*, 18 Aug. 1912, p. 6.

13 *Min-li-pao*, 18 Aug. 1912, p. 7.

14 'Kuo-min-tang ch'eng-li hsüan-yen', *Min-li-pao*, 18 Aug. 1912, p. 2.

15 'T'ung-meng-hui pen-pu tsung-wu-pu t'ung-kao hai-wai kung-han', Tsou Lu, *Tang-shih-kao*, Vol. I, pp. 106-7.

16 Sun Yat-sen, 'Chieh-chieh min-sheng wen-t'i', *Kuo-fu ch'üan-shu*, p. 528.

17 *Min-li-pao*, 27 Aug. 1912, p. 3.

18 'Sung Chiao-jen chih ko-pao shu', *Min-li-pao*, 16 Sept. 1912, p. 7; 'Sun Chung-shan chih Sung Tun-ch'u han', *Min-li-pao*, 22 Aug. 1912, p. 7.

19 Tsou Lu, *Tang-shih-kao*, Vol. I, p. 120; *Kuo-fu nien-p'u*, Vol. II, p. 338.

20 Li Chien-nung, *Chung-kuo chin-pai-nien cheng-chih-shih*, Vol. II, p. 370; Tsou Lu, *Tang-shih-kao*, Vol. I, pp. 106, 120; Ch'en Hsu-lu, 'Lun Sung Chiao-jen', *Hsin-hai lun-wen-chi*, Vol. I, p. 370.

21 Li Chien-nung, *Chung-kuo chin-pai-nien cheng-chih-shih*, Vol. II, p. 380.

22 'Sung Chiao-jen fu Sun Wu shu', *Min-li-pao*, 4 July 1912, p. 2; 'Kuo-min-tang huan-ying-hui yen-shuo-tz'u', un-der 'Sung Yü-fu yen-shuo-tz'u', in Yeh *et al.* (eds.), *Sung Yü-fu.*

23 'Chih nan-yang t'ung-chih shu kuo-nei cheng-ch'ing han', *Kuo-fu ch'üan-shu*, pp. 516-17.

24 'Min-kuo yüan-nien pa-yüeh erh-shih-wu jih hsia-wu i-shih tsai pei-ching Kuo-min-tang ch'eng-li ta-hui yen-chiang', 25 Aug. 1912, *Kuo-fu ch'üan-shu*, p. 528; 'Fu T'ung-meng-hui nü-t'ung-chih lun nan-nü p'ing-ch'üan han', 2 Sept. 1912, ibid., p. 516.

25 'Chang Chia-shen chih Jen-kung shu', 25 Dec. 1911, in Ting, *Liang Jen-kung*, Vol. I, pp. 372-3; also 'Chih Yüan Hsiang-ch'eng shu', ibid., Vol. II, pp. 380-3.

26 Yü-fu, 'She-hui chu-i chih shang-chio', *Min-li-pao*, 1 Aug. 1911, p. 1.

27 Ts'en Hsüeh-lü, *San-shui Liang Yen-sun hsien-sheng nien-p'u*, Vol. I, p. 122.

28 'Ch'en Ch'i-mei chih Huang Hsing shu', Tsou Lu, *Tang-shih-kao*, Vol. I, pp. 273-81.

29 'Cheng-t'an ch'ieh-t'ing lu (5 Oct. 1912)', *Yüan-sheng i-chu*, Vol. I, pp. 245-9; 'Tsin-men t'ung-hsin (12 Oct. 1912)', ibid., pp. 249-52.

30 Li Chien-nung, *Chung-kuo chin-pai-nien cheng-chih-shih*, Vol. I, p. 380; 'Chih ko-sheng t'ung-kao Lu tsung-li tz'u-chih', Hsü Yu-p'eng, *Yüan ta-tsung-t'ung shu-tu hui-p'ien*, Vol. V, p. 17.

31 'Lu tsung-li yen-shuo ho chih cheng-chieh (30 July 1912)', *Yüan-sheng i-chu*, Vol. I, pp. 188-93; 'San-jih kuan-t'ien chi (1 August 1912)', ibid.,

Vol. I, pp. 194-200; Li Chien-nung, *Chung-kuo chin-pai-nien cheng-chih shih*, Vol. II, pp. 373-6; Li Shou-k'ung, 'Min-ch'u chih kuo-hui yü tang-cheng', in H. H. Wu (ed.), *Ts'ung-k'an*, Vol. V, Taipei, 1964, pp. 140-1.

32 'Min-kuo cheng-fu yü cheng-tang shou-ling chih hsieh-ting cheng-ts'e', *Min-li-pao*, 1 Oct. 1912. See also *Yüan ta-tsung-t'ung shu-tu hui-p'ien*, Vol. V, pp. 31-2.

33 'Cheng-t'an ch'ieh-t'ing lu (5 Oct. 1912)', *Yüan-sheng i-chu*, Vol. I, pp. 245-9; 'Tsin-men t'ung-hsin (12 Oct. 1912)', ibid., pp. 249-52.

34 *Yüan-sheng i-chu*, Vol. I, pp. 251-2.

35 Sung Chiao-jen, 'Yü Liu Keng-ch'en shu', *Nan-she ts'ung-k'e: Wen-lu*, Vol. XVI, p. 6a.

36 'Kuo-min-tang i ch'üan-li tsan-chu cheng-fu', *Kuo-fu ch'üan-shu*, p. 540.

37 Tsou Lu, *Tang-shih-kao*, Vol. I, p. 120; Yang Yu-chiung, *I-hui lun-ts'ung*, p. 311.

38 *Yüan-sheng i-chu*, Vol. I, p. 249.

39 Li Shou-k'ung, 'Min-ch'u chih kuo-hui yü tang-cheng', in H. H. Wu (ed.), *Tsung-k'an*, Vol. V, p. 154.

40 Yang Yu-chiung, *Chung-kuo cheng-tang-shih*, p. 61; Hsieh Pin, *Min-kuo cheng-tang-shih*,

pp. 51-2. Ku Chung-hsiu, *Chung-hua min-kuo k'ai-kuo-shih*, Appendix III supplies an incomplete list of 588 names for the Lower House and 261 names for the Senate.

41 Ch'ou Ngao, 'Hsin-hai ko-ming ch'ien-hou tsa-i', *Hsin-hai hui-i lu*, Peking, 1961, Vol. I, pp. 450-1.

42 Hsieh Pin, pp. 49-50, collated with Tseng Yen, 'Chung-hua min-kuo ti-i-chieh kuo-hui shu-yao', in Yang Yu-chiung *et al.*, *Min-ch'u kuo-hui*, Taipei, 1962, p. 63.

43 'Min-kuo erh-nien i-yüeh shih-chiu-jih tsai Shanghai kuo-min-tang ch'a-hua-hui yen-chiang', *Kuo-fu ch'üan-shu*, pp. 556-7; Ts'en Hsüeh-lü. *San-shui Liang Yen-shun hsien-sheng nien-p'u*, Vol. II, p. 418.

44 Wen Yen, 'Min-chu cheng-chih tsai chung-kuo', *I-hui tsa-chih*, No. 16, July 1958; Li Chien-nung, *Chung-kuo chin-pai-nien cheng-chih shih*, Vol. II, p. 389.

45 'Nung-lin tsung-tsang Sung Chiao-jen ts'u-chih ch'eng', *Yüan ta-tsung-t'ung shu-tu hui-p'ien*, Vol. IV, pp. 9-10; *Min-li-pao*, 19 Oct. 1912; Wu Hsiang-hsiang, *Sung Chiao-jen*, p. 213.

46 Huang Tsun-san, *San-shih-nien jih-chi*, Aug. 1912; 'Hsüan-t'ung san-nien shih-yüeh nien-szu jih Wu Kuan-

ying chih Jen-kung hsien-
sheng shu', in Ting Wen-
chiang, *Liang Jen-kung hsien-
sheng nien-p'u chang-p'ien ch'u-
kao*, Vol. I, pp. 368-9.

47 Ting Wen-chiang, Vol. II,
pp. 393-5, 406-11.

48 'Yü Liu Keng-ch'en shu
(29 Dec. 1912)', *Nan-she-
ts'ung-k'e: Wen-lu*, Vol. XVI,
pp. 5b-6b.

49 'Chih Huang Hsing wang
chieh-chi Peking Kuomin-
tang pen-pu ching-hui tien',
Kuo-fu ch'üan-shu, p. 522; Wu
Hsiang-hsiang, *Sung Chiao-
jen*, p. 248, notes 90, 91.

50 'Yu Liu Keng-ch'en shu
(29 Dec. 1912)', *Nan-she
ts'ung-k'e: Wen-lu*, Vol. XVI,
pp. 5b-6b.

51 *Min-li-pao*, 20 Jan. 1913, p. 7.

52 'Sung Tun-ch'u chih wei-
yen', ibid., 13 Feb. 1913.

53 Sung Chiao-jen's speeches in
Shanghai and Nanking, *Min-
li-pao*, 20 Feb. 1913, p. 3,
and 10 March 1913, p. 3.
For Sung's movements in
this period see *Min-li-pao*, 14,

16, 22-4 Feb., 10, March
1913.

54 Yang Yu-chiung, *I-hui lun-
ts'ung*, p. 319. For Yüan Shih-
k'ai's opposition to cabinet
government see 'Yüan yü ko
cheng-t'uan tai-piao Yao Yü-
p'ing, Hsü Shao-cheng teng
t'an-hua chi-lu', *Min-li-pao*,
22 Nov. 1912, p. 3.

55 Wu Hsiang-hsiang, *Sung
Chiao-jen*, p. 218.

56 Sung Chiao-jen, 'Ta na-
ming-shih po-tz'u', *Min-li-
pao*, 15 March 1913, p. 3, 16
March, p. 2, 17 March, p. 2.
See also 'Sung hsien-sheng po
mou-tang-chü chih shih-shih
t'an', *Min-li-pao*, 12 March
1913, p. 2.

57 'Cheng-shih kuo-hui chih
yin-chien', *Min-ch'üan-pao*, 11
Sept. 1912.

58 'Feng Kuo-chang fan-tui
Huan-ying kuo-hui-t'uan
tien', *Min-li-pao*, 22 Jan.
1913, p. 6.

59 See Wu Hsiang-hsiang, *Sung
Chiao-jen*, pp. 224-6.

60 Morrison Papers, item 178.

13 EPILOGUE

1 Information provided by
Professor C. P. FitzGerald,
letter to the author, 1 Nov.
1966.

2 'Yü-fu hsien-sheng pei hai-
hou shih-jih-chi', in Yeh *et al.*
(eds.), *Sung Yü-fu; Shen
Yun-lung*, 'An-sha Sung
Chiao-jen an ti yao-fan Hung

Shu-tsu', *Hsin-shih-tai*, Vol. I,
No. 5, pp. 50-3.

3 *Min-li-pao*, 22 March 1913.

4 'Chih ko-sheng tutu wei-ch'ih
ta-chü', *Yüan ta-tsung-t'ung
shu-tu hui-p'ien*, Vol. VII, pp.
2-3; 'Fu Wang Ching-wei lun
Sung-an', ibid., Vol. VII,
pp. 5-6.

5 Li Chien-nung, *Chin pai-nien cheng-chih-shih*, Vol. II, pp. 390-1, 384.

6 Ibid., pp. 391-4; T'an Jen-feng, 'P'ai-tz'u', *CTSTL*, Vol. III, 1956, p. 69; 'Tsung-li chih nan-yang t'ung-chih shu' and 'Ch'en Ch'i-mei chih Huang Hsing shu', in Tsou Lu, *Tang-shih-kao*, Vol. I, pp. 272-81; 'Yü Huang Hsing lun kuei-ch'ou shih-pai chih yu ping ch'ien ch'i kuei-kuo han (1914)', *Kuo-fu ch'üan-shu*, pp. 590-1.

7 Tsou Lu, *Tang-shih-kao*, Vol. I, p. 123; Li Chien-nung, *Chin pai-nien cheng-chih-shih*, Vol. II, p. 401.

8 'The Murder of Mr. Sung', *NCH*, 29 March 1913 or *NCH* collection, p. 904.

9 The second revolution occurred in mid-July 1913. For details see Li Shou-k'ung, 'Min-ch'u chih kuo-hui yü tang-cheng', *Chung-kuo hsien-tai-shih ts'ung-k'an*, Vol. V, pp. 179-209.

10 Information provided by Professor C. P. FitzGerald, letter to the author, 1 Nov. 1966.

11 'Tsun-yin', *Kung Tzu-chen ch'üan-chi*, 2nd ed., Shanghai, 1961, p. 88.

12 'Confucianism and the Republic in China', *The Times*, 24 Sept. 1912.

13 *Japan Foreign Office Records* (Gaimushō kiroku): *Kakkoku Naisei zassan, Shina no bu—kakumeitō kankei (Shina bō-meisha wo fukumu)*, Vol. 4, pp. 450156-450157.

14 Chang Chi, 'Hsiang chung-hsün-t'uan tang-cheng-pan chiang Kuomintang shih-tai, ti-erh-chiang', 9 Nov. 1943, *Chang Chi Collection*, pp. 32-3. See also his 'Tzu-chuan nien-p'u', 1912, ibid., p. 239.

15 *Kuo-fu nien-p'u*, Vol. I, p. 172. The first two stages laid down in the Plan of Revolution (Ko-ming fang-lüeh) were intended to last for three and six years respectively.

16 'Statecraft at the Capital', *The Times*, 29 April 1913.

17 'Tsung-li fu Yang Han-sun lun t'ung-i tang-ch'üan yü fu-ts'ung ming-ling shu', *KMWH*, Vol. V, pp. 613-14; *Kuo-fu ch'üan-shu*, pp. 594-5.

18 Chiang Kai-shek, 'Wei shih-mo yu-tang', *Chien-kuo yüeh-k'an*, Vol. I, No. 2, p. 8.

19 Ch'ien Tuan-sheng, 'Min-chu cheng-chih hu, chü-ch'üan kuo-chia hu?', *Tung-fang tsa-chih*, Vol. 31, No. 1, 1934, pp. 24-5.

SELECTED BIBLIOGRAPHY

Only major works and collections used for this study are listed here. Others may be found in the notes.

PUBLISHED SOURCES

Bland, J. O. P., *China, Japan and Korea*, New York, 1921.

——, *Recent Events and Present Policies in China*, Philadelphia, 1912.

Brunnest, H. S. and Hagelstrom, V. V., *Present Day Political Organization of China*, trans. A. Beltehenko and E. E. Moran, photo. reprint, Taipei, n.d.

Cameron, M. E., *The Reform Movement in China 1898-1912*, Stanford, 1931.

Chang Chi (張繼), *Chang P'u-ch'üan hsien-sheng ch'üan-chi* (張溥泉先生全集), Taipei, 1951.

——, *Chang P'u-ch'üan hsien-sheng ch'üan-chi pu-chi* (張溥泉先生全集補集), Taipei, 1952.

Chang Ch'i-yün (張其昀) (ed.), *Kuo-fu ch'üan-shu* (國父全書), 1st ed., Taipei, 1950; 3rd ed., Taipei, 1963.

Chang Chung-fu (張忠紱), *Chung-hua min-kuo wai-chiao-shih* (中華民國外交史), Vol. I, 1st ed., 1943; reprint, Taipei, 1957.

Chang Chung-li, *The Chinese Gentry: Studies on Their Role in Nineteenth Century Chinese Society*, Seattle, 1951.

Chang Hsiang-wen (張湘文), *Nan-yüan ts'ung-kuo* (南園叢稿) Peking, 1929, 15 vols.

Chang Hsiao-jo (張孝若), *Nant'ung Chang Chi-chih hsien-sheng chuan-chi* (南通張季直先生傳記), reprint, Taipei, 1965, 6 vols.

Chang Kuo-kan (張國淦), *Hsin-hai ko-ming shih-liao* (辛亥革命史料), Shanghai, 1958.

Chang Nan (張枏) and Wang Jen-chih (王忍之) (eds.), *Hsin-hai ko-ming ch'ien shih-nien chien shih-lun hsüan-chi*, Series 1 and 2 (辛亥革命前十年間, 時論選集第一, 第二), Peking, 1962, 2 vols.

Chang Nan-hsien (張難先), *Hu-peh ko-ming chih-chih-lu* (湖北革命知之錄), Shanghai, 1946.

Chang Ping-lin (章炳麟), *T'ai-yen wen-lu hsü-p'ien* (太炎文錄續編), Taipei, 1956.

——, *Chang-shih ts'ung-shu chih-i: T'ai-yen wen-lu ch'u-p'ien pei-lu* (章氏叢書之一 : 太炎文錄初編別錄), Shanghai, n.d.

Chang Shih-chao (章士釗), *Chia-yin tsa-chih t'sun-kao* (甲寅雜誌存槁), 1st ed., Shanghai, 1922; 3rd ed., Shanghai, 1925, 2 vols.

Chang Wen-hsiang kung ch'üan-chi (張文襄公全集), 1st ed., 1928; photo. reprint, Taipei, 1963, 6 vols.

Chang Yü-lan (張郁蘭), *Chung-kuo yin-hang-yeh fa-chen shih* (中國銀行業發展史), Shanghai, 1957.

Ch'en, Jerome, *Yuan Shih-k'ai 1859-1916*, London, 1961.

Chiang Yung-ching (蔣永敬), *Hu Han-min hsien-sheng nien-p'u kao* (胡漢民先生年譜稿), in H. H. Wu (吳相湘) (ed.), *Chung-kuo hsien-tai-shih ts'ung-k'an* (中國現代史叢刊), Vol. III, pp. 79-320.

Chien Po-tsan (翦伯贊), *Chung-kuo-shih-lun-chi* (中國史論集), 2nd ed., Shanghai, 1947, 2 vols.

Ch'ien Chi-po (錢基博), *Hsien-tai chung-kuo wen-hsüeh-shih* (現代中國文學史), 1st ed., Shanghai, 1933; 3rd ed., Shanghai, 1935.

Chü Cheng (居正) (ed.), *Ch'ing-tang shih-lu* (清黨實錄), n.p., n.d., microfilm, Hoover Library, Stanford.

——, *Chü chüeh-sheng hsien-sheng ch'üan-chi* (居覺生先生全集), Taipei, 1954, 2 vols.

——, *Mei-ch'uan p'u-chi* (梅川譜偈), Taipei, n.d. Preface dated August 1949.

Chü Chüeh-sheng (居覺生) (Chü Cheng), *Hsin-hai cha-chi*

Mei-ch'uan jih-chi ho-k'an (辛亥簡記梅川日記合刊), Taipei, 1956.

Chung-hua min-kuo k'ai-kuo wu-shih-nien wen-hsien, Second Series (中國民國開國五十年文獻, 第二編), *Wuchang shou-i* (武昌首義), Taipei, 1961.

Chung-hua min-kuo k'ai-kuo wu-shih-nien wen-hsien, First Series (中華民國開國五十年文獻, 第一編), *Chung-kuo T'ung-meng-hui* (中國同盟會), Taipei, 1964, 4 vols.

Chung-hua min-kuo k'ai-kuo wu-shih-nien wen-hsien, Second Series (中華民國開國五十年文獻, 第二編), *Ko-sheng kuang-fu* (各省光復), Taipei, 1964, 3 vols.

Chung-kuo jen-min cheng-chih hsieh-shang hui-i ch'üan-kuo wei-yüan-hui wen-shih tzu-liao yen-chiu wei-yüan-hui (中國人民政治協商會議全國委員會文史資料研究委員會) (ed.), *Hsin-hai ko-ming hui-i-lu* (辛亥革命回憶錄), Vol. I, Peking, 1961; Vols. II, III, IV, Peking, 1962; Vols. V, VI, Peking, 1963.

Chung-kuo kuo-min-tang chung-yang tang-shih shih-liao p'ien-tsuan wei-yüan hui (中國國民黨中央黨史史料編纂委員會) (ed.), *Ko-ming hsien-lieh chuan-chi* (革命先烈傳記), Chung-king, 1941.

——, *Ko-ming wen-hsien* (革命文獻), Vols. I-VI, Taipei, 1953-6.

Chung-kuo shih-hsüeh-hui (中國史學會) (ed.), *Chung-kuo chin-tai shih tzu-liao ts'ung-k'an: Wu-hsü pien-fa* (中國近代史資料叢刊:戊戌變法), Shanghai, 1957, 4 vols.

Feng Tzu-yu (馮自由), *Chung-hua min-kuo k'ai-kuo ch'ien ko-ming-shih* 中華民國開國前革命史), Taipei, 1954, 2 vols.

——, *Ko-ming i-shih* (革命逸史), Vol. I, Changsha, 1939; 3rd reprint, 1947; Vol. II, Chungking, 1945; 2nd reprint Shanghai, 1946; Vol. III, Chungking, 1945; 2nd reprint, Shanghai, 1946; Vol. IV, Shanghai, 1946; Vol. V, Shanghai, 1947.

——, *Chung-kuo ko-ming nien-liu-nien tsu-chih-shih* (中國革命廿六年組織史), Shanghai, 1948.

——, *She-hui chu-i yü Chung-kuo* (社會主義與中國), Hong Kong, 1920.

FitzGerald, C. P., *Revolution in China*, London, 1952.

Harvard East Asian Research Centre, *Harvard University Regional Studies: Papers on China*, Mass., 1949-69, 20 vols.

Hewlett, Meyrick, *Forty Years in China*, London, 1944.

Hou Wai-lu (侯外廬), *Chung-kuo tsao-ch'i ch'i-meng ssu-hsiang shih (1600-1840)* (中國早期啟蒙思想史1600-1840), Peking, 1956.

Hsieh Pin (謝彬), *Min-kuo cheng-tang-shih* (民國政黨史), reprint, Taipei, 1962.

Hsü Shih-shen (許師愼), *Kuo-fu ko-ming yüan-ch'i hsiang-chu* (國父革命緣起詳註), 1st ed., 1947; 2nd ed., 1954, Taipei.

—— (ed.), *Kuo-fu tang-hsüan lin-shih ta-tsung-t'ung shih-lu* (國父當選臨時大總統實錄), Taipei, 1967, 2 vols.

Hsü Yu-p'eng (徐有朋), *Yüan ta-tsung-t'ung shu-tu hui-p'ien* (袁大總統書牘彙編), reprint, Taipei, 1962.

Hsüeh Chün-tu, *Huang Hsing and the Chinese Revolution*, Stanford, 1961.

Huang Tsun-san (黃遵三), *San-shih-nien jih-chi* (三十年日記), n.p.; 1933, Vol. I, *Liu-hsüeh jih-chi* (留學日記) 1905-12; Vol. II; *Kuan-i jih-chi* (觀奕日記), 1912-24; Vol. III, *Hsiu-yang jih-chi* (修養日記), 1924-8; Vol. IV, *Pan-hsüeh jih-chi* (辦學日記), 1928-30.

Huang Yüan-yung (黃遠庸), *Yüan-sheng i-chu* (遠生遺著), reprint, Taipei, 1962, 2 vols.

Hummel, Arthur W. (ed.), *Eminent Chinese of the Ch'ing Period*, Washington, 1943-4, 2 vols.

Hunan-sheng-chih p'ien-chi wei-yüan-hui (湖南省誌編輯委員會) (ed.), *Hunan-sheng-chih, series one: Hunan-sheng chin-pai-nien ta-shih chi-shu* (湖南省誌第一編:湖南省近百年大事記述), Changsha, 1959.

Hupeh sheng che-hsüeh she-hui k'o-hsüeh hsüeh-hui lien ho-hui (湖北省哲學社會科學學會聯合會) (ed.), *Hsin-hai ko-ming wu-shih chou-nien chi-nien lun-wen-chi* (辛亥革命五十周年紀念論文集), Peking, 1962, 2 vols.

I Kuo-kan (易國幹) *et al.* (eds.), *Li fu-tsung-t'ung cheng-shu* (黎副總統政書), 1st ed., Shanghai, 1915; reprint, Taipei, 1962.

Jansen, Marius B., *The Japanese and Sun Yat-sen*, Cambridge, Mass., 1954.

Jung Meng-yüan (榮孟源) (ed.), *Chung-kuo chin-tai-shih tzu-liao hsüan-chi* (中國近代史資料選集), Peking, 1954.

Katsuo Yoshihisa (葛生能久), *Tōa senkaku shishi kiden* (東亞先覺志士記傳), Tokyo, 1935, 3 vols.

Kayano Chōchi (萱野長知) *Chūka minkoku kakumei hikyū* (中華民國革命秘笈), Tokyo, 1914.

Kita Ikki (北一輝), *Kita Ikki chosaku-shū: Shina kakumei gaishi* (北一輝著作集:支那革命外史), Tokyo, 1960, 2 vols.

Ko Kung-chen (戈公振), *Chung-kuo pao-hsüeh-shih* (中國報學史), reprint, Taipei, n.d.; Preface in original ed. dated June 1926.

Ku Chung-hsiu (谷鍾秀), *Chung-hua min-kuo k'ai-kuo-shih* (中華民國開國史), reprint, Taipei, 1962.

Kung Tzu-chen (龔自珍), *Kung Tzu-chen ch'üan-chi* (龔自珍全集), Shanghai, 2nd ed., 1961.

Li Chien-nung (李劍農), *Chung-kuo chin-pai-nien cheng-chih-shih* (中國近百年政治史), 3rd reprint, Taipei, 1962, 2 vols.

——, *The Political History of China 1840-1928*, trans. Teng and Ingalls, Princeton, 1956.

——, *Tsui-chin san-shih-shih-nien chung-kuo cheng chih-shih* (最近三十年中國政治史), Shanghai, 1930; 3rd ed., 1931.

Li Lien-fang (李廉方), *Hsin-hai Wuchang shou-i chi* (辛亥武昌首義記), Taipei, 1960.

Li Shih-yüeh (李時岳), *Hsin-hai Ko-ming shih-ch'i liang-hu ti-ch'ü ti ko-ming yün-tung* (辛亥革命時期兩湖地區的革命運動), Peking, 1957.

Li Yün-han (李雲漢), 'Huang K'e-ch'iang hsien-sheng nien-p'u-kao' (黃克強先生年譜稿), in H. H. Wu (吳相湘) (ed.), *Chung-kuo hsien-tai-shih ts'ung-k'an* (中國現代史叢刊), Vol. IV, Taipei, 1962, pp. 143-422.

Liang Ch'i-ch'ao (梁啟超), *Ch'ing-tai hsüeh-shu k'ai-lun* (清代學術概論), Shanghai, 1920.

——, *Intellectual Trends in the Ch'ing Period*, trans. and ed. Immanuel C. Y. Hsü, Mass., 1959.

——, *Wu-hsü cheng-pien-chi* (戊戌政變記), Peking, 1954.

Lin Chih-chün (林志鈞), *Yin-ping-shih ho-chi: chuan-chi* (飲冰室合集:專集), Shanghai, 1936, 16 vols.

Lin Yu-t'ang, *Public Opinions in China*, Chicago, 1936.

Liu Hou-sheng (劉厚生), *Chang Ch'ien chuan-chi* (張謇傳記), 1st ed., Shanghai, 1958; photo. reprint, Hong Kong, 1965.

Liu K'uei-i (劉揆一), *Huang Hsing chuan-chi* (黃興傳記), Taipei, 1953.

Liu Yü-sheng (劉禺生), *Shih-tsai-t'ang tsa-i* (世載堂雜憶), Peking, 1960.

Lo Chia-lun (羅家倫) *et al.* (eds.), *Huang K'e-ch'iang hsien-sheng shu-han mo chi* (黃克強先生書翰墨跡), Taipei, 1956.

——, *Kuo-fu nien-p'u* (國父年譜), Taipei, 1958; 2nd ed., 1959, 2 vols.

MacMurray, John V.A., *Treaties and Agreements with and Concerning China*, Vol. I, New York, 1921.

Nowell, Charles E., *A History of Portugal*, Princeton, 1958.

Pan Kung-chan (潘公展), *Ch'en Ch'i-mei* (陳其美), Taipei, 1954.

Pei-ching-shih li-shih hsüeh-hui (北京市歷史學會) (ed.), *Pei-ching-shih li-shih hsüeh-hui ti-i ti-erh chieh nien-hui lun-wen hsüan-chi* (北京市歷史學會第一第二屆年會論文選集), 1961-2, Peking, 1964.

Powell, Ralph L., *The Rise of Chinese Military Power 1895-1912*, Princeton, 1955.

Reid, John Gilbert, *The Manchu Abdication and the Powers*, Berkeley, 1935.

Reinsch, Paul S., *Intellectual and Political Currents in the Far East*, Boston and New York, 1911.

Saggitarius, *The Strange Apotheosis of Sun Yat-sen*, London, 1939.

Sanetō Keishiū (實藤惠秀) *Chūkokujin nihon ryūgaku-shi* (中國人日本留學史), Tokyo, 1960.

Shang Ping-ho (尚秉和), *Hsin-jen ch'un-ch'iu* (辛壬春秋), 1st ed., 1924; reprint, Taipei, 1962.

Sung Chiao-jen (宋教仁), *Chien-tao wen-t'i* (間島問題), Shanghai, 1908.

——, *Erh-pai-nien lai chih O-fan* (二百年來之俄患), Taipei, 1952.

——, *Wo-chih-li-shih* (我之歷史), 1st ed., Hunan, 1920; reprint, Taipei, 1962.

Tai Chi-t'ao (戴季陶) *Sun Wen chu-i chih che-hsüeh ti chi-ch'u* (孫文主義之哲學的基礎), Taipei, 2nd ed., 1954.

Teng, S. Y., and Fairbank, J. K., *China's Response to the West*, Mass., 1954; New York, 1963.

Ting Wen-chiang (丁文江) (comp.), *Liang Jen-kung hsien-sheng nien-p'u chang-p'ien ch'u-kao*(梁任公先生年譜長編初稿) Taipei, 1962, 2 vols.

Ts'ai Chi-ou (蔡寄鷗), *O-chou hsüeh-shih* (鄂州血史), Shanghai, 1958.

Ts'ao Ya-po (曹亞伯), *Wuchang ko-ming chen-shih* (武昌革命眞史), Shanghai, 1903, 3 vols.

Ts'en Hsüeh-lü (岑學呂), *San-shui Liang Yen-sun hsien-sheng nien-p'u* (三水梁燕孫先生年譜, 1st ed., n.d., n.p.; reprint, Taipei, 1962, 2 vols.

Tso Hsun-sheng (左舜生), *Chung-kuo chin-pai-nien-shih tzu-laio ch'u-p'ien* (中國近百年史資料初編), Taipei, 1958.

Tsou Hai-pin (鄒海濱), *Ch'eng-lu wen-chi* (澄廬文集), Canton, 1934, 2 vols.

Tsou Lu (鄒魯), *Chung-kuo kuo-min-tang shih-kao* (中國國民黨史稿), Shanghai, revised ed., 1947, 3 vols.

——, *Kuang-chou san-yüeh erh-shih-chiu ko-ming shih* (廣州三月廿九日革命史), Changsha, 1939.

Wang Yün-sheng (王芸生), *Liu-shih-nien lai Chung-kuo yü Jih-pen* (六十年來中國與日本), Shanghai, 1932-8, 6 vols.

Wu Hsiang-hsiang (吳相湘), *Sung Chiao-jen Chung-kuo min-chu hsien-cheng ti hsien-ch'u* (宋教仁中國民主憲政的先驅), Taipei, 1964.

Wu Tse-chung (吳則中) (ed.), *Chih-hui hsien-sheng i-p'ien tsung-yao hui-i* (稚暉先生一篇重要回憶), Taipei, 1964.

Yang Yu-chiung (楊幼炯), *Chung-kuo cheng-tang-tang-shih* (中國政黨史), 2nd ed., Shanghai, 1937.

——, *Chung-kuo chin-tai fa-chih-shih* (中國近代法制史), 2nd ed. Taipei, 1962.

—— (ed.), *I-hui lun-ts'ung* (議會論叢), Taipei, 1964.

—— *et al.* (eds.), *Min-ch'u kuo-hui* (民初國會), Taipei, 1962.

Yang Yü-ju (楊玉如), *Hsin-hai ko-ming hsien-chu-chi* (辛亥革命先著記), Peking, 1958.

Yeh Ch'u-ts'ang (葉楚傖) *et al.* (eds.), *Sung Yü-fu* (宋漁父), Shanghai, 1913; rcprint, Taipei, 1963.

Young, C. Walter, *The International Relations of Manchuria*, Chicago, 1929.

Periodicals

Chekiang-ch'ao (浙江潮), Tokyo, 1903-4.

Chien-kuo yüeh-k'an (建國月刊), Vol. I, No. 1—Vol. XV, No. 1, Shanghai and Nanking, 1929-36.

Chin-tai-shih tzu-liao (近代史資料), Peking, 1954.

Chin-tai-shih tzu-liao: Hsin-hai ko-ming tzu-liao (近代史資: 辛亥革命資料), Peking, 1961.

Chuan-chi wen-hsüeh (傳記文學) Vol. VII, No. 5, Taipei, Nov. 1965.

Erh-shih shih-chi chih-chih-na (式抬世紀之支那), Tokyo, 1905.

Han-sheng (漢聲), Tokyo, 1903.

Hsiang-hsüeh-pao (湘學報), Changsha, 1897-8.

Hsiang-tao chou-pao (响導週報), No. 86, Shanghai, Oct. 1924.

Hsin-min ts'ung-pao (新民叢報), Nos. 1-96, Yokohama, 1902-7.

Hsing-shih (醒獅), Nos. 1-4, Tokyo, 1905-6.

Hupeh hsüeh-sheng chieh (湖北學生界), 7 issues, Tokyo, 1903.

Kiangsu (江蘇), 8 issues, Tokyo, 1903.

Kuo-shih-kuan kuan-k'an (國史館館刊), Vol. I, Nos. 1-4; Vol. II, No. 1, Nanking, 1947-9.

Min-pao (民報), 26 issues, Tokyo, 1905-10.

Nan-she ts'ung-k'e (南社叢刻), Nos. 3-20, Shanghai, 1911-17.

Nineteenth Century China, The, Hankow Collection: Collected Papers, Vol. 41, Hong Kong University Library.

Shinshu daigaku kiyo (信州大學紀要), No. 2, Shinshu, 1952.

Ta-lu (大陸), Shanghai, 1902-3.

Tang-shih shih-liao ts'ung-k'an (黨史史料叢刊), Nos. 1-4, Chungking, 1944; renamed *Ko-ming wen-hsien* (革命文獻), Nos. 5-7 Nanking, 1947.

Tung-fang tsa-chih (東方雜誌) (*The Eastern Miscellany*), Shanghai, 1904-48.

Yu-hsüeh i-p'ien (遊學譯編), 12 issues, Tokyo, 1902-3.

Newspapers

Asahi Shimbun (朝日新聞), Tokyo, issues for December 1905.

Chinese Mail, The, Hong Kong, 1911-13.

Chinese Times, The, (*Ching-tung hsin-pao,* 警東新報), Melbourne, 11 Feb. 1905-Dec. 1914; continuation of the *Ai-*

kuo-pao (愛國報), founded by Cheng Lu (鄭祿) in Oct. 1901.

Chung-hsing jih-pao (中興日報), Singapore, 1907-10.

Lin-shih cheng-fu kung-pao (臨時政府公報), Nanking, Feb.-April 1912.

Min-ch'üan-pao (民權報), Shanghai, May-Nov. 1912.

Min-kuo-pao (民國報), Shanghai, 1911.

Min-li-pao (民立報), Shanghai, 1910-13.

Ni-roku Shimbun (二六新聞), Tokyo, Dec. 1905.

North China Herald, Shanghai, 1912-13.

Su-pao (蘇報) Shanghai, 1900-3.

T'ien-to-pao (天鐸報), Shanghai, 1910-13.

Times, The, London, issues for 1912-13.

Tokyo Nichinichi Shimbun (東京日日新聞), Tokyo, issues for Nov. 1911, Meiji, 44th year.

Tung Wah Times (weekly), Sydney, 1902-36.

Unpublished Sources

Cheng, Shelley Hsien, 'The *T'ung-meng-hui,* Its Organization, Leadership and Finance', 1905-1912, Ph.D. dissertation, University of Washington, Seattle, March 1962.

Chung-kuo T'ung-men-hui chang-ch'eng ch'ao-an (中國同盟會章

程草案), Taichung: Nationalist Party Archives, MSS. Cat. No. 335/94.

Japan Foreign Office Records (*Gaimushō Kiroku*): *Kakkoku naisei zassan Shina no bu—Kakumeitō Kankei* (*Bōmeisha wo fukumu*), *Mon 1 Rui 6 Kō 1 Gō 4-2-1* (外務省記錄: 各國內政雜纂, 支那の部: 革命黨關係 (亡命者含む)門 1 類 6 項 1 號 4-2-1), 6 vols.

Morrison, G. E., Morrison Papers, Mitchell Library, Uncat. Mss./Set 312, 183 Items. Items used for this study are 1-45 (newspaper cuttings) 1896-1915; 59-113 (diaries 1899-1920); 146-147 (memos.); 172-183 (correspondence).

Waseda University Student Record, *Meiji szu-shih-erh-nien san-yüeh Ta-ch'ing-kuo kung-shih-kuan shao-chieh hsüeh-sheng so-yin-pu chao-t'ao t'ien ta-hsüeh Ch'ing-kuo liu-hsüeh-sheng-pu* (明治四十二年大清國公使館紹介學生索引薄早稻田大學清國留學生部), Waseda University, Tokyo, March, 1909.

GLOSSARY

Akasaka 赤坂
All Men are Brothers (Sui-hu-chuan)
水滸傳
Alliance League for Regions
North and North of the Great
Lake (Ta-chiang nan-pei t'ung
meng-hui) 大江南北同盟會
An-Chün Prefecture Association
for the Promotion of the Public
Good (An-chün kung-i-she) 安郡
公益社
An-lu Prefecture (An-lu-chün) 安
陸郡
Anhwei 安徽
Annam 安南
Anthology of Translation (I-shu hui-
p'ien) 譯書彙編
Antung 安東
Armoury, The (Wu-ku) 武庫
Association for National Military
Education (Chün-kuo-min chiao-
yü-hui) 軍國民教育會
Awakening Lion (Hsing-shih) 醒
獅

Black Dragon Society (Hakuryū-
kai) 黑龍會
Bureau of General Affairs (Shu-
wu-pu) 庶務部

Central China Office of the
Chinese League (Chung-kuo
t'ung-meng-hui chung-pu tsung-
hui) 中國同盟會中部總會
Central Command (T'ung-ch'ou-
pu) 統籌部

Central Executive Council
(Tsung-wu-hui) 總務會
Chang Chi 張繼
Chang Chia-shih 章駕時
Chang-chiang College (Chang-
chiang shu-yüan) 漳江書院
Chang Chih-tung 張之洞
Chang Ch'ien 張謇
Chang Feng-hsiang 張鳳翔
Chang Hsün 張勳
Chang Huang-ch'i 張篁溪
Chang Ping-lin 章炳麟
T'ai-yen 太炎
Chang Shao-tseng 張紹曾
Chang Shih-chao 張士釗
Chang Tou-shu 張斗樞
Chang Tzu 章梓
Chang Yao-tseng 張耀曾
Chang Yü-k'un 章裕昆
Changsha 長沙
Ch'ang-te 常德
Chao Er-hsun 趙爾巽
Chao Feng-ch'ang 趙鳳昌
Chao Ping-chün 趙秉鈞
Chao Sheng 趙聲
Po-sheng 伯生
Ch'ao-chou 潮州
Chekiang 浙江
Chen-chiang 鎮江
Ch'en Ch'i-mei 陳其美
Ch'en Chin-t'ao 陳錦濤
Ch'en T'ien-hua 陳天華
Ch'en Tso-hsin 陳作新
Ch'en Tu-hsiu 陳獨秀
Cheng Tsan-ch'eng 鄭贊丞
Chengchow 鄭州
Ch'eng Chia-sheng 程家檉

Ch'eng Te-ch'üan 程德全
Hsüeh-lou 雪樓
Chiang I-wu 蔣翊武
Chiang Kai-shek 蔣介石
Chiao Ta-feng 焦達峰
Chien-tao 間島 (Kantō in Japanese)
Ch'ien Tuan-sheng 錢端生
Chihli 直隸
Ch'i-hua Translation Bureau (*Ch'i-hua i-shu-chü*) 啟華譯書局
China Daily, The (*Chung-kuo jih-pao*) 中國日報
China Resurgence Society (*Hua-hsing-lui*) 華興會
Chinese Educational Society (*Chung-kuo chiao-yü hui*) 中國教育會
Chinese Flag (*Han-chih*) 漢幟
Chinese League (*Chung-kuo t'ung-meng-hui*) 中國同盟會
Chinese Mail, The (*Chung-kuo hua-tzu jih-pao*) 中國華字日報
Chinese National (*Kuo-min-pao*) 國民報
Chinese Nationals' Association (*Kuo-min-hui*) 國民會
Chinese Nationals' League (*Chung-kuo kuo-min t'ung-meng-hui*) 中國國民同盟會
Chinese Revolutionary Party (*Chung-hua ko-ming-tang*) 中華革命黨
Chinese Scholars' League (*Chung-Kuo chiao-hsüeh t'ung-meng-hui*) 中國教學同盟會
Chinese Students' Association (*Chung-kuo hsüeh-sheng-hui*) 中國學生會
Chinese Students' League (*Chung-kuo hsüeh-sheng t'ung-meng-hui*) 中國學生同盟會

Chinese Youths' Society (*Chung-kuo ch'ing-nien-hui*) 中國青年會
Ching 井
Ching-cheng School (*Ching-cheng hsüeh-t'ang*) 經正學堂
Ching wu-mo 井勿幕
Ch'ing dynasty (*Ch'ing-ch'ao*) 清朝
Ch'ing-wu, see Huang Hsing
Chü Cheng 居正
Chu Chia-pao 朱家寶
Ch'uan-shan, see Wang Fu-chih
Chung-shan, see Sun Yat-sen
College of Hunan and Hupeh (*Liang-hu shu-yüan*) 兩湖書院
Commercial News (*Shang-wu-pao*) 商務報
Comparative Finance, The (*Pi-chiao-ts'ai-cheng-hsüeh*) 比較財政學
Comrades' Association for Petitioning for a Parliament (*Li-hsien ch'ing-yuan t'ung-chih-hui*) 立憲請願同志會
Consultative Assembly of Representatives of Provincial Military Governments (*Ko-sheng tutu-fu tai-piao lien-hu-hui*) 各省都督府代表聯合會
Co-operation for Kwangtung Independence Society (*Kwang-tung tu-li hsieh-hui*) 廣東獨立協會
Council of Review (P'ing-i-pu) 評議部
Current Affairs Academy (*Shih-wu hsüeh-t'ang*) 時務學堂

Democratic Party (*Min-chu-tang*) 民主黨
Disciplinary Department (*P'ing-i-pu*) 評議部

East Asia News (*Tung-ya hsin-wen*) 東亞新聞

Journal of Pure Discourse (*Ch'ing-i-pao*) 清議報

K'ang Pao-chung 康保忠
K'ang Yu-wei 康有爲
Kansu 甘肅
Kantō, *see* Chien-tao
Katsura Tarō 桂太郎
Kayano Chōchi 萱野長知
Kiangsi 江西
Kiangsu 江蘇
Kiangsu News (*Su-pao*) 蘇報
Kiangsu News case (*Su-pao-an*) 蘇報案
Kita Ikki 北一輝
Kiukiang 九江
Kōbun gaku-in 弘文學院
Kōzai Tadao 高材世雄
K'o Feng-shih 柯逢時
Kuang-hui Mining Company (*Kuang-kui k'ang-wu kung-ssu*) 廣惠礦務公司
Kuanghsü 光緒
Kueichow 貴州
Kuo-min-tang 國民黨
Kuo Yao-chieh 郭堯階 or 郭瑤皆
Kwangsi 廣西
Kwang-tung 廣東
Kweichow, *see* Kueichow

Lan T'ien-wei 藍天蔚
Li Chao-fu 李肇甫
Li Chien-nung 李劍農
Li Chun 李準
Li Hsieh-ho 李燮和
Li Lieh-chün 李烈鈞
Li Lien-fang 李廉方
Li-ling 醴陵
Li Ya-tung 李亞東
Li Yüan-hung 黎元洪
Liang Ch'i-ch'ao 梁啟超
Liang Shih-yi 梁士詒
Lin Chao-tung 林肇東
Lin Shu-ch'ing 林述慶

Literary Society (*Wen-hsüeh-she*) 文學社
Liu Ch'eng-yü 劉成禺
Liu-chou 柳州
Liu Hou-sheng 劉厚生
Liu Jen-hsi 劉人熙
Liu Kuang-han 劉光漢
Liu Kung 劉公
Liu K'uei-i 劉揆一
Liu Wen-chin 劉文錦
Liu Yao-cheng 劉堯澂
Lu Cheng-hsiang 陸徵祥
Lu Hao-tung 陸浩東

Ma Chün-wu 馬君武
Ma Fu-i 馬福益
Ma Yü-pao 馬毓寶
Macao (Ao-men) 澳門
Military Studies Promotion Society (*Chen-wu hsüeh-she*) 振武學社
Miyazaki Torazō 宮崎寅藏
Mounted Bandits (*Ma-tsei*) 馬賊
Mutual Advancement Society (*Kung-chin-hui*) 共進會
Mutual Encouragement Society (*Li chih-hui*) 勵志會

Nanking 南京
National Advisory Assembly (*Tzu-cheng-yüan*) 資政院
National Assembly (*Kuo-hui*) 國會
Nationalism and Education (*Min-tsu chu-i chih chiao-yü*) 民族主義之教育
Nationalist Mutual Advancement Party (*Kuo-min kung-chin-hui*) 國民共進會
Nationalist Party (1912), *see* Kuo-min-tang
Nationalist Public Party (*Kuo-min kung-tang*) 國民公黨

Shih Chao-chi 施肇基
Shinjuku-ku 新宿區
Sian 西安
Sinkiang 新疆
Sino-Japanese Student Association (*Jih-hua hsüeh-sheng-hui*) 日華學生會
Society for the Daily Increase of Knowledge (*Jih-chih-hui*) 日知會
Society for the Protection of the Emperor (*Pao-huang-hui*) 保皇會
Society for the Realisation of Constitutional Government (*Hsien-cheng shih-chin-hui* 憲政實進會
Society for the Recovery of China (*Kuang-fu-hui*) 光復會
Society of Common Hostility to the Manchus, The (*T'ung-ch'ou-hui*) 同仇會
Soochow 蘇州
South Road Higher Primary School (*Nan-lu kao-teng hsiao-hsüeh-t'ang*) 南路高等小學堂
Southern Study Society (*Nan-hsüeh-hui*) 南學會
Structural Outline of the Provisional Government of the Republic of China (*Chung-hua min-kuo lin-shih cheng-fu tsu-chih ta-kang*) 中華民國臨時政府組織大綱
Sun Wu 孫武
Sun Yat-sen 孫逸仙
   Chung-shan 中山
   Wen 文
Sung Chia-jen 宋家仁
Sung Chiao-hsin 宋教信
Sung Chiao-jen 宋教仁
   Ch'ien 謙
   Kung-ming 公明
   Lien 鍊

Tun-ch'u 鈍初
Yü-fu 漁父
Sung Lu-ch'ih 宋魯池
Szechuan 四川

Tai Chi-t'ao 戴季陶
T'ai-yuan 太原
Tan T'ao 但燾
T'an Jen-feng 譚人鳳
T'an Yen-k'ai 譚延闓
T'ang Liu-yang 唐瀏陽
T'ang Shao-yi 唐紹儀
T'ang Ts'ai-ch'ang 唐才常
T'ao Ch'eng-chang 陶成章
T'ao-yüan 桃園
Teng Tzu-yü 鄧子瑜
Three Principles of the People (*San-min chu-i*) 三民主義
Tibet 西藏
Tide of Chekiang (*Che-chiang-ch'ao* or *Chekiang-ch'ao*) 浙江潮
Tientsin 天津
T'ien T'ung 田桐
Ts'ai Chi-min 蔡濟民
Ts'ai Chi-ou 蔡寄鷗
Ts'ai O 蔡鍔
Ts'ai Yüan-p'ei 蔡元培
Ts'ao Ya-po 曹亞伯
Tseng Ching-chou 曾靖州
Tseng Kuo-fan 曾國藩
Tseng Po-hsing 曾伯興
Ts'en Ch'un-hsüan 岑春萱
Ts'en Wei-sheng 岑偉生
Tsou Yung 鄒容
Tsou Yung-ch'eng 鄒永成
Tsung-li 總理
Tuan-fang 端方
Tumen-chiang 圖門江
Tung-t'ing-hu 洞庭湖
T'ung-hua 通化
Twentieth-Century China (*Erh-shih shih-chi chih Chih-na*) 弌拾世紀之支那

INDEX

Abdication, Manchu, *see* Manchu
Academics, 182
Agriculture, 170–1
Akasaka, 46, 47, 242
Alaha, Dr, 80
All Men are Brothers (*Shui-hu-chuan*), 35, 61
Alliance League for Regions North and South of the Great Lake (Ta-chiang nan-pei t'ung-meng-hui), 40, 106, 242
An-Chün Prefecture Association for the Promotion of the Public Good (An-chün kung-i-she), 106, 242
Anhwei, 11, 43, 69, 70, 77, 92, 96, 100, 101, 116, 127, 242
An-Lu Prefecture (An-lu-chün), 106, 242
Annam, 77, 242
Anthology of Translation (*I-shu hui-p'ien*), 21, 242
Antung, 64
Armoury, The, 26, 242
Association for National Military Education (Chün-kuo-min chiao-yü-hui), 27, 28, 242
Attorney-General, 140, 141
Australia, 147
Austria, 60
Awakening Lion (*Hsing-shih*), 36, 40

Belgium, 165, 166
Bentham, Jeremy, 22
Bismarck, Prince Otto von, 60
Black Dragon Society (Hakuryū kai), 46, 242
Bland, J.O.P., 143
Boer Republic, 128
Boxer Uprising, 10, 25, 26, 38, 85, 145, 149

Britain, 4, 10, 27, 60, 69, 81, 86, 87, 131, 145, 146, 147, 173, 186
Buck, Pearl, 35n
Bureau of General Affairs (Shu-wu-pu), 47
Burma, 10, 77, 86, 87

Cabinet: Sung Chiao-jen and, 139, 140, 148, 151, 160, 163, 168–70; responsible, 152, 153, 161, 162, 163, 179; first (composition), 160–9 *passim*, 180
Cabinet Party, 180, 181
Canton, 52, 84–95 *passim*, 103; uprising, 52, 88–99 *passim*, 110, 111, 112, 121, 127, (of 1910), 87, (of 1911), 88, 91, 112
Cantonese, 48, 50, 56, 69, 73, 89, 93, 156, 157
Cavour, Camillo, 60
Central China Office of the Chinese League (Chung-kuo t'ung-meng-hui), 4–5, 34, 158, 175, 194–5, 198, 242; origin, 91–2, 93, 95; aims and organisation, 96–100; activities, 100–5; support for, 109, 111, 112, 116; ascendancy, 125–6; threat to leadership, 154; re-amalgamation within the Chinese League, 155; importance, 195
Central Command (T'ung-ch'ou-pu), 88, 101, 242
Central Executive Council (Tsung-wu-hui), 97, 98, 112, 113, 242
Chambers of Commerce (of Shanghai and Hong Kong), 147
Chang Chi, 48, 50, 72, 77, 158, 242
Chang Chia-shih, 133, 242

250   *Index*

Designed by Cathy Akroyd
Text set in 10 pt. Monotype Baskerville, one point leaded, and printed on 85 gsm Esparto paper by Cathay Press Limited, Aberdeen, Hong Kong